Exploring the Bias

Exploring the Bias

Gender and Stereotyping in Secondary Schools

Edited by

Elspeth Page and Jyotsna Jha

Commonwealth Secretariat

Commonwealth Secretariat
Marlborough House
Pall Mall
London SW1Y 5HX
United Kingdom

Published by the Commonwealth Secretariat
Edited by editors4change Limited
Designed by SJI Services
Cover design by Tattersall Hammarling & Silk
Printed by Hobbs the Printers Ltd, Totton, Hampshire

Views and opinions expressed in this publication are the responsibility of the authors and should in no way be attributed to the institutions to which they are affiliated or to the Commonwealth Secretariat.

Wherever possible, the Commonwealth Secretariat uses paper sourced from sustainable forests or from sources that minimise a destructive impact on the environment.

Cover photo credit: Commonwealth Secretariat/Jyotsna Jha

Copies of this publication may be obtained from

The Publications Section
Commonwealth Secretariat
Marlborough House
Pall Mall
London SW1Y 5HX
United Kingdom
Tel: +44 (0)20 7747 6534
Fax: +44 (0)20 7839 9081
Email: publications@commonwealth.int
Web: www.thecommonwealth.org/publications

A catalogue record for this publication is available from the British Library.

ISBN: 978-1-84929-007-4 (paperback)
ISBN: 978-1-84859-042-7 (downloadable e-book)

Contents

List of Tables, Figures and Boxes

Acronyms and Abbreviations

ADB	Asian Development Bank
CABE	Central Advisory Board of Education (India)
CARICOM	Caribbean Community
CPE	Compulsory primary education
CSO	Central Statistical Office (Trinidad and Tobago)
CXC	Caribbean Examinations Council
DEO	District Education Officer (Malaysia, India)
ECCE	Early childhood care and education
EDI	Education Development Index
FGN	Federal Government of Nigeria
FTT	Food and textiles technology
GEM	Gender Empowerment Measure
GER	Gross Enrolment Ratio
GOI	Government of India
GoS	Government of Samoa
GPI	Gender Parity Index
HDI	Human Development Index
HDR	Human Development Report
HOD	Head of Department
IGCSE	International General Certificate of Secondary Education
LSE	Life skills education
MCS	Muslim Community School (Pakistan)
MDGs	Millennium Development Goals
MESC	Ministry of Education, Sports and Culture (Samoa)
MOE	Ministry of Education (Malaysia)
MWFCD	Ministry of Women, Family and Community Development (Malaysia)

NER	Net Enrolment Ratio
NGO	Non-governmental organisation
NMP	Ninth Malaysia Plan
OBC	Other backward classes (India)
OECD	Organisation for Economic Co-operation and Development
PE	Physical Education
PSE	Personal and social education
PTA	Parent–Teacher Association
PTI	Physical training instructor
QA	Quality Assurance (service, Seychelles)
QSS	Quaid Secondary School (Pakistan)
SC	Scheduled castes (India)
SEA	Secondary Education Assessment (Trinidad and Tobago)
ST	Scheduled tribe (India)
SUHAKAM	Suruhanjaya Hak Asasi Manusia, Malaysia (Human Rights Commission, Malaysia)
UNDP	United Nations Development Programme
UNESCO	United Nations Educational, Scientific and Cultural Organization
UNICEF	United Nations International Children's Emergency Fund

Acknowledgements

Jyotsna Jha and Elspeth Page

We would like to thank all the contributors for their patience and co-operation. A huge thank you to all of them for responding to numerous queries and demands on short notice. We are also grateful to all those who participated in the research: students, teachers, principals, other school staff, educational managers and policy planners for spending time and sharing their views and experiences. Thanks are also due the publication section colleagues and editors for their co-operation and support.

Mahrookh Pardiwalla

I would like to sincerely thank all of the following:

- The Ministry of Education, Seychelles and the principal of the Independent School for actively supporting the project and giving permission for the study to be carried out in selected schools.

- The head teachers, staff and students of the four case study schools, who all provided valuable insights into the research topic and helped make sense of this complex issue.

- Mrs Nella Belmont, Mrs Margaret Adam and Mr Justin Valentine for participating in the fieldwork and data collection.

- The Commonwealth Secretariat for funding and co-ordinating the study and providing opportunities for exciting cross-fertilisation of ideas among participating countries.

Jeniffer Mohammed

I am grateful to all the school researchers, students, principals, teachers and students who generously gave their time and goodwill so that this baseline data could be collected. My appreciation also extends to the Ministry of Education who granted permission for the research, acknowledging that gender is a significant issue and that we need to know more about how it is making an impact on schools.

Maria Chin Abdullah

I would like to express my warm thanks to Jyotsna Jha and the Education Section, Social Transformation Programmes Division of the Commonwealth Secretariat, United Kingdom. Thank you for giving my study team and me the opportunity to be part of this project. I extend warm thanks to the study team who have given me their utmost help and encouragement. Very special and deep appreciation to Yunus Ali, who not only helped to document the data and conduct the interviews, but went beyond to help write parts of the interviews and share his analysis. To Eddie Wong and Alvina Tan who both literally 'jumped' into this survey as the data was getting overwhelming, and never once complained. Sincere thanks and warm appreciation to the following people and institutions for their crucial support and constructive feedback:

- Ministry of Education and the Economic Planning Unit for their approval of this project,

- Dr Soon, Head of the Planning and Research Unit and Puan Zaleha Hamid, Gender Focal Unit of the Ministry of Education for their support,

- The Kedah Education Department and the Sungai Petani Education Department for their approval and willingness to be part of the interview,

- All the head teachers, principals and teachers of the four schools for their patience and feedback,

- All the students who participated in the focus group discussions and gave their frank opinions.

Finally, on a personal note, my warmest thanks to the staff and friends of Empower for their full support to this project.

Gatoloai Tilianamua Afamasaga

Sincere thanks are due the chief executive officer of the Ministry of Education, Sports and Culture, the Directors of the Congregational Christian Church Schools and the Methodist Schools in Samoa for allowing the researchers access to their schools.

Much gratitude is also due to all the principals, deputy principals, teachers and students of the schools for allowing the researchers into their classrooms and staffrooms. The researchers gained much pleasure from spending time in the schools, forging new links and continuing long-standing relationships with colleagues and friends in the front line for secondary schooling in Samoa. Finally, the research in Samoa would not have been possible without the generous assistance of Dr Silipa Silipa, Leiataua Iosefa Leiataua and Fitiao Susan Faoagali in data collection, and together with Gatoloai Tili Afamasaga collectively analysing the data and collaborating in writing the report

Shobhita Rajagopal

I am grateful to all the students, teachers, principals and staff members of the government schools covered in this study, for giving their time and sharing their insights on the various dimensions of gender and schooling processes. I also acknowledge the support provided by the officers of the Education Department, Government of Rajasthan who readily gave their time and discussed various issues at length. I gratefully acknowledge the research support rendered by Shri Radheyshyam Sharma and Tanwar Singh during fieldwork and data analysis. Finally, I wish to thank, Dr Jyotsna Jha for giving me this opportunity to further explore the dimensions of gender in secondary schooling in Rajasthan.

Dilshad Ashraf

I wish to acknowledge my colleague Sultana Ali's contribution to the study.

Salihu Girei Bakari

We wish to show our gratitude to all those who made this research work possible. These include Felicia Ibkwe, Felicitas Ibkwe, Dauda Bello and Jiddere M Kaibo, IE Anyanwu and CC Agomoh who did all the tours and fieldwork with us. We are also grateful to Mana Akaiku who assisted in data analysis. We also specifically extend our appreciation to the Universal Basic Education Commission for providing additional funds for effective conduct of this study. We are equally grateful to the Kogi State Ministry of Education for allowing this research to be carried out in the state and for its immeasurable support in the process. In the same way, we extend our gratitude to the inspectors, supervisors, principals, teachers and all those involved in conducting this study.

Foreword

Gender equality in education is about both girls and boys having equal entitlements to access education. It is about the processes in education facilitating the realisation to provide a range of equal opportunities to expand capacities of all children to the fullest. This in turn will contribute to the development of a just, responsible and compassionate society. Equality of opportunity refers to access to schooling, learning and other experiences within schools and to the wider opportunities that are available through education and schooling.

The present book, based on case studies of selected schools in seven Commonwealth countries: India, Malaysia, Nigeria, Pakistan, Samoa, Seychelles, and Trinidad and Tobago, attempts to unpack issues of gender equality within schools. Gender analysis of classroom and other schooling processes is an under-researched area and this book makes a modest attempt to address this. Although all stages of schooling are important for the formation of gender-related ideas and norms, the secondary stage of education is important in that it targets an age group which is at a critical stage of identity formation and the development of decision-making skills. This is the stage that provides a link between childhood and adulthood, and so issues related to empowerment and relations can be addressed more effectively. The research explored in this publication focuses on gender analysis of schooling processes in secondary schools.

Of particular interest is that the book covers countries with diverse contexts and situations. For example India, Pakistan and Nigeria are struggling to achieve gender parity in school enrolment and completion figures, and in these countries girls continue to have lower participation rates than boys at all stages of education. Other countries such as Malaysia, Samoa, Seychelles, and Trinidad and Tobago have achieved near universal primary education with therefore almost complete gender parity at that level. However, these countries face gender disparity at secondary level, with boys often having lower rates of participation and tending to relatively under-perform. The research therefore set out to undertake gender analysis of school processes in this diversity of contexts in order to consider similarities and differences.

The case studies aim to provide interesting and useful insights into many issues related to classroom and other schooling processes. Schools considered in the study were found to be often reinforcing gender stereotypes, norms and attitudes. A pilot action project was designed as a follow up to the study in a small number of schools in four of the seven countries (India, Malaysia, Seychelles, and Trinidad and Tobago). Its objective was to develop school-based solutions to help make schooling processes more gender-responsive. The documented experiences from these pilot projects have also formed the basis for another publication: *The Gender-responsive School: An Action Guide*. This guide identifies a range of possible actions at various levels that can help a school to become more gender responsive and as such have a positive impact on the learning, experiences and achievements of both girls and boys. The action guide can therefore be read alongside this publication, as this would combine a situational analysis with a discussion of potential action orientated responses.

Caroline Pontefract
Director,
Social Transformation Programmes Division.
Commonwealth Secretariat

Contributors

Mahrookh Pardiwalla	mpardiwalla@seychelles.sc
Jeniffer Mohammed	Jeniffer.Mohammed@sta.uwi.edu
Maria Abdullah	maria29chin@gmail.com
Tili Afamasaga	t.afamasaga@nus.edu.ws
Shobhita Rajagopal	shobhita@idsj.org
Dilshad Ashraf	dilshad.ashraf@aku.edu
Salihu Bakari	sgbakari@yahoo.co.uk
Jyotsna Jha	j.jha@commonwealth.int
Elspeth Page	elspethpage@yahoo.com
Janet Raynor	janet.raynor@gmail.com

Mahrookh Pardiwalla

Mahrookh Pardiwalla, MEd in Educational Leadership, currently works as a freelance consultant and trainer on Education and Gender in Seychelles. Previously she worked for over 25 years with the Ministry of Education, as teacher, teacher trainer, head of teacher training and staff development co-ordinator. Her last position within the Ministry of Education was Director of the School Improvement Programme, a national project that was selected as one of the finalists of the Commonwealth Good Practice Awards in 2006. Mahrookh Pardiwalla has wide experience in teacher training, curriculum development, educational leadership, distance education, project development, human rights and gender.

Jeniffer Mohammed

Jeniffer Mohammed is a lecturer at the School of Education, University of the West Indies, St Augustine, Trinidad and Tobago. She holds a BSc in Geography from the University of the West Indies, Mona, Jamaica and postgraduate qualifications in the Sociology of Education. For many years she taught at the secondary level in Trinidad and Tobago. Dr Mohammed now lectures in the Sociology of Health and Education, the Teaching of Social Studies and Qualitative Research. Her research interests include gender and education, the analysis of textual materials and teaching and learning in the social studies.

Maria Chin Abdullah

Maria Chin Abdullah is a women's rights activist and researcher, specialising in gender and development, human rights, local governance and democracy. She has been with the women's movement for more than 20 years. Her involvement with women's issues in Malaysia began with the first workshop on Violence Against Women in 1985, which set the national agenda for women's rights. She is a keen advocate for policy and legal reforms on gender equality and non-discrimination for all. Maria Chin Abdullah is involved in coalition building, such as the Joint Action Group for Gender Equality (JAG), a vocal women's coalition; the Coalition against Privatisation of Health Services; All Petaling Jaya Action Coalition, a coalition of 44 local residents associations fighting for local democracy and also chairs the Coalition on Good Governance with 14 taskforces.

Maria Chin Abdullah's work is published in books and articles on women's rights, democracy and local governance. She develops training manuals on feminism, rights and democracy and sits as an adviser to the gender think tank of the Welfare, Women's Affairs, Science, Technology and Innovation under the Selangor State Government. Her other interests include promoting women's political participation and decision-making powers. She has a bachelor's degree in Applied Economics and a Master of Science in Urban Planning at the University College, London.

Gatoloai Tilianamua Afamasaga

Gatoloai Tili Afamasaga has spent the last 31 years in education in Samoa as second-ary schoolteacher, teachers' college principal, Dean of the Faculty of Education and since 2006 as the Director of the Oloamanu Centre for Professional Development and Continuing Education at the National University of Samoa. Her education has been in Samoa, Victoria University and Christchurch Teachers College (New Zealand) and Macquarie University (Australia). Gatoloai Tili Afamasaga's research interests have been in the management of change, curriculum implementation, women and gender issues and in education for sustainable development. She is married with five children and three grandchildren.

Shobhita Rajagopal

Shobhita Rajagopal is Associate Professor at the Institute of Development Studies, Jaipur, specialising in gender and education. She has been researching in the area of gender and development and has been closely involved in studying processes of rural women's empowerment for over two decades. Dr Rajagopal has actively worked on mainstreaming gender in policy, has published extensively both nationally and inter-nationally and has contributed to the *Annotated Bibliography on Gender in Secondary Education* compiled by the Commonwealth Secretariat in 2007.

Dilshad Ashraf

Dilshad Ashraf is an Assistant Professor at the Aga Khan University Pakistan's Insti-tute for Educational Development (AKU-IED). Her specialisations in teaching and research include gender and curriculum studies, teacher development, school improvement and education and development. She has conducted research projects and has also published on the issues of gender and education across primary, secondary, and tertiary levels. Dr Ashraf is also engaged in conducting workshops for public and private sector stakeholders to help them build their capacity to integrate gender perspective in teaching/learning and organisational policies and practices. Other important areas of her work include organisational evaluation (and school audit) and education in emergencies. She supervises a reconstruction project focussed on education in the earthquake-hit areas of Northern Pakistan. She technically supports another similar project in Azad Jammu and Kashmir Pakistan.

Salihu Girei Bakari

Salihu Bakari holds a doctorate degree in Gender and Education at the University of Sussex and has over ten years teaching and managerial experience in teacher education institution in Nigeria with research interests in gender, education and development. He worked with the Universal Basic Education Commission in Abuja, a Nigerian agency responsible for achieving Education For All (EFA) for all school-age children. He also worked with the Education Trust Fund in Abuja and was also the Co-ordinator for Projects and International Training and Support for Adamawa State. Dr Bakari was the founding Director-general, Special Projects also in Adamawa State, a position he held until his recent appointment as the Executive Chairman, Adamawa State Universal Basic Education Board, a body responsible for management and control of primary and junior secondary schools in the state.

Jyotsna Jha

Jyotsna Jha works as Adviser, Education and Gender, and Education and HIV and AIDS at the Commonwealth Secretariat in London. Her work on gender and education in the Secretariat has focused on research and advocacy on various aspects including the issues of promoting schooling practices that promote respect for equality and diversity, empowerment-focused girls' education and boys' underachievement. Prior to joining the Secretariat, Dr Jha was based in India where she undertook several research, evaluation and implementation-support projects for both government and non-government organisations, and for national and international agencies. She has worked with educational policy planners, administrators, teachers and professionals at various levels.

With a PhD in Economics of Education, Dr Jha has several publications to her credit. These include two books, *Elementary Education for the Poorest and other Deprived Groups: The Real Challenge of Universalization* (Manohar, India: 2005) and *Boys' Underachievement in Education: An Exploration in Selected Commonwealth Countries* (Commonwealth Secretariat, London: 2007). Dr Jha is the editor of *An Annotated Bibliography on Gender in Secondary Education: Research from Selected Commonwealth Countries* (Commonwealth Secretariat, London: 2007) and has written chapters in *Gender and Social Policy in a Global Context* (Palgrave, London: 2006) and *Reinventing Public Service*

Delivery in India: Selected Case Studies (Sage, India: 2006). Most of her recent writings have focused on equity issues in education.

Elspeth Page

Elspeth Page is an independent consultant with over 20 years experience in Africa, South Asia and Europe and a doctorate in Education, Gender and International Development. Her interests span pre-primary, primary and elementary and youth and adult non-formal levels, focusing on pedagogy, curriculum, gender, marginalised groups, inclusion and empowerment. Her work encompasses capacity building, skill transfer, empowering partner organisations, networking, project cycle management, project conceptualisation and planning, formative and summative monitoring and evaluation approaches, institutional learning and knowledge management. Dr Page has worked with varied stakeholders, managing relationships between international development agencies, governments, NGOs, academics and local communities.

Dr Page's doctoral thesis explores the social construction of gender identities and the factors influencing pupils' gendered enrolment, persistence, achievement and desire for greater equality and public-sphere participation (available at: www.elspethpage.feeuk.com). Publications include 'Negotiation and compromise: an exploration of gender and government elementary education' in *Educational Regimes in Contemporary India* (eds. R. Chopra and P. Jeffrey, Sage, New Delhi: 2005) and 'Unsettling caste-bound gender orders: the convergence of teacher commitment and pupil aspiration in two schools in Madhya Pradesh' in *Educate*, 3, 35–52 (2003).

Janet Raynor

Janet Raynor has worked as an independent consultant in various countries in South Asia and Africa in areas related to gender and education. She has contributed chapters on this theme to recent books, including *Women teaching in South Asia: an edited collection* (ed. J. Kirk, Sage, New Delhi: 2008), *Gender Education and Equality in a Global Context: Conceptual frameworks and policy perspectives* (ed. S Fennell and M Arnot, Routledge: 2007), *Sen's Capability Approach and social justice in education* (ed. M Walker and E Unterhalter, Palgrave: 2007), and *Beyond Access: Transforming Policy and Practice for Gender Equality in Education* (ed. S Aikman and E Unterhalter, Oxfam: 2005). She has also made a number of contributions to publications from the *Beyond Access: Gender, education and development* project (DfID/Institute of Education/Oxfam).

CHAPTER 1

School, Gender and Stereotypes: Despair and Hope

Jyotsna Jha, Elspeth Page and Janet Raynor

The issue of gender equality occupies a central place in global policy discourse on education, human and social development. Gender equality in education has several dimensions.

Equal access to schooling has to be a foremost concern: a first step. Despite notable progress in recent years, a good number of countries, especially in South and West Asia, and sub-Saharan Africa, are still facing gender disparity against girls in terms of access to schooling. This is a major hindrance in achieving universal primary education. Girls still constitute about 55 per cent of the estimated 75 million children who are not enrolled in primary education (UNESCO, 2009). The situation is different at secondary stage. While the disparities in access and enrolment at secondary level are generally high and against girls in most South and West Asian and sub-Saharan African countries, disparities are also visible against boys in many countries in the Caribbean and the developed part of the world.

Another important dimension of gender equality in education pertains to educational processes. Gender equality in education not only implies that both girls and boys have equal access to schooling, but also that the process of education provides all girls and boys with a range of equal opportunities and experiences for expanding their capacities to the fullest potentials in a manner that they are able to contribute to the making of a just, responsible and compassionate society. This dimension of gender equality in education raises questions about the role of educational and schooling processes in promoting substantive equality. Is education necessarily a process of change? What is the role of schools in this process of transformation? Are educational processes geared towards change? Are schools conscious of the responsibility and do they have the necessary wherewithal to make the processes gender responsive and the learning experiences empowering? These questions are especially relevant at secondary stage. Secondary education caters to an age group that is critical for identity formation and for developing the critical skill of decision-making. This is the stage that provides a link between childhood and adulthood.

Schooling processes refer to all that happens in a school: the ways in which teachers treat their children, the language that is used, the methods of teaching that are practiced, the ways in which the responsibilities are distributed – in classrooms and outside classrooms, the ways in which sports and other outside-classroom activities are organised. Overall, these are the practices that lead to knowledge and learning of skills and shape attitudes and beliefs among the learners. In the past, schooling processes have largely been considered an issue of quality and the definitions of quality have not always included attention to equality and gender. This is changing with newer perspectives and more comprehensive definitions of gender equality in education.

The Global Monitoring Report 2003/04 highlighted the fact that the achievement of full gender equality in education would imply:

- *'Equality of opportunities, in the sense that girls and boys are offered the same chances to access school, i.e. parents, teachers and society at large have no gender-biased attitudes in this respect,*

- *Equality in the learning process, i.e. girls and boys receive the same treatment and attention, follow the same curricula, enjoy teaching methods and teaching tools free of stereotypes and gender bias, are offered academic orientation and counselling not affected by gender biases, profit from the same quantity and quality of appropriate educational infrastructures,*

- *Equality of outcomes, i.e. learning achievements, length of school careers, academic qualifications and diplomas would not differ by gender,*

- *Equality of external results, i.e. job opportunities, the time needed to find a job after leaving full time education, the earnings of men and women with similar qualifications and experience etc would all be equal.*

The last condition, while not strictly part of a notion of educational equality, is nevertheless entailed by it: the perspective of gender discrimination in labour market prevents the attainment of equality of access, treatment and outcomes in education by affecting the relative costs and perceived benefits of educating girls and boys' (UNESCO, 2003).

Different groups have defined quality differently. Critical approaches are significant to understand the issue of equality in quality, and also in the context of acknowledging the role of education in reproducing or questioning the existing social order. The focus here is on empowerment and therefore makes it especially relevant in the context of gender. Although the cognitive aspects and easily measurable learning outcomes have received greater focus, there has recently been an emphasis on including the empowerment agenda within the definition of quality. Aikman and Unterhalter, for example, suggest that quality:

'... entails more than the attainment of equal numbers in school, or parity in examination results: it implies a fuller meaning of equality, which includes conditions in school and post-school opportunities... ... ...(and) concerns to improve quality include the framing of curriculum, the content and form of learning materials, the nature of the pedagogy, and teacher-student relations' (Aikman and Unterhalter, 2005: p. 4).

A deeper understanding of schooling processes from the perspective of gender is also essential if the wider goal of gender equality in society is to be achieved. Education is central to social development, critical for achieving greater participation of women in political activities, and for their social and economic empowerment. Amartya Sen, in his keynote speech at the Commonwealth Conference of Education Ministers in 2003, clearly articulated the connection:

> '... the relative respect and regard for women's wellbeing is strongly influenced by women's literacy and educated participation in decisions within and outside the family. There is also much evidence that women's education and literacy tend to reduce the mortality rates of children – of boys and girls both. These and other connections between basic education of women and the power of women's agency indicate why the gender gap in education produces heavy social penalties' (Sen, 2003).

The agency of women, however, gains real strength only when the process of education leads to empowerment. Research into boys' underachievement has also underlined the need for greater enquiry in schooling processes. Boys' relative underachievement at the secondary stage, in terms of participation or performance, is a growing trend in some countries that have largely succeeded in addressing the issue of access and nearly wiped out the gender disparities at primary stage. A study conducted by Commonwealth Secretariat Education Section illustrated how boys face tremendous pressure to conform to 'masculine' gender identities and that this is closely linked with their relative underachievement (Jha and Kelleher, 2007). The study suggested that gender analysis of classroom and schooling processes would help in understanding this trend and finding an answer to the required changes at classroom and school levels.

Educational processes are also important for their contributions to the attainment of quantitative goals and targets. In their study on boys' underachievement, Jha and Kelleher (2006) illustrated that schooling processes are critical to understand and influence the issues of numbers, i.e. issues dealing with gender disparities in education. Although it is difficult to apportion, it is increasingly being recognised that a significant proportion of dropouts, especially at secondary stage, may be related to 'non-access' issues such as teacher–child relationships, peer behaviour and expectations, etc. In the past, access has been seen as an issue of quantity and educational processes an issue of quality. This is changing and the crucial link between enabling classroom processes and attaining the goals for gender parity in access, completion and achievement are being better understood.

Despite some shifts in redefining quality and recognising the importance of the nature of educational processes in moving towards substantive gender equality in education, the evidence indicates that the issue has received less attention in the efforts made to improve classroom processes.

> 'Education reform since the 1990s has tended to emphasise students' performance and achievement. Consequently most efforts to improve classroom and teacher practices

concentrate on teaching reading and mathematics. Less attention has been devoted to incorporating a gender development dimension in teacher training' (Skelton 2005, cited in UNESCO Global Monitoring Report, 2007: p. 88).

In 2006, the Commonwealth Secretariat Education Section published an annotated bibliography of existing works in gender and education with special emphasis on secondary education in five countries: Ghana, Kenya, Nigeria, India and Pakistan (Jha, 2007). These Commonwealth countries are reported to have high levels of gender disparity and inequality. A perusal of the entries to the annotated bibliography illustrated that there are a large number of studies exploring access, but a dearth of studies looking at processes within schools. The need for further research to obtain a more nuanced understanding of school processes in developing countries was obvious: to inform policy and programmatic decisions as well as teacher-training and support activities.

Prompted by these findings and recommendations, the Commonwealth Secretariat Education Section initiated a research study on gender analysis of classroom and other processes in India, Malaysia, Nigeria, Pakistan, Samoa, Seychelles and Trinidad and Tobago. These countries were selected in order to represent the four main regions of the Commonwealth (Africa, Asia, the Caribbean and the Pacific); a diverse selection of economic, geographical, social and cultural contexts; very different gender environments; and marked educational gender disparities, either against boys (as in Seychelles, Trinidad and Tobago, Malaysia and Samoa) or against girls (as in India, Pakistan and Nigeria).

The Conceptual Frame

If education processes and opportunities are geared to question unequal gender relations and established notions of femininity and masculinity, inequalities may be challenged. If not, they continue to exist. Equal access does not guarantee equality in treatment: it does not guarantee equality in educational processes. Unequal treatments are more likely to be more prevalent in situations where there is disparity in access. Gender analysis of classroom and schooling processes is relevant in all kinds of situations.

The conceptual bases and beliefs that lie underneath this gender analysis of classroom and schooling processes are outlined below.

The process of education or schooling that facilitates imparting of knowledge and skill on one hand, and acts as a course of socialisation on the other, has tremendous potential for empowerment and transformation. It is important to recognise this possibility, and shape education in a manner that helps realise this potential. This would also require recognition of the fact that there is always a likelihood of education and schooling to become 'status quoist' and conforming unless consciously ensured otherwise.

The concepts of equity and empowerment are critical in the context of gender equality. This means that quantitative measures alone are not adequate to capture progress towards gender equality in education. Kabeer (2001) defines empowerment as 'the expansion in people's ability to make **strategic** life choices in a context where this ability was previously denied to them'. It is important to differentiate strategic life choices from others as 'strategic life choices help to frame other, second order and less consequential choices which may be important for the quality of one's life but do not constitute its defining parameters'. Also important to note is the fact that 'empowerment entails a process of change'. People who exercise a great deal of power may be very powerful but not necessarily empowered, as they were not disempowered before.

Inequality needs to be separated from difference. To quote Kabeer (2001), 'we have to disentangle differentials which reflect differences in preferences and priorities from those which embody a denial of choice'. The denial of choice asks for affirmative action to help mitigate unequal positioning in many cases. It may include measures to address gender stereotypes and creation of differentiated opportunities and treatment in order to impact traditional gender relations, roles and positioning. In the context of inequalities, affirmative action is not indicative of unequal treatment in a negative sense. Rather, they are indicative of a negotiation of inequality and a deliberate creation of opportunities to move away from it, towards equality.

Gender inequality cannot be viewed completely in isolation from other forms of inequality that exist in various societies and systems. It is often embedded in other forms of inequalities, e.g. caste, class, race, religion or location. The impact of gender differentiated norms and practices are often sharper and more complex for groups that also face other forms of marginalisation and vulnerability. It is important to understand and acknowledge this phenomenon, and appreciate the linkages and implications in the context of education. Gendered enquiry in education can be enriching and useful only when it works in tandem with other forces and divisions, taking note of the shifting configurations over time and space.

There are certain universally defensible values[1] that guide the concept of equality and justice, and are applicable to the issue of gender as well.

Each individual irrespective of caste, class, colour, gender, religion or location has a right to have all entitlements and opportunities for development of capacities so as to live with basic human dignity and without discrimination leading to autonomy of mind and action while caring for others at the same time is a universally desirable goal. The context as determined by polity, culture, society, economy or geography does not alter this principle. How this principle is achieved in practice and mediated through different institutions or processes – political, social, cultural and economic – is an issue of contextualisation. In other words, the broad goal remains the same; the roadmap to reach the goal may take different shapes and directions depending upon the context. This assumption helps in resolving some of the dilemma of public policy and social choice in a plural society.

These five broad and fundamental assumptions form the conceptual base of our enquiry. These are consistent with the 'Rights Framework' that emphasises achieving gender equality in its broadest sense.

It is also important to mention that equality is a relative concept, freedom being a more absolute term. Gender equality, in a broad sense does not refer only to equality of treatment and opportunity but also of ensuring the minimum desirable freedom for everyone, boys and girls belonging to all socio-economic, religious, ethnic groups in all locations, rural or urban.

Approach and Methodology

Approach

The research followed a qualitative approach, focussing on a small sample of secondary schools within their local and national education systems.

The foundational question of the study was whether education processes and opportunities reproduce or challenge unequal gender stereotypes. The study focused on:

- Processes both within the classroom and outside it, in the wider school environment,
- School management policies and processes, and
- Education system policies and processes.

The exploration of all processes also included a focus on expectations, aspirations, perceptions, behaviour and language use.

The study was conducted to analyse existing situations and provide pointers for addressing gender-related issues. Its objective was to analyse school and classroom processes to understand:

- If school and classroom processes reproduce or challenge dominant gendered stereotypes, identities and relationships,
- How these processes reproduce or challenge dominant gendered stereotypes, identities and relationships, and
- If these processes were found to reproduce dominant gender stereotypes, identities and relationships, what is being done, or what might be done, to interrupt the patterns and move towards more equitable processes.

Three questions were thus asked in each focus area, as illustrated in Table 1.1 below.

The research was conducted through a variety of qualitative approaches, including:

- Textbook analysis,
- Observations, both within and outside the classroom,

Table 1.1. Research questions

Focus areas	Question 1	Question 2	Question 3
• Classroom processes • School processes • School management processes • Education system processes	Do they reproduce or challenge dominant gendered stereotypes, identities and relationships?	How do they reproduce or challenge dominant gendered stereotypes, identities and relationships?	If they reproduce dominant gender stereotypes, identities and relationships, what is being done, or what might be done, to redress the situation?

• Interviews with teachers and principals,

• Focus group discussions with students, teachers, administrative staff and school inspectors/support officials, and

• Focus group discussions or interviews with senior education managers.

The research instruments were collaboratively developed by in-country researchers and the Commonwealth Secretariat Education Section. The basic design and instruments were kept constant across all countries, to facilitate the synthesis of the country studies and allow a comparative analysis.

The school-based research was conducted in five secondary schools in Trinidad and Tobago and Nigeria, and four schools in the other countries. Table 2.1 shows the distribution of schools across intake and management types. Eighteen out of 30 schools were co-educational. All schools in Seychelles were co-educational, whereas in the other countries at least one or two schools were single-sex, taking either only girls or only boys, the former being more common. Responding to a demand from parents, one boys-only school in Pakistan had started admitting girls, though formally it still remained a single-sex school. Another co-educational school in Pakistan had started using single-sex classrooms from grades 6 to 9, responding again to pressure from parents to segregate the students. The later analysis reveals some interesting insights into how the understanding of gender unfolds differently in varying contexts of single-sex and co-educational contexts.

Of the 30 schools, 21 were state schools, fully managed and financed by the government. Two out of five schools in Trinidad and Tobago were privately managed denominational schools with full aid from the government for teachers' salaries and certain other maintenance expenses. In Samoa, two out of four schools were church schools and in Pakistan, one out of four was a community-based faith school while another was community-based, government supported school. Table 1.2 lists schools' student intake (whether co-educational, boys or girls) and management type.

Table 1.2. Intake and school management

	School 1		School 2		School 3		School 4		School 5	
	Intake	*Mgt.*	*Intake*	*Mgt.*	*Intake*	*Mgt.*	*Intake*	*Mgt.*	*Intake*	*Mgt.*
1 Seychelles	C	S	C	S	C	S	C	P		
2 T and T	G	PDA	B	PDA	C	S	C	S	C	S
3 Malaysia	G	S	C	S	C	S	C	S		
4 Samoa	C	S	C	S	C	PC	G	PC		
5 India	C	S	C	S	B	S	G	S		
6 Pakistan	G	S	B+G	S	CS	PMCS	C	CBF		
7 Nigeria	B	S	C	CGS	G	S	C	S	C	P

Intake C – co-educational (co-ed), B – boys only, G – girls only, B+G * – Boys, girls now admitted, CS – co-ed (single-sex rooms for G6-9)

Mgt.: Management S – state/government, PC – private, church, PDA – private, denominational, aided, CGS – community, government supported, CBF – community-based faith school, MCS – Muslim community school

In Seychelles, with only 13 secondary schools in the country, this sample represents a significant percentage of all schools. In other higher-population countries such as India, the percentage would barely register and therefore, the generalisation of the findings should be avoided. The actual teaching and learning process is always unique to a particular teacher and learner and therefore no two classes are ever conducted the same way. To that extent, it is difficult to generalise the findings of any process-based studies, even if the samples are large. The purpose of this study was to have an in-depth gender analysis of schooling processes in varying contexts rather than presenting the country profile per se; the country papers should be read and interpreted accordingly.

The field studies were conducted in different months of 2007, depending on the school calendar in different countries. The lead researchers developed their initial reports based on a suggested format provided by the Secretariat. These draft reports were shared and peer-reviewed in a workshop held in Seychelles, which was also attended by the government officials from respective countries. Barring Samoa, the rest of the countries were represented in this workshop. It was strongly felt and agreed upon that the reports should explore similar parameters but need not follow the same reporting structures. This was to retain the variety of context, perspective, approach, emphasis, detail and character. A synthesis of the country reports, following a common style and structure would have sacrificed this depth and variety, and the voice of the country authors. Therefore it was decided to have an introductory chapter providing an overview of the analysis, rather than a synthesis of the country papers. The following sections of this chapter provide that overview.

Limitations

Researching any social issue addressing power and privilege is always complex, often emotive and laden with potential for confrontation. These challenges are easily magnified when researching gender, as it cuts across every societal institution, from the family to parliament: no one is exempt. In some instances, researching gender does become confrontational, pitting women against men, focussing on blame and generalisations and reinforcing the gender dichotomies that the pursuit of gender equality seeks to dismantle. Factors of power and of performance may have policed the discussion in all focus groups, including those with teachers and with students. However, this is a challenge that any research of this kind faces and hence not unique. Nevertheless, it is important to remember this limitation while interpreting the observations and findings.

Although some references have been made to the issues of ethnicity, caste, poverty and socio-economic parameters, the analysis mainly limits itself to gender disaggregation. Therefore, except in a few instances it has not been possible to deeply explore the issue of intersection of gender with other inequality issues. The small number of schools makes it difficult to compare and contrast across different kinds of schools, except some comments regarding single-sex and co-educational. The study design did not include exploration of parental views. Interactions with students provided an understanding of parental attitude as perceived by boys and girls. Although the study explored the issue of aspirations among boys and girls, it did not explore post-school choices and outcomes of education.

An important challenge of qualitative research is that it is much more researcher-dependent than quantitative research. This at times leads to significant variations in analytical perspectives and interpretations, which is also true for this study. However, this can be turned into an advantage, as reading of one chapter provides a perspective which can then be applied to another context by the reader, even if the author themselves has not used it.

Statistical Overview: Development, Gender and Education in the Case Study Countries

The seven case study countries comprise a varied sample: two are from Africa, two from Asia, two from the Pacific and one from the Caribbean. In 2005, according to the 2007–2008 Human Development Report (HDR)[2] of the United Nations Development Programme (UNDP), Seychelles and Samoa had very small populations of around 100,000; Trinidad and Tobago had a population of about 1.5 million and Malaysia had one of 26 million. In comparison, Nigeria's population was around 141 million, Pakistan's was 160 million, while that of India was over 1,000 million (a billion). Table 1.3 provides background information on geography, population, date of independence and major religions.

Table 1.3. Geography, population, independence and major religions

Country	Continent	Reg.	Geography	Area km2	Popul'n	Ind. Date	Main religions
1 Seychelles	Africa	SSA	4 major islands	451	100,000	1976	Christianity
2 Trin & Tob	Caribbean	LAC	2 major islands	5,128	1.3m	1962	C & H
3 Malaysia	Pacific	EAP	Divided by ocean[3]	329,847	25.7m	1957	I, B, H, C
4 Samoa	Pacific	EAP	2 main islands	2,831	100,000	1962	Christianity
5 India	Asia	SWA	Varied	3,287,240	1,134.4m	1947	H, I, B, J, S, C
6 Pakistan	Asia	SWA	Varied	803,940	158.1m	1947	Islam
7 Nigeria	Africa	SSA	Varied	923,768	141.4m	1960	I, C

Notes:

1. SSA – sub-Saharan Africa; LA&C – Latin America and the Caribbean; EA&P – East Asia and the Pacific; S&WA – South and West Asia.
2. Population data from 2005, unless otherwise indicated
3. B-Buddhism, C-Christianity, H-Hinduism, I-Islam, J-Jainism, S-Sikhism

Sources: Population data from the UNDP 2007–2008 Human Development Report; population, independence and religions, Wikipedia; others – various.

These countries have a diverse social context. While India, Malaysia, Nigeria, Seychelles and Trinidad and Tobago are multi-religious, multi-ethnic countries, Pakistan has only one religion, Islam, and Samoa only Christianity. Religion, traditions and social contexts have significant impact on gender notions and relations. Samoa is an interesting case as the village, district and national government political systems as well as protocols and procedures in all areas of life continue to be governed by the notion of *Fa'aSamoa*. '*Fa'aSamoa*' means 'the Samoan Way' and is an all-encompassing concept that dictates how Samoans are meant to behave. It refers to the obligations that Samoans owe their family, community and church and the individual's sense of Samoan identity. Each individual within *Fa'aSamoa* can have many roles and responsibilities, which are determined by several factors including locality, holder of *matai* title, age and gender.

As illustrated in Table 1.4 below, the 2007–2008 HDR indicates a clear rank in terms of Gross Domestic Product (GDP) per capita, from Seychelles, through Trinidad and Tobago, Malaysia, Samoa, India and Pakistan to Nigeria. Amongst the case study countries, the GDP per capita rank correlates exactly with the UNDP's Human Development Index (HDI).[4] Following this approach, three countries are classified among the high human development group, three as medium human development and one as low human development.

Exploring the Bias: Gender & Stereotyping in Secondary Schools

Table 1.4. Selected development indicators for the case study countries

Country	GDP per capita US$	Human dev. category	HDI rank: of 177	Value	GDI rank: of 157	Value	GEM rank: of 93	Value
1 Seychelles	16,106	High	50	0.843	NA	NA	NA	NA
2 Trin & Tob	14,603	High	59	0.814	56	0.808	23/93	0.685
3 Malaysia	10,882	High	63	0.811	58	0.802	65/93	0.504
4 Samoa	8,677	Medium	77	0.785	72	0.776	NA	NA
5 India	3,452	Medium	128	0.619	113	0.600	NA	NA
6 Pakistan	2,370	Medium	136	0.551	125	0.525	82/93	0.377
7 Nigeria	1,128	Low	158	0.470	139	0.456	NA	NA

Source: UNDP 2007–2008 Human Development Report

The GDP per capita/HDI ranking also correlates with that for UNDP's Gender-related Development Index (GDI),[5] for six of the seven case study countries. No GDI value is given for Seychelles. The Gender-specific EFA Index (GEI) and the Gender Parity Index (GPI)[6] for both primary and secondary Net Enrolment Ratios (NERs) of the UNESCO 2009 Education For All (EFA) Global Monitoring Report (GMR) suggests that Seychelles' GDI and HDI ranks **may** correspond. Seychelles is therefore assigned first place in the GDI ranking, as ranking the countries helps to provide a loose framework for analysis and comparison. Following the convergence of the GDP, HDI and GDI rankings, the case study countries are thus always addressed in the following order: Seychelles, Trinidad and Tobago, Malaysia, Samoa, India, Pakistan and Nigeria.

The comparative ranking of the case study countries against the UNDP's Gender Empowerment Measure (GEM)[7] would give a more definitive indication of the gendered outcomes of education, as it assesses parliamentary representation, economic participation and actual income. Unfortunately, however, and in common with 84 of the 177 countries in the 2007–2008 HDR, there is no GEM data for Seychelles, Samoa, India or Nigeria.

In the absence of a full set of GEM data, the study can be contextualised with an overview of progress towards achievement of the second and third Millennium Development Goals (MDGs). Table 1.5 provides such data for the case study countries, available for all but one indicator.

The presentation of this data illustrates the complexity of ranking countries against any indices. It also underlines the need to treat all macro data as at best, loosely indicative and at worst, potentially misleading. While this MDG data broadly replicates the HDI/GDI rank patterns in that the first four countries (Seychelles, Trinidad and Tobago, Malaysia and Samoa) outperform the following three (India, Pakistan

Table 1.5. Country progress against MDG 2 and MDG 3

Country	MDG 2: achieve universal primary education			MDG 3: promote gender equality and empower women					
	Primary NER % (2005)	Proportion (%) of students starting grade 1 who reach grade 5 (2004)	Literacy rate (%) of 15–24 years olds (Most recent of 1995–2005)	Ratio of girls to boys in primary education (using GER)	Ratio of girls to boys in secondary education (using GER)	Ratio of girls to boys in tertiary education (using GER)	Ratio of literate women to men 15–24 years old	Share of women in wage employment in the non-agricultural sector	Proportion of seats held by women in national parliament
1 Seychelles	99	99	99.1	1.00	1.03	1.39	1.01	NA	23.5
2 Trin & Tob	90	90	99.5	1.01	0.99	NA	1.00	NA	25.4
3 Malaysia	95	95	97.2	0.97	1.04	1.27	1.00	NA	13.1
4 Samoa	90	94	99.3	1.00	1.14	1.31	1.00	NA	6.1
5 India	89	73	76.4	1.00	1.12	0.93	0.80	NA	9.0
6 Pakistan	68	70	65.1	0.94	0.80	0.70	0.69	NA	20.4
7 Nigeria	68	73	84.2	0.76	0.74	0.88	0.94	NA	NA
HDR table	T12	T12	T12	T30	T30	T30	T30	T31	T29

Sources: UNDP 2007–2008 Human Development Report, Tables 12, 29, 30 and 31

and Nigeria), the data against certain indicators return surprises. Examples of this are the low primary Net Enrolment Ratio (NER) for Trinidad and Tobago; Nigeria's relatively high youth and adult literacy rates; India's apparently high ratio of girls to boys in secondary education and Pakistan's high representation of women in parliament. One of the discrepancies might be partly due to the fact that the female to male ratios in primary, secondary and tertiary education are calculated using the highly imprecise measure of Gross Enrolment Ratios (GERs) to allow comparison against the three levels (as there is as yet no full set of NERs for tertiary education). These apparent surprises remind us that quantitative indicators for global comparison must be contextualised with more problematised, country-specific explorations.

As there is no GEM data for Seychelles, Samoa, India and Nigeria, and the single MDG 3 indicator tracking economic activity has no entries, other data on women's economic activity and political participation is explored. Table 1.6 provides more information on female economic activity for Nigeria, and some for Samoa and India, but there is still no new information for Seychelles.

When ranked according to the percentage of women engaged in economic activity, or women's economic activity as a percentage of the male rate, all countries except

Exploring the Bias: Gender & Stereotyping in Secondary Schools

Table 1.6. Gender inequality in economic activity

| Country | Female economic activity (Aged 15 and over) | | | Employment by economic activity (%)[8] | | | | | | Contributing family workers (%) | |
| | Rate (%) 2005 | Index (1990= 100) 2005 | As % of male rate 2005 | Agriculture | | Industry | | Services | | | |
				Women 1995– 2005	Men 1995– 2005	Women 1995– 2005	Men 1995– 2005	Women 1995– 2005	Men 1995– 2005	Women 1995– 2005	Men 1995– 2005
Seychelles	NA	NA	NA	NA	NA	NA	NA	NA	NA	NA	NA
Trin & Tob	46.7	112	61	2	10	14	37	84	53	NA	NA
Malaysia	46.5	105	57	11	16	27	35	62	49	NA	NA
Samoa	39.2	97	51	NA	NA	NA	NA	NA	NA	NA	NA
India	34	94	42	NA	NA	NA	NA	NA	NA	NA	NA
Pakistan	32.7	117	39	65	38	16	22	20	40	NA	NA
Nigeria	54.4	95	53	2	4	11	30	87	70	NA	NA

Source: UNDP 2007–2008 Human Development Report, Table 31, pages 338–341

Nigeria retain the default order. Nigeria returns the highest (given) rate of female economic activity and the third rank in the female rate as a percentage of the male rate, placing it before Samoa, India and Pakistan. This change in Nigeria's rank reorders Pakistan at the bottom of the gendered economic activity scale, a fact rendered more interesting as Pakistan's 'employment by economic activity type' patterns diverge from those for the other countries with data. In all cases apart from Pakistan, data on employment by economic activity type duplicates recognised gender patterns: more men than women in agriculture and industry, and more women than men in the service industry.[9] In Pakistan, however, there are more women than men in agriculture, and more men than women in services.

Table 1.7 provides historical background with the year women received the right to vote, to stand for election, the year when the first woman was elected or appointed to parliament and the percentage of women at ministerial level, in the lower and upper houses. Against these categories, country rankings change significantly.

If we take the first year that women received the right to vote or stand for election, India and Pakistan were the earliest, followed by Trinidad and Tobago, Seychelles and Samoa, then Malaysia and finally Nigeria. In most cases, the right to vote came when countries were governed by colonial administration. A ranking against the year that a woman was first elected to parliament puts India first, followed by Malaysia, Trinidad and Tobago, Pakistan, Samoa, Seychelles and then Nigeria. A third ranking, against the percentage of women in government at ministerial level has Trinidad and Tobago in the lead, followed by Nigeria, Seychelles, Malaysia, Samoa, Pakistan and then India. Finally, a ranking against the percentage of seats in the

Table 1.7. Women's political participation

| Country | Year women received the right to: | | First year woman elected (E) or appointed (A) to parliament | Women in government at ministerial level (%) 2005 | Seats in parliament held by women (% of total) | | Upper house or senate |
| | Vote | Stand for election | | | Lower or single house | | |
					1990	2007	2007
Seychelles	1948	1948	1976 E&A	12.5	16.0	23.5	NA
Trin & Tob	1946	1946	1962 E&A	18.2	16.7	19.4	32.3
Malaysia	1957	1957	1959 A	9.1	5.1	9.1	25.7
Samoa	1948 & 1990	1948 & 1990	1976 E	7.7	6.6	6.1	NA
India	1935 & 1950	1935 & 1950	1952 E	3.4	5.6	8.3	10.7
Pakistan	1935 & 1947	1935 & 1947	1973 E	5.6	10.1	21.3	17.0
Nigeria	1958	1958	1994 E	17.6	NA	22.0	NA

Source: UNDP 2007–2008 Human Development Report, Table 33, pages 343–346

lower house held by women puts Seychelles in the first place, followed by Nigeria, Pakistan, Trinidad and Tobago, Malaysia, India, then Samoa. These statistics present intriguing, and sometimes apparently contradictory patterns: patterns that the country chapters explore, contest and frame.

When we turn to deeper exploration of the macro statistics on education, using the more focussed, sector-specific EFA Global Monitoring Report, the different data sources and dates[10] introduce further inconsistencies. As outlined in Table 1.8, the Education Development Index (EDI) ranks Malaysia above Trinidad and Tobago and

Table 1.8. Country ranking by EDI and GEI[11]

EDI	Country	Rank	Value	GEI	Country	Rank	Value
1	Seychelles	34/129	0.974	1	Seychelles	11/129	0.991*
2	Malaysia	45/129	0.965	2	Trin & Tob	51/129	0.974*
3	Trin & Tob	64/129	0.941	3	Malaysia	77/129	0.952*
4	Samoa	NA	NA	4	Samoa	NA	NA
5	India	102/129	0.794	5	India	108/129	0.834
6	Nigeria	113/129	0.752	6	Nigeria	113/129	0.815
7	Pakistan	118/129	0.652	7	Pakistan	118/129	0.714

Notes: *Indicative of inequality at the expense of boys and/or men
Source: UNESCO GMR (2009)

Exploring the Bias: Gender & Stereotyping in Secondary Schools

Nigeria above Pakistan. (There is no data for Samoa: it has been placed fourth in both ranks).

The default/HDI rank is maintained in the Gender-specific EFA Index, and here we begin to see the negative gender balance turning from girls and women: the GEIs for Seychelles, Trinidad and Tobago and Malaysia are indicative of gender disparities at the expense of boys and men in secondary and/or tertiary level.

Table 1.9 provides data to contextualise the difference between countries' HDI and EDI ranks, ordering them against *net* primary and secondary enrolment and *gross* tertiary enrolment. This data changes the ranking in each case, highlighting interesting patterns for deeper exploration. Of particular note are the primary NER for Trinidad and Tobago and the tertiary GER for India.

Finally, data presented in Table 1.10 below ranks countries against the Gender Parity Index (GPI) for enrolment at the three levels (not the NER or GER itself). Ranking against the GPI at the primary and secondary levels puts Nigeria before Pakistan, but ranking at the tertiary level puts Pakistan before India and Nigeria.

Table 1.9. Country ranking by primary, secondary and tertiary enrolment

P	Country	NER	GPI	S	Country	NER	GPI	T	Country	GER	GPI
1	Malaysia	100	1.00	1	Seychelles	94	NA	1	Seychelles	NA	NA
2	Seychelles	99	1.01	2	Malaysia	69	1.10	2	Malaysia	29	1.29
3	Samoa	90	1.00	3	Samoa	66	1.14	3	India	12	0.72
4	India	89	0.96	4	Trin & Tob	65	1.04	4	Trin & Tob	11	1.28
5	Trin & Tob	85	1.00	5	India	NA	NA	5	Samoa (1999)	11	1.04
6	Pakistan	66	0.78	6	Pakistan	30	0.77	6	Nigeria	10	0.69
7	Nigeria	63	0.86	7	Nigeria	26	0.84	7	Pakistan	5	0.85

Source: UNESCO GMR 2009

Table 1.10. Country ranking, GPI of primary, secondary and tertiary enrolment

P	Country	NER	GPI	S	Country	NER	GPI	T	Country	GER	GPI
1	Seychelles	99	1.01	1	Seychelles	94	NA	1	Seychelles	NA	NA
2	Malaysia	100	1.00	2	Samoa	66	1.14	2	Malaysia	29	1.29
2	Samoa	90	1.00	3	Malaysia	69	1.10	3	Trin & Tob	11	1.28
2	Trin & Tob	85	1.00	4	Trin & Tob	65	1.04	4	Samoa (1999)	11	1.04
5	India	89	0.96	5	India	NA	NA	5	Pakistan	5	0.85
6	Nigeria	63	0.86	6	Nigeria	26	0.84	6	India	12	0.72
7	Pakistan	66	0.78	7	Pakistan	30	0.77	7	Nigeria	10	0.69

Source: UNESCO GMR 2009

All these quantitative analyses and rankings highlight many areas for investigation and challenge. They do provide, however, an 'indicative' background or framework for the country-based qualitative enquiries, and the challenge.

The analyses suggest a good overall level of development and education in Seychelles, Trinidad and Tobago, Malaysia and Samoa, gender disparity at the expense of boys and men at secondary and tertiary levels, and 40–50 per cent of women engaged in economic activity. It is not possible to know the status and pay of women's economic activity, but their political participation is limited, despite the other indicators. The percentage of seats held by women in national parliament ranges from 6 per cent to 25 per cent (all using UNDP HDR 2008 data). Women are persisting to higher levels of education, but the statistics do not enable us to make an assessment of the outcomes of their education.

In contrast, the analyses suggest progressively less robust development in India, Pakistan and Nigeria respectively; gender disparity against girls and women at primary, secondary and tertiary levels, and 32 per cent of Indian women, 33 per cent of Pakistani women and 55 per cent of Nigerian women engaged in economic activity, again of unknown status. There is a surprising range in the percentage of seats held by women in national parliament. Most significantly, 20 per cent in Pakistan: greater than Malaysia, Samoa and India[12] (using UNDP HDR 2008 data). The data needs deeper contextualised exploration.

Addressing the Research Questions

The study was conducted to explore (i) whether school and classroom processes were reproducing or challenging dominant gendered stereotypes, (ii) how these processes were operating, and (iii) if processes were reproducing stereotypes, what was being done, or might be done, to interrupt the patterns and move towards more equitable processes.

The country case studies were broad and exploratory, the national contexts and the school samples were highly varied, and the analysis and report writing were conducted independently. The resulting reports contained such depth and variety: of perspective, approach, emphasis, detail and character. A synthesis of the country reports, following a common style and structure, would have sacrificed this depth and variety, and the voice of the country authors. This section thus presents a synthesis of insights on the **areas** that should be explored to address the research questions, rather than a detailed synthesis of the findings from each country. The country studies assigned different emphasis and order to the various areas, and not all chapters addressed all areas.

Do school processes reproduce or challenge gendered stereotypes?

The first question of the study was whether school and classroom processes were reinforcing or challenging dominant gendered stereotypes. To address this question, it was found necessary to explore the social, ethnic and religious mix of national populations, to determine if gendered stereotypes were common across all groups or specific to some. Having established this foundation, it was then necessary to explore the nature of the stereotypes themselves. Some countries grounded this exploration in a literature review; all included it as a major focus of data collection. In this case, the sample was restricted to the perspectives of educational bureaucrats, school managers, principals and head teachers, teachers and students who had reached class 9 or 10.

Gendered stereotypes and national policy

Analysis of dominant gender stereotypes, of the 'gender order and gender regimes' (Connell, 2002: p54) within each country highlights a constant refrain: from Seychelles, with its high levels of human development and female education; from Trinidad and Tobago, with its high levels and its large number of female-headed households to countries with lower human development ratings and evident gender disparities against women. The refrain, the dominant gender order of each country, was that of difference, of boys and girls, men and women being different and differently suited to different spheres. In each case, regardless of patterns of women's educational, economic or political achievements, researchers felt this difference contained an inequality, in both power and in authority. Notwithstanding these broad similarities, the notions of what is masculine and what is feminine have some stark differences. The two most contrasting examples are Trinidad and Tobago, where the notion of hegemonic masculinity goes to the extent of viewing education itself as a feminine activity, and Pakistan, where femininity is synonymous with being totally submissive and unquestioning, signifying family and community honour.

This did not, however, mean that boys and men always benefitted. Contained within each national gender order were notions of 'ideal types', of privileged, hegemonic forms of masculinity and of relationships between men and women. In contrast to the restricted range of acceptable male identities, girls' options were much wider. In both cases, assumed traits and behaviours could not radically contravene established gender orders, but the acceptable range, especially that acceptable to peers, was broader for girls than it was for boys. Girls may have had to act out different identities in different settings, to project themselves differently to satisfy various 'audiences', but girls and women could more easily display traits and behaviours stereotypically associated with boys and men than vice versa. Does national policy support or contest the dominant gender order?

The broad brush-strokes outlining national gender orders suggest persistent inequality and inequitable treatment between men and women, as well as between men. In somewhat stark contrast, however, many countries have national or policy engagement with, and commitment to gender equality, as enshrined in the human development discourse and encapsulated in the third Millennium Development Goal. Countries have signed up to the major significant declarations and conventions, most had revised national policies or reform packages with some mention of gender, and some had full education and gender policies. In these cases, there is often commitment to the achievement of societal and educational gender equality. There are few inclusions, however, of broad strategic plans suggesting how it might be pursued.

School processes and reproduction or challenge

Having established the nature of dominant gender stereotypes, as well as the gender visions underlying national policies, the studies were able to address the question of whether school and classroom processes were reproducing or challenging them. The response across all countries was that the reproduction of dominant gender stereotypes and regimes was immediately evident across numerous educational, school and classroom processes. This does not mean that some of these processes, or other less obvious ones, did not entail challenges to dominant stereotypes, but that the patterns of reproduction of these stereotypes were both numerous and almost always immediately apparent.

Despite the inevitably generalising nature of analysis, there were some examples of challenge to the dominant gender order: most obviously in the statements and practices of girls and women, less regularly, but significantly, in those of some boys and men. Due again to the limited nature of the student data, it was not possible to identify correlations with socio-economic group, ethnicity and/or religion. In comparison with processes of reproduction, those who challenged gendered stereotypes were few, and often hidden – sometimes consciously, often subconsciously. This fact is indicative of the sometimes aggressively gendered environment of sample schools.

How do these processes reproduce or challenge stereotypes?

The country analysis identified four arenas where processes might contribute to or challenge the school-based reproduction of dominant gender orders. These arenas were those of attitudes, environments, curriculum and materials, and teaching, learning and classroom processes.

Attitudes, expectations and aspirations

While attitudes, expectations and aspirations are not in themselves processes, their centrality to all processes necessitates their detailed exploration. The analysis explored how people intuitively feel that gender identities are formed: whether they feel that people are 'essentially' male or female, or if gender identities and relationships are constructed through their socio-cultural experiences. And, if they feel the latter, whether they think concepts of gender equality, or tradition, religion or any other value framework should set the parameters for this construction. It explored whether livelihood and educational expectations of men and women (or boys and girls) are set by (i) essentialist notions, (ii) recognition, acceptance or resigned submission to the gendered status quo, or (iii) by a commitment to gender equality and equity. Analysis attempted to determine how those committed to equality respond to the reality of the gendered status quo and whether people's attitudes applied equally to all socio-economic or ethnic groups.

In nearly every country context, the focus on gender was emotive, for both men and women: the research always prompted strong, sometimes defensive or aggressive reactions. For some, who felt various levels of 'gender frustration', the research seemed to offer the opportunity to vent it. Others may have felt guilty that they were not doing anything to implement or pursue gender equality strategies, or that their thoughts, actions or practices contributed to the perpetuation of inequality. In other cases, individuals were threatened by the debate, did not see the perspective of the researchers and could not see what it had to do with the enterprise of schooling. Whatever the causes, the level of administration- or school-wide intellectual engagement with the issue of gender and its importance to their professional roles was minimal.

Due to their power over schools, school management and teachers, the attitudes of education bureaucrats and administrators, both of government and non-government organisations (private, religious and community-based) are crucially important. Individuals of this group who are committed to gender equality can initiate a virtuous cycle of gender-opportunity. If they not, they can contribute to the opposite. On the whole, attitudes within this group reflected stereotypes of the gendered status quo. Individuals in these senior positions, with considerable power and influence to affect change, seemed 'stranded' without the analytic or strategic tools to understand, appreciate or implement any policy frameworks addressing the pursuit of gender equality. It did not appear as if they reflected on the fact that these frameworks should affect their practice, or on how they might do so. Attitudes about head teachers or principals and teachers reflected essentialised dichotomies about the characteristics of each sex and the impacts of this on their professional conduct. There was no generalised notion across the countries that men were always better at leadership than women, but the stereotypes were always gendered. There was regular reference to the ways in which women's domestic roles interfered with their professional ones, and occasional mention of how men's non-educational activities and commitments took them away from school and their duties during the teaching day.

The attitudes of the principal or head teacher and the way in which they contributed to the schools' vision and mission (either written or unarticulated) were probably even more significant than those of educational administrators, bureaucrats, funders or even school management boards. A capable and strong head teacher, committed to gender equality, whether a woman or a man, could be one of the most critical factors in determining a school's gender regimes. With support, they could create enabling environments for like-minded teachers as well as those who have not yet engaged with the issues. Given the contentious nature of gender, however, such leaders often face isolation, resistance and/or hostility and such reactions can undermine the opportunity, courage or energy for change. Across the country studies, none of the principals or head teachers felt zealously committed to progressing gender equality in their schools as one of the most important features of their role. Women often (though not always) had 'gut' feelings about gender equality and some took principled stands (a female principal in Pakistan who supported her teacher's autonomy in her choice of head-gear being a particular case in point). There were examples of 'would-be' transformative men, inclined to review inequitable school processes and procedures. If these leaders had reflected deeply on these issues, it had not yet resulted in any strategic plans for action or for addressing real or anticipated opposition.

Although head teachers and principals committed to equality have the potential to determine the ethos of the whole school, they were enabled or undermined by the presence or absence of likeminded teachers among their staff. Teachers committed to gender equality could also make a difference (albeit one that is constrained) even in schools with no likeminded colleagues. It was the teachers who came into regular contact with the students, the teachers whose attitudes, expectations, practices and interactions could count for so much, or so little, in their students' lives and imaginations.

Teachers' viewed girls' role in contributing to 'care work' at school and home was viewed as non-problematic: both acceptable and unavoidable. In Trinidad and Tobago, boys' leisure-time activities were seen as detrimental to their academic success and school lives. Teachers' academic expectations were higher for girls in Seychelles, Trinidad and Tobago, Malaysia and Samoa; differentiation was not so clear in the other countries. In Seychelles, Trinidad and Tobago, Malaysia and Samoa, girls were considered more responsible and hardworking, while boys were considered indifferent and ill disciplined. In India and Pakistan, boys were seen as more naturally intelligent, but more inclined to be lazy, while girls were seen as hardworking, conscientious grafters. Also common was the perception that 'girls learn by rote learning' and 'boys are more active learners' based entirely on the fact that girls outperformed boys in areas where rote learning was considered necessary and not on any real experiences of trying out active learning processes with either boys or girls. Boys were also invariably perceived as the ultimate leaders, although girls were increasing in their assertiveness in leadership roles in Seychelles and Trinidad and Tobago.

The students, always the greatest number of any group in a school, constitute a powerful source of influence, inspiration and sometimes, control. In every school, when asked to list the traits of boys and girls, men and women, the students recognised and often repeated gendered stereotypes. When they were asked to describe themselves, and their future aspirations, the boys more readily upheld these stereotypes. Boys generally believed they would be the main breadwinner (even in Trinidad and Tobago, where there is such a large percentage of female-headed households) and saw girls as 'weaker' and in need of protection.

In many cases, the girls upheld some traits and aspirations, but rejected those associated with weakness, secondary status and dependency; even when they spoke of independence, some admitted that they felt they needed protection. A lack of realism in career or work aspirations was common to both boys and girls (in terms of a mismatch between subjects under study and those required for stated career preferences), not just the few girls who aspired to careers in male-dominated fields. Students' parents and their home environments appeared to reinforce gender stereotypes, but the research did not interview parents or visit homes, so such inferences were derived from discussions with students and school staff.

Identities are rarely only 'formed' by external influences: individuals are at the centre of the construction and negotiation of their own identities. While this research did not focus specifically on less obvious student cultures and peer-group processes, boys' reduced enrolments, poor achievement and increased dropout constituted a significant marker of student resistance to school regimes. Other, less high-profile incidences of resistance can be gleaned from focus group discussions and observations. Two incidents of students' undermining any transgression of their accepted gender regimes are both from Trinidad and Tobago. In one, boys who were interested in academic subjects and in doing well were regarded as effeminate by their peers. In the other, girls on the sideline of a netball match referred to the only boy on the pitch as a 'faggot'.

This first section has addressed the importance of attitudes, expectations and aspirations in the processes of identity formation. The next section addresses the actual environments of the school and the messages that these environments convey.

Environments: school visions and messages

The primary feature of a school's environment, raised by all country studies, was that of the actual physical environment. Schools were more appealing and enabling for all students if they were maintained and cared for, regardless of resources; if they offered at least basic facilities, with toilet blocks and water supply; if they provided an encouraging environment; and, vitally, if girls, boys and staff were safe from psychological bullying, or physical, sexual or reputational harm, within the school or while on school-assigned tasks. In the most extreme case of an unsafe school, Nigerian girls were subject to the threat and reality of sexual abuse while on school errands to collect water. Even one such occurrence undermines the entire purpose of schooling.

The issue of girls' reputational and physical safety was a major issue in all countries, Seychelles to Nigeria, often for very different reasons – sometimes with different consequences, but always highly gendered ones. As has been shown, Nigerian girls were exposed to unacceptable risks: they were more openly involved in voluntary relationships with student peers. In India and Pakistan, girls' education could be arrested even on parental suspicion of involvement with boys, and the inclusion of sex or HIV education was usually considered inappropriate in schools. Schools in Trinidad and Tobago and Seychelles tried to adapt codes of conduct and versions of personal and social education (PSE) to address high rates of teenage relationships and pregnancy.

The importance of this need for a safe environment, particularly for girls, often resulted in gender-segregation during certain tasks and activities. This, like many other issues explored in the chapters, was seen from a variety of perspectives. Some researchers saw it as protecting and enabling the girls; others saw it as an example of the reproduction of gendered dichotomies. Each case has to be assessed in its own context.

The school purpose, ethos and mission, both the explicit and the hidden versions, had a major impact on identify formation, even in the absence of explicit commitment to gender equality. If the schools were committed to quality, equality and the success of every student, they were more likely to present all students with a broader range of life-options. Some schools in the study, generally those with greater resources and more successful or affluent student populations, provided such inspiration.

Beyond the creation of a baseline of quality, the school vision and mission statements (where they existed) could determine which types of gender identities and interactions were encouraged, and which were discouraged. Almost all principles and head teachers of single-sex schools, whether in Trinidad, Samoa, India or Pakistan perceived gender as a non-issue in their schools, as they were single-sex. This reflects the fact that gender is widely perceived as a boy versus girl issue, which prevents a more holistic understanding. In almost all cases, girls-only schools were more conformist in protecting and promoting the dominant notions of feminine behaviour and image. This is in contrast with a number of experiences in literacy and women development programmes where single-sex experiences have been used to promote empowerment-based approaches and question unequal gender relations. The issue of a large number of girls underperforming within the situation where boys' underachievement is the average occurrence, and vice versa, also gets lost where gender is perceived only in terms of boys versus girls.

In practice, even a vision and mission statement based on gender equality might be undermined. School management, principals and teachers may want to treat girls and boys in a gender-equitable way, but they may feel that this will have detrimental results for the girls. In India, Pakistan and Nigeria, for example, teachers or principals with visions of equality/equity are caught between these and those of the parents or communities whom they serve, if they have different aspirations for their daughters. Such schools or teachers have to tread a fine line to inspire their pupils and yet not jeopardise the same girls' chances of staying in school. The larger school system, in most cases, does not provide the desired tools and support to these teachers and principals to deal with such issues.

In another complex situation, in all country cases, not just those with educational gender disparities against boys, there was a disjuncture between the school system (with its endorsement of hegemonic masculinities) and the aspirations, identities and imaginations of some of the male student population. The student data did not allow in-depth analysis by socio-economic, ethnic or religious background, but other research suggests this percentage constitutes large numbers of boys from disadvantaged groups. These disaffected boys tended to either not enrol, or to underachieve, misbehave and/or drop out, compounding their disadvantage. In the pursuit of equity, the dynamics of these situations demand analytic attention and exploration, rather than the anecdotal apportioning of blame on women teachers, as reported in Trinidad and Tobago.

Another feature identified by the country studies as critical in setting guidelines for the pursuit of equity, was the identification of which groups (if there are identifiable groups, among both girls and boys) were achieving and which ones were underperforming. If groups could be and were identified, by staff or students, the underperformance itself was seen as an essential 'trait' associated with that group. In many cases, teachers labelled students from lower socio-economic/ethnic groups (boys or girls or both, depending on the setting) as 'weak' purely by the fact of their background. An extension of this, raised in the Pakistan study, was the affect on groups or individuals by the messages communicated about which families and communities were valued: by what interaction took place, and by who was involved in that interaction. Schools encouraged performance and aspiration where they engaged the support and involvement of parents and communities, especially those of marginalised students or groups.

All country studies identified areas of the school environment of co-educational schools, where the gendered dimensions were immediately apparent: those of gender differentiation in authority, responsibility, subject choice tasks, sports, clubs, break-time activities and disciplinary procedures.

The first of this category was the gendered allocation of authority and responsibility, among both the teachers and students. Given the very small size of the teacher sample, and the small percentage of each national teaching force they represented, the analysis could only highlight localised patterns. These patterns point to an increasing female majority among the teaching staff, but a persistent minority in management structures. There were many variations on the gendered patterns associated with positions of responsibility assigned to students, often related to whether the school in question was single-sex (in name and practice, as one boys' school in Pakistan admitted girls) or co-educational. There were discernable patterns, however. Jobs were assigned to girls and boys depending on management's gendered perception of their appropriateness and head boys were sometimes vested with authority over head girls.

In some countries, the second clear separation was related to teacher and student distribution across subjects. While there were exceptions in almost all instances, there was a persistence of women teaching, and girls selecting, arts subjects, and men teaching, and boys selecting, science subjects. In some schools, these patterns were gradually beginning to change.

The researchers identified clear examples where boys and girls were generally segregated around the school: before and after lessons; at break-times; doing teacher-assigned tasks; in sports activities, and sometimes in clubs and extra-curricular activities. The gender issues associated with sports and physical activities were so numerous that they alone deserve a separate study. Not only was the choice of and participation in sports highly gendered, sport **itself** was, as a phenomenon. Apart from in Seychelles, sports were regularly seen as an area of male preserve and excellence.

In the co-educational schools in Pakistan, boys and girls rarely interacted. One of the Pakistani co-educational schools even segregated the students from grades 6 to 9 into different classrooms. There were numerous justifications for these segregations, ranging from management techniques, notions of appropriateness, girls' reputational and physical safety, to concessions to comply with parental wishes and expectations. These are all complex areas, which required careful exploration and assessment of their impact, but no school teams appeared to be engaged in such activity.

The final area of differentiation was in the setting and enforcing of school rules. Rules were often framed by schools' understanding of appropriate behaviour and relationships between boys and girls. While this sometimes resulted in what appeared to be unnecessarily restricted interaction and the reproduction of dominant gender dichotomies, such strategies often appeared to be the only option available to the school staff. School management, principals and teachers may have had some aspiration to treat girls and boys equitably, but they may have not found any way to do so and maintain discipline in situations of limited resources, limited training and experience, and seriously disruptive students. Some teachers might have decided on balance between ideals and aspirations on the one hand and school or classroom control on the other.

The consequences of breaking the rules were often more gendered and severe than the rules themselves. In most cases, boys received more physical punishment, generally of a more harsh nature, which sometimes appeared to constitute assault. The punishment of the extreme cases of disruption by disenfranchised boys presented an acute gender contradiction. Whilst schools and education systems are often founded on academic masculinities that align poorly with those of disengaged boys, they resort to highly gendered management techniques which are responses to the boys' more 'macho' masculinities.

In many cases, girls' punishment included more public humiliation than physical violence, shocking examples being the cases of teachers' humiliation of Malaysian girls in incidents related to menstruation. In other situations, Nigeria's being a particular case in point, school rules were deeply, inequitably gendered. Not only were some cases of bullying and intimidation left unpunished, but in situations of pregnancy arising through rape or teacher-student relationships, the girl was punished and excluded from school, while the boy or the teacher continued with his education or job.

The second section explored school environments and the messages that they convey. The following section will explore the curriculum, syllabus, exams, textbooks and learning materials.

Curriculum, syllabus, exams, textbooks and learning materials

The nature – not exclusively the gendered nature of the curriculum, any syllabi, exams, textbooks and other learning materials was identified as a significant factor in processes of reproduction or challenge to the gendered status quo. Attention was drawn to the epistemic foundations of the curriculum, whether it was based on the reproduction of a body or bodies of knowledge defined by others, or on the creation of knowledge; on rote learning and memorisation, or on exploration, independent thinking and questioning. It was felt that in Seychelles, Trinidad and Tobago and Malaysia, where elements within the curriculum and materials appeared to encourage knowledge creation rather than reproduction, there was a greater likelihood of challenge to stereotypical gender norms. This seemed significantly reduced in India, Pakistan and Nigerian, however, where the curriculum and materials tended to lean towards reproduction.

Another curriculum-related issue was whether all schools offered an 'equitable' breadth of subjects to all its students, or whether some were restricted, based on either lack of availability of funds or teachers, or assumptions reflecting gender or social class stereotypes. One or both of these scenarios existed in schools in the case study countries.

The final major theme in this area was the composition and nature of textbooks and learning materials. The researchers explored (i) whether the textbooks and materials encouraged, required or rewarded rote learning and reproduction, or exploratory learning and questioning, (ii) their foundational societal and gender regimes, evident though text and illustration, and (iii) whether teachers were provided with the tools to use them in ways that encouraged critical and independent thinking and broader social equity. Following the patterns of the curriculum foundations, the textbooks of Seychelles, Trinidad and Tobago and Malaysia tended to present fewer stereotypical gender images than those of India, Pakistan or Nigeria.

In Seychelles, most of the textbooks were recently published books and were gender-friendly. In India and Malaysia, there was an effort to depict women in non-traditional roles and portray them as capable of making choices. In India, there have been token 'shifts' such as an added chapter on women's status. In Pakistan, the visibility of women was very low; women and men were often identified with stereotypical attributes: men as brave, heroic, honest and strong; women as caring, loving, kind and self-sacrificing. Also in Pakistan, members of textbook review panels and authors are almost all men. In one instance, however, a team of female authors and reviewers was able to produce a comparatively gender-inclusive textbook.

Teaching, learning and classroom processes

This final section deals with actual teaching, learning and classroom processes.

Replicating the first themes under the issues of environment, the factor of teaching and learning processes to have the most significant impact on equality of achievement was quality. This was not an obviously, immediately apparent gendered issue, and certainly not one that could be linked with the success of either girls, or of boys, but it was a **baseline** issue. If lessons were conscientiously taught, and if teachers demonstrated a degree of professionalism, then this provided a baseline for broadening achievement **for all**. In an absence of such a baseline, schools did not have much leverage against any established inequalities. Key elements of quality included whether the full teaching cycle (of planning and preparing, delivering sessions, marking and re-planning) was commonly observed; whether teachers knew students' names and areas of strength and weakness; whether they differentiated, even within streams, and whether students ever shared concerns about areas of weakness, and, if they did, if teachers responded. In situations where some boys were underperforming, as in Seychelles, Trinidad and Tobago, Malaysia and Samoa, then such boys would have benefitted. If the situation was reversed, and girls were underperforming, then such girls would have benefitted. The country research, however, reported the regular absence of such a baseline in some schools and some classes: again, most noticeably in Nigeria.

The next major non-specifically gendered factor identified that had the potential to have a significant impact on students' achievement, aspirations and goals was the teachers' engagement with individuals. Important areas for exploration were whether (i) teachers had a sense of a pastoral role with their students – whether they attempted to inspire and encourage them; (ii) they engaged with student interests and the things they felt were important; (iii) they tried to overcome generational, socio-economic, ethnic or any other gaps; (iv) they engaged with students' home/ neighbourhood realities and encouraged to overcome external challenges, and (v) they adjusted their teaching and interaction with students so that they might succeed despite home/neighbourhood challenges. Most chapters reveal few instances of teachers engaging with students in these ways: it is possible teachers lost numerous opportunities for inspiration and motivation. The nature and duration of the fieldwork did not allow time for in-depth exploration of these factors, so the researchers could not be sure that more 'personal' interaction rarely took place, but little took place during the fieldwork.

Lessons in Seychelles, Trinidad and Tobago and Malaysia were teacher-led with some opportunities for student participation. Those in India, Nigeria, Pakistan and Samoa were passive and highly teacher-dominated. Teacher-led lessons may have been the only option in very large classes with minimal resources. Across the study, there was a wide range of quality, commitment and professionalism and an even wider range of attention, or otherwise, to students. Every country had its share of disengaged teachers; some appeared to teach to the mythical 'average student' with no concern for what any student might be learning, while there were those who demonstrated energy and interest. After these two baseline factors, there were numerous features of teaching, learning and classroom processes where the gendered nature was more immediately evident.

The first of these was the number of male and female students in co-educational classrooms. The pattern of more men teaching and boys selecting science subjects, and more women teaching and girls selecting arts subjects has been addressed in the previous section on school environments. Where this pattern was sustained, its maintenance perpetuated existing gender and subject stereotypes. As an extension of this was the issue of numbers of boys and girls within a class, and the gender patterns among the obvious achievers within the same class. In classes where boys were in the significant majority, as in India and Pakistan, some girls tended to be more reticent and subdued than they were in classes with a more even gender mix. In classes where girls were in the majority (as in some case in the first four HDI-ranked countries), boys either competed to show themselves as 'good as the girls' or tended to 'act out' more assertive, careless masculinities to avoid 'losing face'.

An extension of this exploration, gendered dominance in classroom role was that of gendered patterns in 'streamed' sets. Year groups in nearly all schools were streamed within subjects, even in one school where a principal/member of the management team wished to phase it out: such an approach was deemed unavoidable. Streaming became gendered and (arguably) doubly inequitable, when the top sets were dominated by either boy or girls, and the lower sets by the inverse. Such patterns, replicating the wider societal gender orders and gender regimes, were recognisable in almost all cases. Again, this was not a phenomenon that only disadvantaged girls: the process was disempowering to significant numbers of boys.

The next very obviously gendered feature of most classrooms (in co-educational schools) was gender-segregated seating arrangements. There were exceptions, but in the majority of cases, whether students were seated at a desk or on the floor, boys and girls sat separately. Furthermore, in most instances, teachers had no involvement in determining seating: students organised themselves in this way. In Samoa, where most lessons were didactic and teacher centred, with their movements restricted to the front of the room, girls always sat nearer the teacher. This might have been a result of the influence of *Fa'aSamoa*, wherein boys treated girls as sisters, ensuring their wellbeing by offering them the opportunity of sitting nearer the centre of teaching activity. Whatever the causes and justification of gender-segregated seating, the consequences were sometimes theorised, but not always substantiated by the data. In order to assess any long-term implications on achievement and identity, the study would have had to be longer and more classroom focussed.

Another clearly gendered feature of all classrooms was teachers' use of gender as a management tool. Students were grouped by sex in registers, queues/lines, tasks, the collection of books, marks or money – or in the 'pitting' of boys against girls in competitive group work. In one Pakistani school, it was found that boys performed better when there were girls in the class, whereas the inverse was observed in Trinidad and Tobago. Another Pakistani school, although co-educational, organised all the classes from grade 6 to grade 9 as single-sex, as this was felt to be a more suitable management approach.

Beyond these highly visible differentiations, there were other processes that appeared to be gendered. Although research constraints precluded in-depth exploration of these areas, definite patterns were discernable.

One obvious area was that of physical, verbal and 'eye-contact' interaction between the teacher and the students: they were differently gendered in different settings. In Samoa, the girls interacted more regularly with their teachers, as they sat at the front of the classroom, in the main areas of teacher activity. In other cases, boys were more boisterous, more ready to volunteer ideas and even call out to the teacher (where it was permitted) and girls more reticent, their involvement hampered by their reluctance to get the answer wrong. In classes with an equal number of boys and girls, however, it was sometimes difficult to recognise any highly-gendered interaction patterns. In India, Nigeria and Pakistan, teachers gave greater attention to boys, by providing more opportunities to respond and participate. When Indian and Pakistani girls appeared shy and reticent, there was no teacher effort to draw them into the lessons or increase their confidence.

Another significant area was teachers' language and imagery, and their use of the textbooks and learning materials. Language regularly reinforced gender stereotypes, although this pattern was less marked in Seychelles. There was evidence of teachers repeatedly labelling boys and girls, terming boys as intelligent but irresponsible (in Trinidad), and girls as potentially less intelligent, but hardworking, disciplined and capable of the persistence required to learn by rote (in Pakistan). In many cases, teachers' use of the textbooks either (i) uncritically reflected the foundational, reproductive epistemology of dense, fact-laden books, or (ii) did not exploit the possibility of using less didactic, fact-based books to question and challenge gender stereotypes. Textbooks, materials and their use are one area in particular need of further research.

This final section has explored teaching, learning and classroom processes and their contribution to the reproduction or challenge of the gendered status quo. The arena of classroom processes is one that has a vast potential to create environments that help children to actively challenge the gendered status quo. In these country studies, however, they tended to reinforce it much more regularly. The next section explores the actions that might be taken to help progress more gender equitable school processes and, thus, the pursuit of greater gender equity.

What might advance greater gender equality?

Individual research teams have suggested a range of possible recommendations for various levels: policy to institutional reforms, teacher training to school-based changes. Advancing gender equality in education with a focus on schooling processes means making school a more democratic and equal institution in general and poses a major challenge in most societies. Nevertheless, it is a challenge that needs to be addressed and the study points to a number of possible solutions.

Democratising gender debate and action: going beyond national policies

Most national policies have incorporated the goal of gender equality in their commitments in some manner or the other. However, the action largely remains limited to adoption of access related initiatives. The relational aspects of gender rarely get addressed in a systematic manner. The attitudes, beliefs and views regarding gender among teachers, principals and educational bureaucrats are rarely questioned or challenged. Teacher training courses do not go deep enough into these issues and gender is generally treated only superficially both in pre-service and in-service programmes. In order to change this, it is important to democratise the gender debate taking it to all levels, and developing more nuanced approaches for training of teachers as well as educational administrators. Teachers and principals cannot lead the process of change unless equipped with the right kinds of attitudes and skills, and supported by educational administrators.

Gender mainstreaming at all levels and stages

Schools function as part of hierarchical structures governed by rigid systems and processes. This is largely true not only in the case of state schools but also those run by religious bodies and other school-governing structures. Even in cases where principals and school administrators were very aware of gender issues, they were reluctant to take action as they didn't feel empowered enough. Gender-equal processes in schools demand the presence of a democratic culture and ethos that teachers and principals themselves have not experienced. It is important to democratise the systems, processes and norms that govern schools if the processes and norms within schools have to change. This requires gender mainstreaming based institutional reforms of education systems as a whole. Gender mainstreaming includes adoption of gender-responsive budgeting and monitoring process. Gender-responsive budgeting and monitoring can go a long way in ensuring the gender-responsive school environment and processes.

Gender mainstreaming in education involves integration of gender at all stages and levels: curriculum, syllabus, textbooks, learning materials, teaching and assessment processes both in substance and in practice.

Promoting school-based and school-led research, initiatives and change processes

Change in schooling processes requires change in school ethos, change in class-room processes, change in the ways of interactions between principals and teachers, teachers and students, among teachers and among students. Shared vision and understanding is critical for this kind of change. School ethos and culture cannot be changed without developing shared vision of gender-equal processes and working collectively towards achieving that vision. Similarly, classroom-based changes leading to shifts in teaching/learning practices, styles, the language being used and stereotypes being questioned require a community of teachers who are willing to experiment, reflect, share and learn. A single teacher can initiate some of these, but it would be difficult to go far without support and reinforcement from others. It is important to recognise this fact in order to appreciate the need for promoting school-based and school-led research and change processes, especially when they are linked to bringing change in processes and gender-related attitudes.

Promotion of school-based and school-led research and change process also presupposes faith in the capability of school and recognition of the autonomy of teachers. Gender-responsive teaching/learning processes require a change in school environment and processes that recognise students', both boys' and girls', autonomy and tries to develop healthier, more wholesome notions of masculine and feminine. This is not possible in an environment that does not recognise and value teachers' autonomy. The study makes it clear that most schools would need external help and support to reach that stage where they are capable of developing a shared vision and initiating researches on their own.

The gender responsive school: an action guide

Following the completion of this research in seven countries, the idea of initiating a school-based Action Gender project was discussed and welcomed in the workshop where all researchers met to discuss the draft reports and present the findings to respective governments. The idea was to provide support to selected schools to develop into gender-responsive institutions in a manner that is empowering, documenting that process of change in order to learn lessons for broader application. The Commonwealth Secretariat supported this pilot project titled Action Gender in Schools in a small number of selected schools in four out of these seven countries: India, Malaysia, Seychelles and Trinidad and Tobago. The approach adopted by these four counties varied in many ways and the Secretariat organised a sharing workshop to facilitate exchange of ideas among country teams. The documented experiences of these projects led to the development of an action guide titled *The Gender Responsive School: An Action Guide,* meant mainly for teachers and principals but useful for policy planners and educational administrators as well. The guide was finalised after a trialling workshop where four Southern African countries (Botswana, Malawi, Mozambique and South Africa) participated.

The guide – the result of collaboration among several players, significantly the team leaders and other researchers, teachers and staff of the schools participating in the pilot projects, and participants at the workshops – shows that it is possible to bring some significant changes in schools, if the process is appropriately conceptualised, supported and implemented. This offers practical and tested solutions for action at different levels, especially in schools. What makes this guide distinct is that it is based on real experiences and not merely ideas. It draws on the wealth of practical, well-documented experience in a variety of styles – reflection and analysis, action checklists, summaries of findings and experience – to provide lively and engaging content, with real life examples and voices.

Despair and hope

This research in seven countries looking at various classroom and other processes in selected secondary schools provided concrete indicators towards the fact that schools reinforce rather than question prevalent gender notions, and that learning experiences do not necessarily lead towards more equal gender relations and environment. The pilot Action Gender in School project that followed the study provided enough pointers to believe that schools can be made more gender-responsive if provided with adequate and appropriate support.

Notes

1. See Nussbaum (2000) for an argument for the universality of basic principles.
2. The 2007–2008 HDR presents the most recent data for the period up to 2005: there is no more recent data, as the 2009–2010 report is not due out until September 2009.
3. Peninsular Malaysia (Malaya or West Malaysia) and Malaysian Borneo (East Malaysia): separated by the South China Sea.
4. The HDI is a composite index measuring average achievement in three basic dimensions captured: a long and healthy life, knowledge and a decent standard of living.
5. The GDI is a composite index measuring average achievement in the three basic dimensions captured in the human development index, adjusted to account for inequalities between men and women.
6. See the UNESCO Global Monitoring Report (2009), pages 122 onwards, 248–249 & 250 and 302 onwards.
7. The GEM is a composite index measuring gender inequality in three basic dimensions of empowerment: economic participation and decision-making, political participation and decision-making, and power over economic resources.
8. As defined according to the International Standard Industrial Classification System, revisions 2 & 3.
9. Industry: mining & quarrying, manufacturing, construction and public utilities. Agriculture: agriculture, hunting, forestry & fishing. Services: wholesale & retail trade; restaurants & hotel; transport storage & communications; finance, insurance, real estate & business services, and community, social & personal services.

10. The default date of the UNESCO EFA Global Monitoring Report data is 2006, although data can range from 2004 to 2007.

11. See GMR, 2009, pages 248-249 & 250.

12. UNDP HDR, Page 332.

CHAPTER 2

Unravelling Multiple Dimensions of Gender in Seychelles

Mahrookh Pardiwalla

Introduction

The dominant gender discourse in Seychelles is that the country does not have a serious gender problem and that both boys and girls have equal opportunities to perform well at school. This discourse is supported by impressive gross enrolment ratios (among the highest in Africa) for primary, secondary and tertiary education: the latter standing at 82.5 per cent as per the UNDP 2007/2008 Human Development Report (UNDP, 2008). The research on gender analysis of schools and classroom processes has provided the opportunity to look behind those figures and examine processes, structures and belief systems that show another reality: a reality where boys are underperforming and under-participating and where girls may be limiting their own life chances because of stereotypes and narrow definitions of femininity.

The research was carried out in four secondary schools on Mahé, the main island of Seychelles archipelago. It explored gendered notions of masculinity and femininity among adolescent boys and girls and male and female staff in school. It looked beyond attendance and examined whether boys and girls received equal treatment and support from teachers; had equal opportunities to participate in all spheres of school life; had equal access to all resources available; and performed according to their full potential.

The chapter summarises the findings from this research and concludes that (i) staff in state schools do not actively challenge the existing gender status quo, through lack of awareness, gender training and critical self-reflection, and (ii) there is insufficient leadership and commitment to gender at the school and ministry levels to question this and encourage greater gender equity.

Background

Country profile

The Republic of Seychelles is a small island state located between latitudes 3° and 7° south, and longitudes 45° and 56° east in the South-Western Indian Ocean. It is made up of 115 islands scattered over an exclusive economic zone covering an area of 1.374 million square kilometres. The total land area is 455.3 square kilometres.

Seychelles attained independence from the British in 1976. Following a change of government in 1977, a one-party political system was adopted until 1992. In 1992, Seychelles became a multi-party democracy. The small economy (US$911 million GDP in 2007) is primarily dependent on tourism and fisheries, which provide most of the country's total foreign exchange earnings.

The comprehensive welfare state established since 1977, which was aimed at minimising income and gender disparities, and providing universal access to healthcare and education has ensured that Seychelles has social indicators comparable to many OECD countries and emerging market economies. It is ranked 50th on the United Nation's 2007/08 Human Development Index (the highest African country ranked) with an index of 0.843. Table 2.1 below shows the social indicators alongside countries of a similar per capita income.

Seychelles has met the targets for most of the eight Millennium Development Goals (MDGs). In relation to MDG 2, Seychelles has achieved universal primary education. The literacy rate of youth (15–24) is 98 per cent and primary school completion rate is 100 per cent. There is 100 per cent school enrolment.

In relation to MDG 3, the proportion of seats held by women in parliament is 29.4 per cent, and the ratio of girls to boys in primary and secondary education is 100 per cent. The ratio of young literate female to males in the age of 15–24 years is 99.4 per cent, among the highest in the developing world. Despite the tremendous improvement in the above-mentioned areas, women continue to have lower status jobs and they represent over 60 per cent of job seekers.

Seychelles' population is approximately 81,177, (2002 census) and is characterised by a slow growth rate, low births and low mortality. The total fertility rate has decreased from 2.7 in 1990 to 2.1 in 2000. The crude death rate has also decreased from 7.8 in 1990 to 6.8 in 2000. The population is of mixed origin mainly from African, Asian and European descent. There is a high degree of social cohesion among its people.

Table 2.1. Social indicators for Seychelles and comparators

	Barbados	Seychelles	Mauritius	Cape Verde	Trinidad & Tobago	Fiji	Maldives
Life expectancy	75.4	73	73	70.7	70	68.3	59
Infant mortality*	11	9.5	13	26	17	15.7	75
Under 5 mortality*	12	13	15	35	19	17.9	114
Literacy (%)	NA	96	NA	NA	98.4	NA	61
Primary completion (%)	100	100	97.5	81.4	NA	87	74

Source: World Development Indicators, World Bank (2008) (* per 1000 births)

Seychelles has three national languages: Creole, English and French. Creole, the mother tongue, is the medium of instruction in the early years of schooling. English is the language of government and business and becomes the medium of instruction in all major subjects from primary years 3 or 4 (P3 or P4). French is the third national language. It is taught as a language as from P1.

Education

Ministry of Education's mission statement

Seychelles has opted for an inclusive educational agenda, which is clearly defined in its official policy statement 'Education for a Learning Society', published in 2000.

> 'The mission of the Ministry of Education is to build a coherent and comprehensive system of quality education and training, reflecting shared universal and national values, which will promote the integrated development of the person and empower him/her to participate fully in social and economic development.'

It is based on principles of equity, quality, accountability, education for empowerment, education for productivity, education for social cohesion and education for global participation.

The principle of equity is clearly defined as:

- Equality of access to compulsory education

- Equitable sharing of resources

- Equal opportunity/creating conditions for optimum achievement according to ability and career aspirations

- Ensuring that the context, content and medium of education are equally favourable to boys and girls

- Catering for special needs/working towards greater 'inclusion of the learning disabled'

Until 2002, the Ministry of Education had an active Gender in Education committee. It has also produced a Gender Action Plan (2002–2015) to respond to the 'Education For All' (EFA) goal 5, which aims to eliminate gender disparities and achieve gender equality in education by the year 2015.

The system: an overview

Education is a high government priority and represents 8.5 per cent of GDP. The state provides free, comprehensive co-educational schooling to all Seychellois children from the age of 3+ to 16+. Further and higher education after secondary school is available to all students who meet the criteria appropriate to the particular course of study or training for which the student applies.

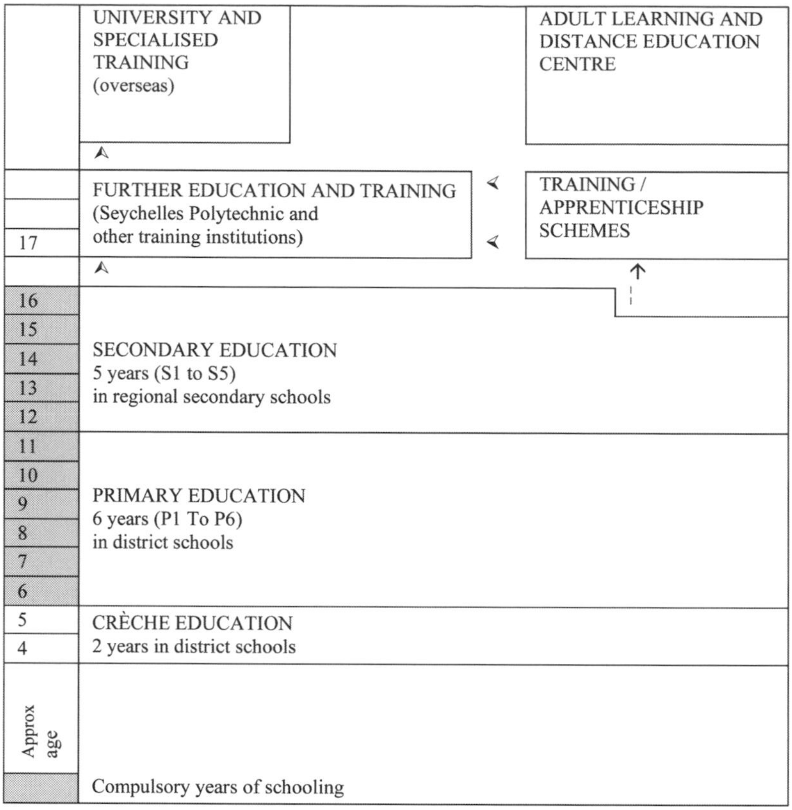

Approx age		
	UNIVERSITY AND SPECIALISED TRAINING (overseas)	ADULT LEARNING AND DISTANCE EDUCATION CENTRE
17	FURTHER EDUCATION AND TRAINING (Seychelles Polytechnic and other training institutions)	TRAINING / APPRENTICESHIP SCHEMES
16		
15		
14	SECONDARY EDUCATION 5 years (S1 to S5) in regional secondary schools	
13		
12		
11		
10		
9	PRIMARY EDUCATION 6 years (P1 To P6) in district schools	
8		
7		
6		
5	CRÈCHE EDUCATION 2 years in district schools	
4		

Compulsory years of schooling

Figure 2.1. The structure of the education system

The country has a small private school system. After the restoration of a multi-party democracy in 1993, the government liberalised its policy on private schools, which started admitting Seychellois children. There are currently three private schools and approximately five per cent of the school population attend private primary/ secondary school.

Distribution of schools

All schools are located on four main granitic islands. Mahé, the main island, has about 88 per cent of the entire school population. Praslin has two primary schools and one secondary school. La Digue has one combined primary and secondary school. A small multi-grade school on Silhouette has 25 students in crèche and primary. Students have to come to Mahé for further education.

Student population

In 2006, the total number of students in full-time education stood at 21,483. The student:teacher ratio is **15:1** at crèche level, **13:1** at primary and secondary levels and **12:1** at post-secondary level.

Curriculum structure in state secondary schools

From secondary 1 to secondary 3, students follow a broad-based curriculum and are introduced to certain vocational subjects such as agriculture/fishing, construction/technology, social economics, art and design, and computer education. At upper secondary, S3 to S5, students follow a core programme of compulsory subjects such as English, French, maths, personal and social education (PSE), religion and physical education. In addition, students are offered a choice of subject groups in relation to their academic ability, career needs and interests.

Teacher population and training

Demand for teachers is high. Eighty-five per cent of teachers at crèche, primary and secondary levels are trained. Fifty-five per cent of teachers at secondary level hold a

Table 2.2. Count of schools, teachers and students (2006) including private schools

Type of School	No. of Schools	No. of Teachers	No. of Students
Crèche	32	186	2,823
Primary	25	692	8,910
Special Education	1	25	63
Secondary	13	590	7,756
Post secondary	9	194	1,931
TOTAL	80	1,687	21,483

Source: Ministry of Education: Education Statistics (2006)

Table 2.3. Number of teachers by gender and origin 2006

	Local			Expatriate			F	M	Both Sexes
	F	M	Total	F	M	Total			
Crèche	169		169		0		169	0	169
Primary	552	97	649		0		552	97	649
Secondary	242	169	411	54	80	134	296	249	545
Post sec.	66	77	143	20	31	51	86	108	194
TOTAL	1,029	343	1,372	74	111	185	1,103	454	1,557

Source: Ministry of Education: Education Statistics (2006)

university degree. Eighty per cent hold a Diploma 2 in Education and above, which is the minimum qualification required to teach at secondary. In spite of the heavy investment in teacher training, there are shortages of Seychellois teachers at second-ary and post-secondary levels because of global competition and emigration of teach-ers. At secondary level, expatriate teachers account for almost 23 per cent of staff.

There are no male teachers at pre-primary (crèche) level. Women account for the majority of teachers at primary and secondary levels, although there are more male teachers at the post-secondary level. There are three male and seven female head teachers in secondary schools. All 10 secondary head teachers have been trained up to master's level in educational leadership.

Gender

Issues affecting women

The Seychelles Constitution ensures equal opportunity and protection for both men and women, and several policies and pieces of legislation are in place to promote gender equality and women's empowerment. Seychelles ratified the Convention on the Elimination of Discrimination Against Women (CEDAW) in 1992.

In spite of facilitative laws, many disparities exist. In education some of the main issues affecting women are stereotyping of subject and career choices at the second-ary level and under-representation in the technical and vocational areas, in spite of girls' good academic performance.

Stereotyping also exists among teachers' subject responsibilities. The majority of lan-guage, religion and personal and social education teachers are female. Men domi-nate in maths, science and physical education. In the technical field, all social economics teachers are female and all construction and technology teachers are male.

Table 2.4. Count of male and female teachers at secondary level by subject

Subject	M	F
English	13	49
French	11	49
Maths	42	21
Science	44	23
Social science	31	29
PSE/Religion	5	48
Technical	57	51
IT	11	7
PE	23	8
Total	237	285

Source: Schools Division Statistics

Women's empowerment and participation in decision-making

Women appear to be highly visible in public life because of the small size of the country, but the full participation of women in decision-making processes at the political and administrative levels has not been achieved.

In 2006, women made up 30 per cent of cabinet of ministers, 41 per cent of all principal secretaries and 30 per cent of parliament. There was only one female magistrate. Women, however, were well represented at local government level, constituting 56 per cent of all district administrators. Although Seychelles is doing well compared to other countries in the region, the full participation of women in the decision-making process has not been achieved and power remains in the hands of the men.

Although many more women are taking up employment, the gendered pattern of male and female labour remains constant. Women continue to have lower status jobs, and are clustered in unskilled and lower-paid occupations. The great majority of women are found in secretarial/typing, domestic service, cleaning, nursing, waitressing, teaching and tourism. Women comprise about 60 per cent of job seekers and 30 per cent of employers (2002 census).

Pockets of poverty, where they exist, affect women more than men because of the large number of households headed by women (47 per cent) with limited marketable skills. Women constitute 80 per cent of recipients on government welfare schemes.

In spite of a broad range of reproductive health services, teenage pregnancies remain a problem. In 2004, 15 per cent of all children born were born to mothers under the age of 20, and 27 per cent were born out of wedlock. Unplanned and unwanted pregnancies among teenage girls also result in illegal, unsafe abortions.

Another concern is the spread of HIV. The prevalence rate among youth (15–19) is 0.15 compared to 0.19 in the general population and the number of women diagnosed for HIV/AIDS is on the increase.

Issues affecting men

Gender concerns regarding men are rarely studied, probably because of the political and economic power yielded by certain categories of men, and the influence of a strong patriarchal ideology that continues to portray men as the 'stronger sex'. The traditional reluctance of men to air their problems in public for fear of appearing weak and the lack of men's organisations as opposed to women's organisations (which were very active in the early 1990s prior to the Beijing World Conference on Women) have meant that issues affecting men have not received as much public attention or media coverage.

Some of the main issues affecting men are the underachievement/under participation of boys in schools and a lower life expectancy rate for men (67 as opposed to 76 for women), linked to unhealthier life styles, drug and alcohol abuse. Other issues are a rising trend in domestic violence.

Gender-sensitive data is essential to challenge existing myths about men or women's superiority in Seychelles society. This is not always available. There is also a lack of qualitative research on stereotyped attitudes and perceptions that are impeding progress in spite of facilitative legal frameworks and measures put in place by government.

The Research and Sample

To date there has been very little research on gender in Seychelles schools, apart from two studies that have looked at the differential achievement of boys and girls in primary and secondary schools based on examination results.

Any new gender analysis in Seychelles must (i) encompass a broad, outcomes-based view of equality (not focussing only on access, as in much current reporting); (ii) recognise the value of micro-analysis at school level (and not rely only on country wide ministry statistics based on conventional indicators of equality); not generalise when talking about boys or girls, but ask 'which boys?' and 'which girls?'; and (iv) avoid falling into the boys versus girls trap, wherein girls/women are blamed for boys' relative under performance.

It would have been useful to examine how class intersects with gender to marginalise students. Unfortunately no data on the socio-economic background of students is available at school or national level and issues of class are largely ignored in educational research.

In line with other studies in this series, a qualitative research using case study methodology was undertaken to build understanding of each of the four schools.

Choice of schools

The research was carried out in four secondary schools on Mahé, the main island: three state schools and one private school. The three state schools chosen were average medium-sized secondary schools with an intake of between 600–800 students. Two of the schools are situated in the vicinity of the town, while the third one is situated on the west coast of the island. Regional secondary schools (except for a small combined primary/secondary school on one of the islands) are largely homogenous. The government's policy of equal opportunities has ensured that all schools are equitably staffed and resourced within available resources and all schools follow the same national curriculum. There is in principle very little variation among schools across the country with regards to staffing, facilities and resources. The three schools chosen drew their student intake from primary feeder schools from different regions of Mahé, North, Central and West.

As state schools are largely homogenous, a private school was included. The fourth school was a small co-educational private school also situated in the vicinity of the town. It is a combined primary and secondary school with a total enrolment of around 500 students, and a secondary school enrolment of 239 students. Students come to the school from all parts of the island. Since it is a fee-paying school, it attracts students from more affluent families and those seeking an alternative education to that offered in state schools. Both state and private schools prepare students for the Cambridge International General Certificate of Secondary Education (IGCSE) examinations at the end of the five-year cycle. The private school has a male head teacher and a female deputy head teacher responsible for the secondary section.

State schools face the enormous challenge of providing a co-educational comprehensive education to students of a wide range of ability, from different social backgrounds, all under one roof. Although students attending the private school also have different abilities, the school does not have to cope with the diversity of challenges posed by students from diverse social backgrounds. The focus of the study was, however, not to compare the academic results, but to understand the gender dynamics operating within the different schools.

School profiles

School A

School A is a medium-sized co-educational secondary government-owned school, situated on the west coast of Mahé. It could be classified as rural, situated some 30 kilometres from the capital. The grounds are more spacious compared to the others, situated around town. Security guards control the entrance to the school. It is a five to six streamed school, with a total student population of 771. Secondary schooling in Seychelles is of five years duration and students are organised into five year-levels (S1–S5). Table 2.5 shows the distribution of students at each level.

Table 2.5. School A, students per year level

Level	Girls	Boys	Total
Secondary 1	63	94	157
Secondary 2	79	79	158
Secondary 3	88	81	169
Secondary 4	75	77	152
Secondary 5	78	57	135
Total	383	388	771

Classes are streamed by ability as from secondary 2, with girls outnumbering boys in the top sets.

The school has a total of 60 staff (29 males and 31 females). Language teachers are largely women, while men dominate in maths and sciences. Most non-teaching staff are women, as is the head teacher and the two deputies.

The buildings are old and in need of renovation, but kept relatively clean. Some temporary prefabricated classrooms, built in the early 1980s to accommodate increased student numbers because of rapid expansion in secondary education, are still in use. The school has 27 classrooms, four laboratories, four specialist rooms, two workshops and two staffrooms. There is running water and electricity. The head teacher spoke of frequent water shortages because pipes were old and had burst. Students complained of the desalinated water supply, which they found unpalatable. There were adequate toilets for girls, but two of the boys' toilet blocks were unusable and in need of repair.

School B

School B is a medium-sized co-educational state secondary school, with a total student population of 693 students in 2007. It is situated on the outskirts of Victoria and draws its student population from town and surrounding areas. It occupies the site of one of the first secondary boys' schools established in Seychelles, by the Marist Brothers around 1884. Some of the original buildings are still standing and used as workshops. The school is close to the main road. It is completely fenced in by stone walls. There are security guards posted at the entrance of the school.

Blocks of classrooms had been built over the last 17 years. There are 26 classrooms, five laboratories, eight specialist rooms, two workshops and one staffroom. There are spacious offices for the head teacher and members of the management team. Some parts of the school, including a block of classrooms and toilets, are in poor condition and need repair. There are no wooden frames or glass in the windows and it appears extremely dangerous. Staircases are dark and dingy. The school has running water and electricity.

The school is exceedingly cramped for space. There is only one concrete court in the middle of the school compound, which is used for physical education (PE) lessons and for volleyball and basketball during break times. When PE lessons are on, all neighbouring classes are disturbed. The school does not have a multi-purpose room or auditorium. School assemblies were held on the court and the head teacher had to shout to be heard. There is a very high level of noise in the school at all times.

As in the other case study schools, there is a very large female presence in the school: management and staff are predominantly female. There are 17 women class tutors as opposed to nine men. All five year-tutors are women.

Table 2.6. School B, students per year level

Level	Girls	Boys	Total
Secondary 1	75	58	133
Secondary 2	74	71	145
Secondary 3	68	64	132
Secondary 4	70	83	153
Secondary 5	71	59	130
Total	358	335	693

The school ran a number of clubs: wildlife, Creole festival, care club, ecology ('eco') club and art club. There were many more girls than boys active in the clubs: 71 girls and 18 boys in the first four clubs, but 11 boys and only one girl in the art club.

School C

School C is a medium-sized co-educational state secondary school, with a total student population of 764 students in 2007. The school was originally built in 1977 as a primary school and is situated just outside Victoria, the capital of Mahé, the main island. During the years 1991–1998, a number of new classroom blocks and specialist rooms were built, and the school was gradually converted into a fully comprehensive secondary school in 1999. It is one of the eight regional secondary schools on Mahé and receives its students from three feeder primary schools in the north of the island.

The school has two blocks of classrooms, four science labs, two social economics rooms, one agriculture room, two construction/technology workshops, two art rooms and one computer room. It has six sets of toilets, three sets of three each for boys and girls. Classrooms are bare and unattractive. Fans and electrical sockets are hanging from many classrooms. The toilets have running water. They have recently been renovated and are in good condition. The school has a staffroom that is slightly cramped for the large number of staff, and adequate offices for its management staff.

The school is close to the main road and it is completely fenced in. Close circuit television was installed as additional security measure in 2006. The crèche (preschool section) is in the same school compound. Break times do not coincide and the noise from the crèche can be very disturbing for the block of classrooms facing the crèche.

There are five classes from S1 to S5 and four classes at S5 (24 classes). On entering school in S1, students are streamed by ability based on their performance in the primary 6 national exams. The trend over the last five years has been for girls to outperform boys in all subjects: girls outnumber the boys in the top streams and boys are over represented in the lower streams.

Table 2.7. School C, students per year level

Level	Girls	Boys	Total
Secondary 1	70	79	149
Secondary 2	82	93	175
Secondary 3	72	80	152
Secondary 4	80	85	165
Secondary 5	71	52	123
Total	375	389	764

Although the gender balance in overall school population is fairly equal, there are slightly more boys (between five and eleven) in the S1 to S4 year groups. In S5, there are 19 fewer boys than girls. Compulsory schooling ends at S4. According to the head teacher, there is a tendency for more boys to leave at the end of S4 to find employment. Girls stay on at school longer until the end of the secondary cycle. This may explain the difference in attendance at S5.

On three consecutive mornings, school buses dropped students off at least 15 minutes after the bell had rung. Students strolled into school in small groups; some even diverted via neighbouring shops. This gave a very unsettled beginning to the day.

The teaching staff is made up of 18 men and 35 women. The management team is made up of one head teacher (female) two deputy head teachers (one male and one female) and nine heads of department (three males and six females). There is a very large female presence in the school.

Girls were more 'visible' and participated more actively in clubs and competitions. The school had three sports clubs, one environment club and a care club. While the three sports clubs (including football) attracted both boys and girls, the wildlife club and the care clubs were dominated by girls. During 2006, the national public speaking and quiz competitions were won by exclusively girls' teams. Boys excelled in the national athletics competition by winning 15 medals as opposed to five for the girls.

School D

School D is a medium-sized, fee-paying private school established in 1993, when government liberalised its policy on private schooling and allowed Seychellois children to attend non state-run schools. The school comprises three sections: kindergarten, primary and secondary. A board of directors appointed by the shareholders, a board of governors and a school management team ensure the proper functioning of the school.

There are 240 students in the secondary section, distributed as illustrated in Table 2.8.

Table 2.8. School D, students per year level

Level	Girls	Boys	Total
Secondary 1	26	25	51
Secondary 2	26	22	48
Secondary 3	20	28	48
Secondary 4	20	27	47
Secondary 5	20	26	46
Total	112	128	240

The school buildings are new and the surroundings are clean and well maintained. The classrooms are well ventilated and airy. The laboratories and computer room are well equipped. Lockers and drinking water fountains are provided for students on the ground floor.

There is a shortage of space for sports and play and only one hard court on the central parking space. Students, mainly boys, were observed playing volleyball during break time. Girls were watching from the sidelines.

There are an equal number of male and female teachers (nine males and nine females). Responsibilities are fairly equally shared.

Boys and girls are equally well represented on the student committee: the chair and vice-chair are female. Drama and dancing clubs are dominated by girls, whereas sports clubs are more popular with the boys.

The school has maintained excellent academic standards with 100 per cent pass rates for the IGCSE exams. Boys and girls perform equally well and no significant gender imbalances in performance are recorded. Very few boys opt to do English literature and the number of girls entered for physics is fewer than that of boys. The choice of subject options may be helping to reinforce traditional divisions. Staff had high expectations for both genders.

Analysis

Education system processes and practices

Gender imbalance within the Schools Division

The Schools Division within the Ministry of Education is responsible for the overall management of primary and secondary schools in Seychelles. Its stated mission is to 'provide educational services to state schools to enable students from pre-primary to secondary levels to achieve high standards of learning, (according to ability) and develop into knowledgeable, responsible and productive citizens'.

It has a total staff of 48, of whom nine are men, with only one man on the senior management team. Interviews were held with the director general of the Schools Division, the director for secondary schools and two education co-ordinators who provide support to schools, all of which were women.

One of the main gender issues identified by the education managers was the largely female staff in the Schools Division. Education managers felt that because of the heavy staffing imbalances in the division, the sharing of views on education and schools was done with women only. This could result in a biased point of view and biased proposals. As there was only one man on the senior management team, the 'male' perspective had far less opportunity to be voiced.

The main problems affecting boys was that they underperformed, had more discipline problems and were associated with fights, acts of vandalism and drugs. The main problems affecting girls were teenage pregnancies and a rising problem of associated truancy, although girls were now given a second chance to reintegrate into schools. The lack of male role models in early childhood/primary classes and the emerging problem of sexual harassment were also cited as two gender-related challenges in schools.

Performance of male and female head teachers

There are three male head teachers out of a total of 10 in all secondary schools. Managers did not perceive any difference in performance, although one co-ordinator said that the men were 'smooth talkers' and found the female head teachers to be more authoritative and action-oriented.

Managers described a gender-friendly school as one to which all felt they belonged and were part of. It was a school where staff and management treated everyone according to needs/desires and took care of students. It was a school where everybody felt happy and to which they wanted to come. There were mixed feelings about whether secondary schools were gender-friendly or not. All managers agreed that there was currently much more awareness of gender in the schools. Many schools were analysing exam results by gender. The situation, however, varied from school to school. Not many secondary schools were consciously doing anything to address gender issues. It did not appear on secondary schools' action plans. It was not brought up in the list of major challenges faced by schools in reports and end-of-year presentations.

Education managers appeared very aware of some of the gender issues, including the stigmatising and labelling of boys, the gender-imbalanced classes and the stereotyped attitudes of some teachers. They were aware that boys and male teachers faced many disadvantages, being in a largely female environment, but admitted that there had been no serious reflection on the part of schools and the ministry. One co-ordinator remarked that while it was considered perfectly acceptable for female staff to be surrounded by boys, some schools and staff would be immediately suspicious if male staff were surrounded by girls. This put added pressure on male staff; it was said that some young male teachers felt discouraged and wanted to give up teaching.

Gender training teachers

The ministry did not organise any training centrally for teachers, but helped in running sessions organised by schools, where it was part of their action plans (mostly in primary schools). Managers felt that there was an urgent need to start raising gender awareness at secondary level, but more research was needed to convince secondary teachers. It was considered that attitudes were hard to change. They believed that the National Institute of Education had a key role to play in training teachers and the PSE programmes may need to be reviewed to reflect changing conditions.

The general feeling was that gender needed to be given more attention by placing it on the agenda of all meetings at ministry and school levels. Gender as a social construct was not fully understood by everyone; frequent references were made to the biological make-up of men and women to explain behaviours.

Quality Assurance service

The Quality Assurance (QA) service was set up in 2001 to i) reinforce self-evaluation in schools in the context of the improvement programme and ii) provide input into policy/decision-making through the collection of reliable data on the performance of the school system in Seychelles.

According to staff, gender was taken into account in the analysis of school-based exam results and performance in national and international exams. Performance indicators under attainment require that a gender analysis is carried out and this was done for all schools evaluated.

QA staff also said that gender-friendliness and relevance were considered when judging the quality of test items and examination papers. Issues such as equal treatment of boys and girls, equitable sharing of resources and equal distribution of questions were noted when conducting classroom observations, being reported under quality of teaching where appropriate. Students own perceptions of fair treatment were also captured through students' interviews. Performance indicators under 'ethos' examine relationships between boys and girls and how they treat each other. Where relevant, they would be reported upon. QA also carries out a special analysis of schools where gender gaps are especially high. This was the case in one primary school.

Although gender analysis was carried out in relation to attainment results and was highlighted in the body of the QA reports, no specific gender recommendations or points of action had been made in relation to secondary schools that have been evaluated. This has been confirmed by examining the reports of the six schools. Normally schools are required to develop action plans in response to QA recommendations. The issue of gender was not considered serious enough to warrant action.

In the case of one of the case study schools, the gender analysis reads as follows:

> 'The analysis of students' performance by gender showed on the whole girls performed better than boys in both English and math[s] across all levels. It is clear that the comparatively weaker performance of boys in contrast to girls had a negative effect on the overall results of the school based examinations for English and math[s].'

There is no recommendation for follow-up action by the school. The school in question was not taking any measure to investigate the problem.

Students

Notions of masculinity and femininity

Students' views and perceptions were gathered from 12 focus group discussions held with three groups of students from each case study school. In each school, discussions were held with a mixed group of boys and girls, a girls-only group and a boys-only group. A total of 45 boys and 44 girls took part in the discussions. No major differences were noticed in the responses gathered from single-sex and mixed-sex groups. Boys and girls expressed themselves freely in both types of groups, but discussions were livelier in the mixed groups where girls and boys challenged each other's perceptions.

There was also little variation in the responses from the four schools on the traits of typical Seychellois boys and girls from different socio-economic backgrounds and locations. Figure 2.2 lists some of the terms and expressions used by the students.

Figure 2.2. Notions of masculinity and femininity

How do girls see themselves?	How do boys see girls?	How do boys see themselves?	How do girls see boys?
Mature	Weaker sex	Strong	Proud
Hardworking	In need of protection	Dominant partner	Stubborn
Responsible	Vulnerable to rape	Bread winner	Macho
Role models for	Not free	Provider	Will not admit to
younger students	Burdened by	Head of household	being wrong
Respected	menstruation and	Have more prestige	Hide emotions
Disciplined	childbirth	Proud	Have more freedom
Able to express	Easily influenced	Socialiser	Lazy
themselves well	Change minds easily	Brave	Easily influenced by
Attractive	Orderly	Free	peers – if you don't
Fashionable		Intelligent	drink and smoke
Outgoing		Self-reliant	you are not a man
Friendly		Good politicians	
Sensitive/fragile		Serious	
In need of protection		Emotionally and	
Treated like princesses		mentally stable	
at home			
Limited freedom			

There is considerable consensus on what constitutes typical Seychellois boys and girls. Girls have a very positive image of themselves. They consider themselves to be mature, hardworking, disciplined, attractive and outgoing and good role models for younger students. They are multi-skilled, but physically weak and need protection. They are protected at home and as one girl said 'treated like princesses'.

Boys described themselves using a much narrower range of qualities and traits. They see themselves as strong, brave and intelligent, the providers and protectors. They have more freedom than the girls and are less restricted by their parents. They considered girls to be the weaker sex, burdened by childbirth and menstruation and in need of protection. They were better at sports. They said they had more prestige in society and made better politicians. None of them would like to change their sex.

Both girls and boys admitted to being happy and 'comfortable in their skins'. They thought highly of themselves (using different sets of criteria) and rather more negatively of the opposite sex.

Figure 2.3. Students' likes and dislikes

	Activities liked	Activities disliked
Boys	Partying/socialising Breaking rules Drinking Dancing Cooking Socialising at school Street racing Playing video games Surfing the net Walking around town Going out with girlfriends/chatting up girls Sports/splaying football Water sports Watching movies	Homework Research work Doing household chores/buying gas Sweeping the class Religious activities at school Babysitting Studying Reading Break-dancing
Girls	Going out with friends Watching television Listening to music Knitting and embroidery Singing/dancing Reading Sports (volleyball, badminton tennis water sports) Baking/cooking Drawing Quiz competitions Looking after animals	Cooking (a few) Cleaning louvres Doing household chores Contact sports Violent sports/games Pressured to go to church Babysitting Too much homework

Likes and dislikes

Girls and boys had similar likes and dislikes. Both genders disliked household chores, looking after younger brothers and sisters and excess homework. Boys however appeared to enjoy more physical, outdoor and risky activities. Girls liked 'quieter' and more indoor activities.

Studies

Both girls and boys felt they had equal opportunities to pursue further studies, choose any career they wished and that all doors were now open. In spite of that, the general consensus was that women were more suitable for the 'caring professions' and those that needed 'patience', while heavy work such as being mechanics or bus drivers should be restricted to men. This stereotyping in career choices was more evident among boys.

Boys and girls (including those students from the low-ability groups) had high expectations and wanted to pursue studies up to university level if possible. Both genders perceived no major obstacles in reaching their goals. Girls seemed to be more conscious of the need for hard work and self-sacrifices in order to attain their goals because of the competition for scholarships. On the other hand, boys (from state schools) felt it would be easy for them to get jobs and succeed even if they did not do very well at school. Parents in general supported them in their career choices, except for those who put a bit of pressure on them to take up the family business.

Girls were given a larger proportion of family responsibilities, looking after siblings and doing household chores. They spent on average between 30 and 90 minutes per day helping round the house with cleaning, ironing, cooking and looking after siblings. Boys spent considerably less time (15–30 minutes) on household chores. They were expected to tidy their rooms and do 'outside' work like sweeping the yard. Some helped with cooking because they found it enjoyable. It would appear that boys did considerably more household chores in homes where there were no sisters. This needs further research.

Girls spent on average much more time doing homework and study than boys. Between 1.5 to 4 hours was spent on homework and research projects. Girls from top sets took extra classes in the evenings for 1.5 hours. The majority of boys (except for those in the top sets) said they spent between 5–30 minutes on study. Most of the time homework was done on Sundays, in class or early in the morning. Their evenings were spent doing sport activities (2–3 hours), watching TV, looking after younger brothers and sisters, playing games and surfing the net (3–4 hours). They enjoyed school because it was an opportunity to meet friends and socialise.

In contrast, both girls and boys in the private school said they spent between 2–4 hours on study every night. The little spare time they had was spent watching TV, surfing the net and talking to parents. Their timetables were extremely full. Some of them trained for sports and others took extra classes in music, dance etc. They found their days to be too short. Interestingly, girls and boys in the top sets from state schools had similar study and leisure patterns.

Girls and boys chose a wide range of subjects as their favourites: there was no discernable gendered pattern. Students chose subjects in the first place if they liked their teacher and the teaching approach. Boys appeared to prefer subjects that matched their career choices, while this did not appear to be the case for girls.

Parental expectations

Parents had similar school expectations for boys and girls. They wanted both to study hard and succeed. They appreciated obedience and good behaviour and liked it when both helped at home. The pressure to project an image of obedience, hard work and exemplary behaviour was felt to be stronger on the girls. Figure 2.4 lists the traits or behaviours that parents liked to see, and those they disliked.

As a general rule, neither boys nor girls felt discriminated against in the classroom. They said they received equal attention from both male and female teachers. (This was borne out by the classroom observations). Students' teacher preference was based more on teacher attitude and teaching style rather than on gender.

Teachers expected more from the girls academically. If a boy and a girl got the same mark, the tendency for the teacher was to praise the boy, but tell the girl she could have done much better.

Both girls and boys however agreed that boys got harder punishments from teachers. They were reprimanded more often in class and spoken to more harshly. Male teachers were careful about how they spoke to the girls and tended to be more protective. Girls agreed that they could get away with more than the boys. This was common to all four schools.

Figure 2.4. Parental expectations

	Parents like it when they:	What parents dislike:
Boys	Study well Give priority to studies Are obedient Help with housework Get a good job Keep away from girls	Dress code Laziness Somersaulting in hip-hop dancing Coming home late
Girls	Get good results and are role models in academic areas Are respected for good behaviour and set good examples Study well Are obedient and respectful Do housework	Rudeness and arrogance Disobedience and answering back Not taking studies seriously Giving too much attention to fashion and music Going out with friends Not helping out enough with household chores

Teacher attention and teaching strategies

Both boys and girls preferred lively lessons with a lot of interaction and discussions. They appreciated it when teachers explained carefully instead of dictating a lot of notes, although good notes were considered useful. Girls enjoyed role-plays and group activities more than the boys. Boys liked activities that were fun and where there were experiments and hands-on experiences. They did not like writing notes and reading from books. Both girls and boys did not like it when teachers gave too much homework.

Safety at school

Students said they generally felt safe from outside intruders at school because of protective walls, closed circuit television (CCTV, in one school) and being surrounded by friends. There were potentially unsafe blind spots in all schools (in spite of the CCTV) like toilets, staircases and inside classrooms.

Girls admitted to have experienced gender-based abuse mainly of a verbal nature. Sexual harassment and bullying occurred mainly at S1–S3 in all four schools. Girls were the targets for sexual abuse but boys and girls were the targets of bullying. Bullying and harassment were not major issues at S4–S5 levels. Although all students knew where to report cases of harassment, this rarely happened, as students feared it could get worse and did not have confidence in management. Students from all four schools felt that action was rarely taken and there was no open acknowledgement of the problem from staff in three of the schools.

Teachers

Teacher expectations were gathered from a focus group discussion held with three male and three female teachers in each of the four schools. Individual interviews were conducted with teachers in the three state schools: twelve interviews were conducted with seven male and five female teachers.

Views on gender

Teachers had only a very limited understanding of the concept of gender. Gender was commonly referred to as differences between boys and girls. Gender as a social construct and the school's role in combating stereotyping was not really understood. In many cases, teachers took a resigned and defeatist position for gendered inequality, putting the blame on home or society. The underperformance of boys and the gender imbalance of classes (against boys) were cited as the two most important gender issues in state schools.

Issues related to gender were rarely discussed at staff meetings. Schools had started analysing gender-disaggregated performance data. There was no serious discussion of the results and no strategies had been developed to try to redress the imbalance. One school had gender as one of the targets in its development plan; it was in the early stages of carrying out a gender audit.

Less than one third of the teachers had had any training in gender or human rights education. Personal and social education (PSE) teachers had covered some aspects in their teacher-training courses and a few others had attended sensitisation sessions in in-school professional development.

The majority of teachers felt that gender should be incorporated into teacher-training programmes and all in-service courses. The interviews had forced them to think of issues they had never reflected upon. Such training would help them to cope with situations at school and develop strategies for redressing imbalances where these were identified. They were not specific on the content of the course.

Self perceptions

Views on masculinity and femininity expressed by teachers were diverse and not as clear-cut as those of the students. About half the male teachers interviewed felt that the man was the dominant figure in the household, whose duty it was to direct the running of the house and give protection to the family. The woman's role was to assist the man and be his companion, as stated in the Bible. Her biological make-up made her more suitable for looking after children. The other half felt that society was changing rapidly. Man was no longer considered the domineering figure and there was equal sharing of responsibilities in the house. They gave personal accounts of how responsibilities were shared in their own homes, even the fact that women traditionally were given more priority and rights over children.

Young female graduates felt that working women had an unfair share of the household chores and responsibility for bringing up the children. Their husbands worked late, went out with friends and they were left to shoulder all the responsibilities. They acknowledged feeling stressed and tired, especially if they held responsible posts at school. Like their female students, some said they sometimes wished they were men because of the extra freedom they enjoyed.

Male teachers felt that females made better class tutors because of their 'caring' nature and the fact that they were better organised and able to combine multiple tasks simultaneously. Two female teachers also felt that women made better class teachers because they were strict, reliable and dedicated. They were of the opinion that men 'did not like responsibility and could not take responsibility', as they had left all the work for mothers and sisters at home, so were not in the habit of behaving responsibly. These views were not, however, the general consensus.

In-school equity

There were no written policies on equal opportunities. In all schools, however, teachers reported an equal sharing of responsibilities: neither women nor men felt discriminated against.

One school ensured that both male and female class teachers or assistant class teachers were appointed. Responsibilities for playground supervision, classroom cover, clubs and representation on the different committees were shared equally. Staff volunteered to act on committees depending on their interests and aptitudes. The ministry appointed heads of departments and heads of year, so the school had no control over the number of male or female established positions. There were more female teachers in the three state schools and more women on the management staff, and this tended to give the impression that women held all responsible posts. Responsibilities were more equally shared out in the private school because there were equal numbers of men and women on the teaching staff (nine males and nine females).

Facilities for staff were considered adequate, although staff in two schools mentioned that their staffrooms were too small and cramped. All schools had separate toilets for men and women.

Teachers were generally not aware of cases of sexual abuse, of staff or students, although some of them had heard 'stories' of past incidents in the school. Eight teachers had witnessed incidents of bullying during playground supervision, especially with newcomers to the school. The schools had no special policies on sexual harassment or bullying, although the offences and the accompanying sanctions were specified in schools' codes of conduct. Teachers were not systematically informed of cases of abuse and felt that it was a matter for management and counsellors.

Gendered differentiation

Most teachers stated that they did not differentiate between boys and girls. They said they enjoyed teaching both, that they treated them equally and saw all as **'students'**, not as 'boy' or 'girl' students. Technical teachers, however, acknowledged that they sometimes treated boys and girls differently. Girls would be given plastic to work with instead of wood because of their inability to handle heavy machines. In agriculture, girls would be made to weed and boys to hoe. The lack of protective clothing and appropriate facilities made the teachers protective towards the girls.

In spite of their profession of equal treatment of girls and boys, teachers held very stereotyped views on how they differed in their learning styles and abilities. In general, they felt girls were better at languages and boys at science. In one school, teachers were of the view that boys learned best by discovery, investigation, practical 'hands on' experience, group work and asking a lot of questions. They said that they had more enquiring minds than the girls; that they were better at maths and general concepts and learned through 'manipulative and visuals'. Girls were more reserved and learned by rote, they were more organised and self-motivated and liked to copy notes. They were also more independent learners and liked reading and writing. Their preference was for a 'book-based style'. Many teachers said that teaching boys posed more of a challenge and teachers 'had to go that extra mile' with them.

Teachers in the private school had less polarised views on the learning abilities of boys and girls. They had high expectations of both genders and felt that the boys could be very competitive when challenged. Two teachers said they had a marked preference for teaching boys.

With regards to attitude towards work and behaviour, the majority of staff from state schools spoke very highly of girls who they said were **naturally** more responsible, serious and mature. Girls volunteered to do presentations and help in school. They were punctual and more regular with homework. Teachers thought that girls were more conscientious and made better prefects. They took their classroom supervisory duties seriously and would report cases of misbehaviour.

Teachers generally felt that boys could be disruptive, rude and hard to control, that they liked to rebel and challenge authority, but that many tended to become more serious and pick up at post-secondary level. Boys were reluctant to report on their friends or co-operate with management. They succumbed more easily to peer-pressure. Teachers said that these negative attitudes in boys were inculcated, tolerated at home, in families and there was very little the school could do to combat that.

According to one head teacher, the home culture encourages girls to stay home and study while boys are allowed to run wild. He quoted the example of an Indian boy who was the star student at the school a few years ago. His academic success was attributed to the fact that 'he was brought up the way girls are' in Seychellois society.

Very few teachers admitted to giving harsher punishments to the boys and being gentler with the girls. Large numbers however admitted not thinking along gender lines when they were in front of a class. When allocating tasks, teachers admitted to some gender bias. Girls would be given lighter duties but generally the boys shirked their responsibilities and left the work for the girls to do. The pattern was for girls to sweep the classrooms and boys to empty the bins and lift heavy furniture.

Although teachers from the private schools felt that girls were generally more hard working and regular in handing homework, there were also good role models among the boys. In some classes, the top performers were boys. It was not unusual for the top scorer to be male in the top sets in state schools as well, but the majority of the high fliers were girls. Students in the private school were not required to do cleaning duties. Responsibilities were shared but boys would automatically be chosen to do heavier work, like carrying furniture.

Textbooks and other learning materials

All state schools follow the same national curriculum and use the same recommended textbooks imported by the Ministry of Education. Textbooks are on loan to students. The textbooks reviewed were English, geography, history, biology, physics and maths textbooks for S4/S5 levels. They were mostly recommended books for

IGCSE exam preparation: none was produced locally. The majority were recently published books or new editions of books published from 1996 onwards in the UK.

The English textbooks were generally well balanced, showing pictures of both males and females in a variety of occupations, including non-traditional images of female boxers and male ballet dancers. There was however a preponderance of texts involving male figures such as Martin Luther King, Rasputin and male Internet 'whiz kids'. Many of the passages were modern and thought provoking, with scope for discussions on issues such as equal opportunities, race ethnicity etc. Only two of the textbooks *New Expressway English 4* and *Certificate in English Language* (published in the UK, but intended for a Malaysian and African school audience) were heavily biased in favour of males.

The series of maths textbooks *Mathematics in Action* was also well-balanced, with cartoon illustrations of men and women and male and female names used in exercises and problem-solving activities. This was not the case for one of the physics textbooks, *Physics for You* by Keith Johnson and Stanley Thorpes (1996), where all illustrations and cartoons were heavily biased in favour of males. The biology textbooks had many diagrams, but very few illustrations.

The geography textbook *Wider World Geography* and history textbook *GCSE Modern World History* carried illustrations relevant to the topics and events covered, reflecting the historical and cultural realities of the periods and countries presented. The history textbook, although concentrating on male leaders and politicians, had many posters and cartoons, which highlighted women's important roles during the world wars.

The only local material reviewed was the personal and social education (PSE) programme. A number of the themes covered in this programme contribute directly to the promotion of the universal values of democracy, human rights and sustainable development. The four strands of the PSE programme are 1) moral education, 2) careers education and guidance, 3) education for citizenship and 4) family life and health education (FLHE). The FLHE component is the one that incorporates relevant aspects of growth and development, sexuality education, gender roles, interpersonal and social skills, family role responsibilities and relationships, personal achievement and leisure, population issues and measures for sustainable development. Concerns faced by youth and adolescents in Seychelles, such as high incidence of sexual behaviour, unwanted pregnancies, increasing incidence of HIV/ AIDS, sexual abuse, the growing number of teenage pregnancies and other family problems are adequately addressed in the programme. The programme emphasises the importance of the family, and aims to promote positive attitudes and behaviour towards parenthood, as a basis for better family living, parental care, gender equity and equality. It also raises concern and develops positive attitudes and behaviour towards conservation measures needed for sustainable socio-economic development and improved quality of life of the Seychellois people, in view of the fragile nature of Seychelles ecosystem.

The methods and teaching approaches advocated are highly participatory and inter-active, encouraging students to take control of their own learning. Following these books, the teacher is to act as a facilitator and, through methods such as case studies, role plays, interviews, songs and drama, encourage young people to think, communicate, make decisions, solve problems and adopt positive behaviours. Teachers are encouraged to evaluate not only knowledge, but also personal development, skills, attitudes and values.

The reviewed textbooks were, therefore, considered as reasonable tools that could be exploited by teachers with a concern for gender equality. The PSE textbooks, in particular, and their underlying exploratory, collaborative teaching and learning styles were conducive to approaches promoting greater participation and equity.

Processes within and outside the classroom

Classroom processes

A total of 20 lessons were observed in the four schools. Equal numbers of male and female teachers were observed teaching. Five or six lessons were observed in each of the state schools and four were observed in the private school. The lessons observed were maths (three), history (one), English (three), geography (two), biology (one), PSE/careers (four), PE (four) and agriculture (two). The focus of the observation was on (i) teacher student interaction, (ii) use of instructional language and quality of language and questioning and (iii) student/student interaction.

The lesson observations in general yielded minimal gender data as, in about half of the observations, very little teacher/student interaction took place. Students were either doing individual class work or taking notes. In two of the state schools, the noise level from outside and in the corridors was sometimes so loud that it prevented any meaningful interaction from taking place. It those instances it was almost impossible for researchers at the back of the class to follow the lesson.

In the ten lessons where teacher student interaction could be observed, girls and boys were given equal attention and teachers involved both by asking and inviting questions. Teachers spent roughly equal amounts of time giving attention to boys and girls and helping them with work. Many teachers both in the state and private school had good teaching techniques and delivered lessons efficiently. The majority of the lessons were teacher-directed, but with varying opportunities for discussion and interaction.

Girls participated more actively in English and history lessons in the top sets in state schools. Boys were more active in the maths and single agriculture lessons in the lower sets. In one top English set dominated by girls, the teacher encouraged competition between the sexes. This competition provided an opportunity to attack the other gender. The few boys in this class were vocal and sometimes scathing in their remarks. This pitching of one gender against the other was also evident in the careers lesson on positive attitudes in the workplace. The teacher chose only one case study of a young irresponsible male worker to illustrate her lesson and generate discussion. Boys were labelled for their lack of responsibility, punctuality and discipline in the workplace. The presentation and the ensuing discussion turned out to be very biased against boys.

In classes where there were discipline problems, both male and female teachers reprimanded boys more often and in slightly harsher terms. They were seen as inattentive, liked to disturb others, and did not comply with the dress code. Although boys were in general less well behaved, many teachers were more impatient with boys than with girls.

In the three PSE lessons observed, dealing with sensitive issues such as HIV/AIDS, child abuse and contraception, boys monopolised the lessons by asking the majority of the questions and constantly seeking the teacher's attention. Although two of the teachers dealt with the topics efficiently and in an open manner, the girls seemed to be reluctant to air their views in front of the boys. In the lesson on contraception, the teacher was not well-prepared and confused contraception with abortion. The lesson was delivered in Creole, giving the boys opportunity to use crude language and embarrass the girls.

In state schools, random seating arrangements were a great deterrent to good classroom communication. Students dictated seating arrangements by pulling furniture and seats where they wanted to. There was considerable disruption at the beginning of the lesson while students found desks and chairs and 'convenient' places to sit near windows and doors: preferably at the back of the class. Teachers rarely intervened. Only in one lesson did the teacher spend at least 15 minutes trying to get the students to settle down, rearrange the desks in an orderly fashion, sweep and tidy the room. In this instance, students responded and calmed down.

In many of these classes, boys and girls sat separately, as illustrated in Figure 2.5 below (although the desks were not neatly aligned as in the plans). When invited to work in pairs or in groups, students automatically formed groups of the same sex unless directed otherwise by the teacher. In the lessons observed, teachers ensured that they formed mixed groups (although this may have been largely due to the presence of observers). The large gender imbalance in some classes made it difficult to form balanced groups.

In the three state schools, the classrooms where observations were conducted were dull and unattractive. There were no posters or charts on the walls and the notice boards were torn. Some of the blackboards and fans were unusable and many needed repainting. The classroom atmosphere in the private school was focused, purposeful, and conducive to learning. Boys and girls were mixed and seemed to get on well. They chatted to each other and there seemed to be a good spirit of 'camaraderie'.

During observations, teachers addressed both genders respectfully using appropriate language in the classroom. However, the shouting and loud noises from neighbouring classes and the playground indicated that this might not always be the case. There were no major instances of sexist language being used in classrooms. Almost all teachers knew their students and addressed them by their first names. In two of the lessons observed, one in the state school and one in the private school, the teachers would frequently use the term 'guys' to refer to the whole class ' hurry up guys', 'pick up the books guys'. The girls appeared to be used to this form of address and followed instructions.

Setting, performance and examinations

In line with its policy of inclusive education, the Ministry of Education does not condone rigid streaming, but secondary schools have considerable autonomy to determine student groupings. The usual pattern was (i) for classes to be streamed by

Figure 2.5. Plans of classroom seating arrangements

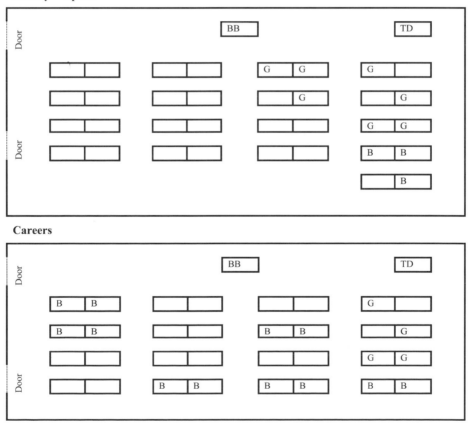

Maths – low set

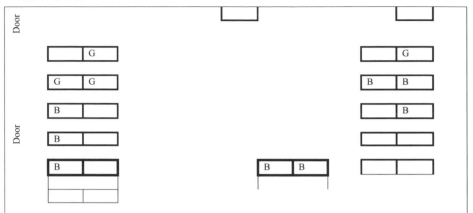

Social sciences – middle set

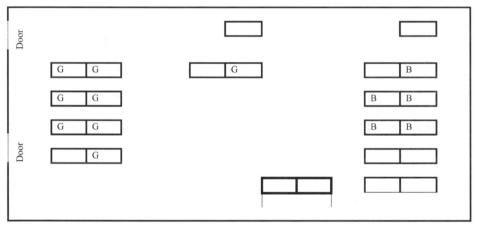

English – top set

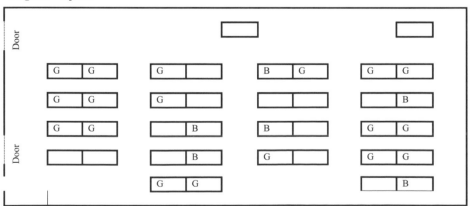

Exploring the Bias: Gender & Stereotyping in Secondary Schools

Agriculture

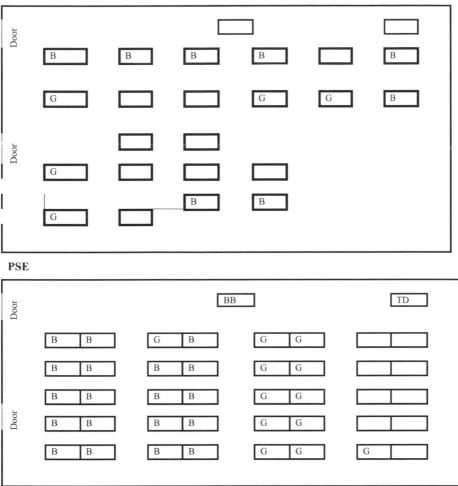

PSE

ability at S1 to S3 levels where students follow a common curriculum, and (ii) to have subject settings at S4 and S5 when students are preparing for the IGCSE international examinations. One of the state schools was starting to implement plans to 'de-stream' at S1 level, but the process was not fully underway so it did not impact on the research. The primary 6 national examination results are used to allocate students to classes in S1 and those of the co-ordinated examinations at S3 are used to confirm student subject options and sets at S4. Table 2.9 below shows the national mean scores for key subjects at primary 6 and secondary 3 from 2000–2004.

Table 2.9. Mean scores of P6 and S3 students, by subject, by gender

Mean scores of primary 6 students, by subject, by gender

	Maths		English		Science	
	Male	Female	Male	Female	Male	Female
2000	36.1	46.0	44.3	56.0	44.6	52.9
2001	33.2	39.9	43.2	55.9	41.0	48.0
2002	25.5	33.5	35.1	47.1	47.2	57.6
2003	31.2	38.3	36.6	48.1	38.9	46.3

Mean scores of secondary 3 students, by subject, by gender

	Maths		English		Science	
	Male	Female	Male	Female	Male	Female
2003	14.9	21.5	33.4	46.6	22.2	28.8
2004	17.5	23.3	39.4	53.3	28.8	35.4
2005	16.5	24.2	39.3	53.0	37.7	35.8
2006	16.7	24.4	40.7	55.7	27.7	34.3

At both P6 and S3 levels, boys' underperformance is consistent across all subject areas. Equally significant is the drop in mean scores between P6 and S3 for boys and girls in maths and science, the slight drop for boys in English and the consistency, and in some cases improvement, in the English scores achieved by girls. Table 2.10 below (using 2006 figures) illustrates by the gender imbalances in S1 to S3 classes in all regional schools.

Across the three state schools, boys constituted about 40 per cent of the top stream and 60 per cent of the lower streams. The pattern remains fairly constant, with small percentage point fluctuations between secondary 1 and secondary 3. Table 2.11 shows the pattern in the three case study schools, but in secondary 5.

Table 2.10. Regional gender distribution among top and low streams, S1–S3

Grade level	Top Stream		Lower Streams	
	M (%)	F (%)	M (%)	F (%)
Secondary 1	45	55	64	36
Secondary 2	41	59	61	39
Secondary 3	46	54	66	34

Exploring the Bias: Gender & Stereotyping in Secondary Schools

Table 2.11. Gender distribution among top and bottom streams, S5 per cent

	Boys (Top)	Girls (Top)	Boys (Low)	Girls (Low)
School A	10	21	16	12
School B	9	23	9	8
School C	16	20	9	12

These figures illustrate interesting patterns, as the gender imbalance in favour of girls continues in the top stream, but the lower streams have become equal. This may indicate that the boys who have dropped out at the end of S4 were those who might have been in the lower streams. This may confirm previous conceptions of the constitution of this especially at-risk group of boys, and merits further investigation.

The private school had two, non-streamed classes from S1 to S5, with setting for maths only at S4/S5 levels. Boys and girls were equally distributed in the two classes in the private school, which had more boys than girls at S5 level. There were ten girls and 13 or 14 boys in each class.

The schools' streaming and setting arrangements undermine boys' chances to sit for international exams. Table 2.12 shows the number of students who have been registered, nationally, for the 2007 IGCSE exam.

There are more girls than boys enrolled for all the examinations both at core and extended levels. The three case study schools show the same pattern of participation. This situation is again not acceptable from an equity point of view and schools may need to examine how their selection and grouping arrangements disadvantage boys through early labelling.

Table 2.12. S5 students' participation in external Cambridge (IGCSE) examination

Subject	Core		Extended	
	Male	Female	Male	Female
English	237	307	157	307
Mathematics	262	368	61	98
Co-ordinated science	120	242	75	127
Combined science	149	227		
History	78	191		
Geography	253	350		

Figures for 2006 from the private school show that all 19 girls and 29 boys were entered for English, French, maths, geography and biology. Because of subject options, more boys than girls took physics and chemistry exams, while more girls chose history and English literature.

Outdoor activities

One PE lesson was observed in each school. Classes were usually combined for PE and conducted by two teachers (two males or one male and one female). In one lesson, girls and boys were separated throughout and had different activities – which were often less physical and strenuous for the girls. The groups came together at the end to evaluate and congratulate each other. In other lessons, there were separate warming-up exercises for boys and girls, but groups were mixed for skills practice and volleyball training. In the private school that was practising for athletics, girls ran one lap less during the warm-up activity, but joined in with boys for long jump and high jump practice.

In all schools, boys and girls wore shorts and T-shirts and those who did not bring their PE kits did not participate. There were more girls sitting on the sidelines. There was good interaction between teachers and students and among students. Teachers encouraged both genders. Girls were less active and complained of the heat, headaches and tasks set for them more often than the boys did. Teachers and boys encouraged them and the atmosphere was friendly.

Facilities for PE were rather cramped in one state school and students were playing on the one hard court in the middle of the school. Facilities in the other two schools were adequate although students could be quite noisy and disturbed classes in the vicinity. Balls and game posts were the only equipment in use. The private school had spacious facilities and transported students to the national stadium for athletics practice. PE lessons were examples of healthy and friendly interactions between boys and girls.

One of the two agriculture lessons, on application of fertilisers, had a practical component conducted outdoors, with a class of six boys and six girls. The agriculture patch was a very small area, with only two beds of lettuce, littered with bottles, boxes and papers. The boys fetched the water in two plastic watering cans while the girls picked up litter. There were two spades, used by the boys to prepare the beds. The teacher demonstrated the application of the fertiliser and handed the fertiliser to the boys only. The girls watched and were accused by boys of being lazy, and not wanting to dirty their 'precious' hands.

Other school activities

Participation in extra curricular activities (ECA) was relatively low and the number of clubs was limited. Head teachers mentioned transport problems as a constraining factor. In two of the state schools for which figures have been provided, boys were more active in the sports and art clubs while care clubs, ecology and wildlife clubs, and Creole festival clubs attracted more girls. Wildlife and other environment clubs are usually very active and enjoy a high profile nationally. In one school, there were 19 girls and only 1 boy in the wildlife club. In the private school, boys were more active in the sports and music clubs and girls in the drama and dance clubs. There was more or less equal participation in the maths club.

Girls were more active in competitions and activities organised at school and national level and won most of the awards at end-of-year prize giving ceremonies as seen in table 2.13 below.

School management processes and practices

The management teams in the state schools consisted of a head teacher and two deputy heads: one for curriculum and one for pastoral issues. There are seven subject departments, headed by heads of departments (HODs). The private school had a much smaller management team consisting of a head teacher, a deputy head teacher and a head of curriculum. There are more females on management teams in all schools. Table 2.14 below lists the distribution of staff across the four schools.

Table 2.13. Gender-wise receipt of best performance awards

	Boys	Girls
School A	15	19
School B	11	21
School C	20	30
School D	11	17
Total	57	87

Table 2.14. Gender profile of school management teams

	School A		School B		School C		School D	
	M	F	M	F	M	F	M	F
Head teacher		1	1			1	1	
Deputy		2		2	1	1		1
HODs	4	5	2	5	3	6		1
Total	4	8	3	7	4	8	1	2

Interviews were held with three head teachers (two females and one male) in the state schools and with the deputy head teacher responsible for the secondary section in the private school. Three staff meetings were observed in the state schools, but it was not possible to observe a staff meeting in the private school.

Gender awareness among management staff

There was greater awareness and understanding of gender among head teachers than among teachers generally. Head teachers from the three state schools were knowledgeable about gender, could identify gender issues in their own schools and admitted concern for issues such as boys' disciplinary problems, lack of motivation, underperformance and classroom gender imbalance. They were aware of gender-unfair practices operating in the school, and some very stereotyped behaviour by teachers. One school had an action plan on gender, although it had not been implemented. The head teacher, who was new to the school, was in the process of sensitising teachers and gathering baseline data to revise and implement the plan. She was committed to gender issues and had undertaken a study on gender as part of her Master of Business Administration (MBA) course in education administration.

Another head teacher, conscious of the large gender imbalance in secondary 1 classes, had replaced setting with mixed-ability teaching. He described his initiatives as a 'hard lonely battle' because teachers were largely opposed to the move. They found it difficult to teach mixed-ability groups because of the large range of abilities and the lack of resources to cater for different needs. Parents were also opposed to the practice, fearing that it compromised their children's education. The head teacher showed great determination to persevere and was equally committed to giving both sexes a fair chance, and he actively encouraged the school's female football team. He felt that the ministry should give more direction to schools and provide research and data to sensitise teachers and parents.

The deputy head teacher from the private school felt that gender was not an issue in the school. Boys and girls performed equally well and the school set high expectations for all. Girls were more conscientious and more regular with homework, but the differing needs of boys and girls were understood and catered for. Management and staff were aware that boys needed the 'extra push' and provided special encouragement and counselling whenever necessary.

Responsible posts

Three of the schools had student councils/committees to ensure participation of students in school activities. Students elected prefects and student committees. The schools set the criteria. In one school, the student committees showed a clear gender bias in favour of girls and an under-representation of boys. The total membership comprised 63 girls and 26 boys; the position of chair was held by ten girls and three boys; vice-chair was held by eight girls and five boys; secretary was held by ten girls and three boys, and 35 girls, as opposed to only 15 boys, were ordinary members. The school has 28 female peer educators as opposed to ten male peer educators. Peer educators are role models for other students. In the two other schools, the practice was to appoint a boy and a girl prefect for each class, resulting in more balanced committees. The two head teachers from state schools said that staff had enormous problems identifying boys with the right qualities to become head boys in their schools.

Some teachers and head teachers seemed to lay more emphasis on the disciplinarian role of prefects, rather than the leadership one. In this frame, a good prefect was one who maintained discipline in the absence of the teacher, who made sure that exercise books were collected and cleaning duties performed. He/she was expected to report instances of misbehaviour to management and act a 'mini teacher'. Girls appeared to be more comfortable in these roles while boys were reluctant to tell on their friends and risk being ostracised by their peers.

Counselling services

All schools had a counsellor and counselling services were available to boys and girls. Girls were more willing to seek advice and made more use of this service, while boys would report to the counsellor only in cases where they were referred, even in the case in the one school with a male counsellor. One explanation given by a head teacher was that boys did not approach counsellors for fear of appearing weak or being teased by their peers. They tried to resolve the problems themselves and often ended up in more trouble.

Peer educators are role models for other students. They receive training in leadership and life skills. They are students who guide and counsel their peers on HIV/AIDS, drug and substance abuse, pregnancies and other adolescence-related problems and lead by example. Some of the qualities required for a peer educator were responsibility, friendliness and commitment. The majority of peer educators in the state schools were girls. Table 2.15 outlines the number of peer educators in the three state schools.

The unequal gender balance suggested to some that girls were more responsible and were better role models. The male counsellor said it was very difficult to persuade the boys to become peer educators and that he had noticed very little change in boys' attitudes during his 12 years as counsellor.

Table 2.15. Number of peer educators in state schools

	Boys	Girls
School A	12	29
School B	9	30
School C	10	28
Total	**31**	**87**

Discipline/suspensions

All schools had a code of conduct: head teachers felt it applied equally to all and that all received fair treatment. They felt that girls were more obedient, responsible and compliant. Boys were more often reported for misbehaviour and breaking rules and were sometimes involved in more serious offences such as alcohol, drugs and gambling. Table 2.16 outlines the number of students suspended in 2006.

Over twice as many boys were suspended from schools in 2006, and over half of both boys and girls suspended were from one school.

Conclusions and Recommendations

Education system processes and practices

There is insufficient leadership on gender at the Ministry of Education and the persistent belief that gender is not a major problem in schools. The ministry should reinstate the Gender in Education Committee, which can champion the cause of gender and lobby policy-makers.

Members of the ministry's Quality Assurance team felt they had sufficient training in order to be able to identify gender issues at school, and gender was not perceived as a major problem in secondary schools. More gender research and data is however needed to help QA staff understand the changing concepts and emerging challenges of gender in Seychelles schools and develop indicators that can measure these effectively. In order to be able to report on the gender dimensions of the hidden curriculum, training in gender analysis and the design of gender-sensitive instruments is also needed. The QA service with its limited staff will not be able to do this on its own.

Students

The research revealed that the way in which many Seychellois boys constructed their masculine identity was problematic. Boys were being brought up with narrow standards of masculinity and associated male identity with physical strength and prowess, social status and dominance. Femininity was equated with childbearing and

Table 2.16. Number of students suspended, 2006

	Boys	*Girls*
School A	12	8
School B	71	24
School C	20	12
School D	3	1
Total	**106**	**45**

womanhood. Hard work, and responsibility were considered feminine traits and not necessary for successful careers. Boys also held more stereotyped attitudes of appropriate jobs for men and women, shying away from the more caring professions like nursing and early childhood education, showing a predilection for more physical and risky activities to demonstrate their manliness.

Boys portrayed themselves as 'breadwinners', 'heads of families' and 'protectors', oblivious to the realities of the Seychellois society and to the fact that 47 per cent of the households were headed by women. It would appear that schools were not helping them to challenge these stereotypes or preparing them for a future where they would not necessarily be the breadwinners and would be expected to participate to a greater extent in household responsibilities.

Boys need to be provided with opportunities at school to reflect the diversity of masculinities that can free them from narrow and limiting possibilities. Careers and personal and social education programmes must be evaluated for their efficiency in changing stereotyped attitudes and developing self-awareness. It is strongly recommended that personal and social education and careers education be delivered by confident teachers who can address emerging challenges boldly.

Girls' expressions of femininity were more rounded, giving them more freedom to express themselves and not overly restricting them. However, the interviews revealed that many girls were caught up in a paradoxical situation attempting to reconcile their wish for greater freedom and economic independence with the need for protection and approval by men.

Gender identities are fixed by early socialisation in the home. Seychellois homes provide girls with a stable, protective and structured environment to learn valuable attributes of responsible and caring behaviour. Many boys were deprived of this opportunity to develop responsible behaviour by being allowed more freedom and a more lenient and unstructured environment at home. This may make them more prone to negative peer pressure, street influences and anti-social behaviour. More research must be undertaken to determine patterns of socialisation in the home, which may be putting boys at risk, and links between the boys' projections of masculinities and the rising incidence of acts of violence, vandalism, bullying and sexual harassment in schools.

The tendency to see the other gender in a more negative light reveals the need for greater understanding and interaction between girls and boys. School processes and practices in state schools, however, seemed to be segregating the students and in some classes observed, putting them in competition against each other. The tendency for many teachers to hold up girls as models of discipline, maturity and hard work can destroy boys' self-esteem even further.

Special intervention and counselling programmes must be developed to engage boys more fully in school. Teachers must develop and use a variety of teaching strategies that answer to the needs and interests of both girls and boys.

Teachers

There are enormous differences in perceptions depending on teacher's gender, age, nationality and subject specialisation in state schools. Such a divergence of views within a small sample indicates that there are different sets of value systems and expectations operating in schools and students may be receiving conflicting messages about appropriate behaviours. There is evidence from classroom observations that this is already taking place. In such situations, it is important that schools make their own position on gender equality and equity very clear.

Gender issues need to be frequently discussed with staff and misconceptions need to be clarified, by producing updated data on student performance and behaviour. Management must take clear leadership for gender and equity issues and the school must have clear written policies to guide all teachers. This was not happening in case study schools and no school had a written policy on equal opportunities. The majority of teachers had not received formal up-to-date training in gender and equated sex with gender.

Many teachers held stereotyped views on girls' and boys' attitudes and performance, which generally went unchallenged. The labelling of boys, and to a lesser extent male teachers, as 'irresponsible' and 'unmotivated' was institutionalised and echoed by all categories of staff male and female in state schools. Such labelling was frequently used as an excuse by men and boys themselves to abdicate responsibilities. Similarly, the belief that 'girls/women are multi-skilled and can cope with more than one thing at a time' placed undue pressure on girls to meet expectations. Management staff lacked expertise, support and strategies to challenge these deep-rooted beliefs and practices. It is evident that repeated messages of low expectations of boys will progressively affect their self-esteem and performance and drive them to rebel against school. There is urgent need to conduct more research and redress this situation.

The pervading negative discourse on boys masked the fact that large numbers of girls in low ability streams were also underperforming and felt threatened by the rough and unruly behaviour of boys. Schools did not adequately cater for their needs. Teachers seemed very reluctant to discuss issues of class or socio-economic status.

Teachers take part in constructing gender through interactions and relationships with students and cannot pretend to be gender neutral. They need to be aware of their influence and the messages they send out daily. The ministry must organise more gender-sensitive training for all its staff and gender must form an integral part of all teacher-training courses

Sexual harassment and bullying are growing concerns in schools. Teachers were not informed or involved in combating this problem. It was not openly discussed or tackled efficiently, and students considered the practice of dealing with isolated cases to be ineffective. Students said they developed their own mechanisms to counter harassment as they grew older and stronger. This leaves the younger and more vulnerable students unprotected at school. Schools need to go beyond the approach of dealing with isolated cases and involve everybody, students, parents and teachers, in preventing and eliminating harassment.

Although male and female teachers reported getting along well with one another and did not feel discriminated against, women teachers appeared to shoulder the major part of responsibilities in state schools in order to get things moving and to avoid confrontation. Management tacitly condoned this arrangement in order to preserve peace, although some young female teachers secretly complained of being overburdened and harassed by long-serving male teachers who refused to do their share of work.

Processes within and outside the classroom

In spite of their stereotyped views and statements, teachers were in general professional in their approach and attentive to both genders. Many teachers also came out very strongly on their 'gender neutral' stance during the interviews. They were convinced that gender was not an issue as far as their teaching was concerned. They wanted to be seen as being gender-fair and non-discriminatory in their practices and were therefore conscious of their own classroom behaviour. They addressed both genders respectfully and asked an equal number of questions. They had mastered all the outward trappings that, in their view, rendered them gender-fair. They did not, however, appear to reflect more deeply on how their teaching might have impacted differently on boys and girls.

The segregated seating arrangements in many classrooms and students' automatic reflex to form single-sex groups when asked to organise themselves for group work may suggest that teachers had a superficial understanding of gender and may not have recognised the gendered contexts within which they operated. Girls were largely 'invisible' in the PSE classes, in the low ability classes and the practical component of the agriculture lesson. Teachers did not seem aware of this situation or adjust their teaching styles. Awareness raising and training could address these issues.

In 11 of the lessons observed in state schools, teachers appeared to conduct their duties in a 'clinical' manner. They entered classrooms, delivered lessons and left oblivious of the noise and litter. Although interactions within the classrooms were correct and acceptable, there was very little friendly interaction with teachers and students outside the classrooms. Teachers did not question their teaching methods or attempt to explain the poor behaviour and performance of boys. They had few strategies or solutions to propose. There is a need for teachers to reconnect with students, and cater for differing learning needs and interests. Action research could be encouraged in schools to promote reflective thinking and action.

All secondary schools (except for the private school) have adopted streaming because it is easier to manage. Setting and subject options require complex timetabling arrangement and adequate numbers of classrooms and teachers. These are not always available in schools. Schools need greater guidance on grouping students to ensure that the ministry's policy of equal opportunities is enforced. It is too serious a matter to be left entirely to schools.

Finally, certain particularly sensitive PSE lessons might be taught in single-sex classes, so that both genders' needs are catered for.

School management processes and practices

Many school management processes and practices are heavily gendered and both girls and boys are affected in their social and academic development. Gender is not considered a serious issue in spite of glaring imbalances in access to certain curriculum areas and participation and performance in examinations.

Although school managers are more gender-aware than teachers, they lack the skills and strategies to address the situation. Gender is insufficiently researched and monitored by education managers.

Schools do not actively challenge gendered behaviours or acknowledge their role in the reconstruction of identities preferring to blame the family, the mass media, female teachers and the society at large. When questioned about the school's responsibilities, many head teachers and teachers admitted 'helplessness' in dealing with the boys. Counselling and persuasion did not appear to work and they considered their efforts to be a waste of time. School practices and processes were unquestioned. Thus it was impossible for them to see how some school practices such as rigid streaming and setting could be alienating boys.

The ministry's policy statement is clear on the principle of equity. The ministry must monitor its implementation in schools and send out clear messages that it is unacceptable for any group to be discriminated against. It must support school management teams in its efforts to create more gender-friendly schools. It must sensitise parents and the public on its policies and choices to deliver on its promise of equity. There is currently stiff opposition from the more vocal parents. Parents however should be made aware of inequalities arising out of rigid streaming practices and engaged in the process of boys' empowerment.

Overall

Making sense of gender in Seychelles schools has proved to be a formidable challenge because of the lack of data and research to guide the process. The Ministry of Education should encourage more debate, training and research in gender so as to deepen teachers' understanding and commitment to gender and 'human rights' education.

Schools will not be able to bring about changes on their own, but trained staff working in partnership with parents, other partners and the ministry can start the process of reflection and reconstruction. The case study schools were willing to take up the challenge.

CHAPTER 3

Sex or Gender Equity: the Organisation of Schooling in Trinidad and Tobago

Jeniffer Mohammed
University of the West Indies, St Augustine

Introduction

Trinidad and Tobago is a twin-island state located at the southern end of the chain of islands in the Caribbean Sea known as the Lesser Antilles. Trinidad experienced Spanish and British colonisation, as well as the influence of French settlers. Tobago was controlled by many different European powers for short periods. In 1899, the British joined both islands into one colony. Trinidad has an ethnically diverse population consisting of the descendants of Africans (39.6 per cent), Indians (40.35 per cent), Chinese (0.4 per cent), Europeans (0.6 per cent) and other groups (0.65 per cent), as well as a significant mixed group (18.4 per cent). In addition, there are many immigrants from other Caribbean countries. Tobago is mainly African in ethnic heritage. Religion reflects this diversity – in Trinidad, Roman Catholics predominate among the Christian religions and there are significant numbers of Hindus and Muslims of different sects. In Tobago, Protestant denominations predominate, while on both islands there are small groups who practice Afro-centric religions such as the Orisha. In 2006, the combined population was 1.29 million, comprising almost equal numbers of males and females. The distribution by age is shown in Table 3.1, further demographic statistics in Table 3.2 and some economic indicators in Table 3.3.

Table 3.1. Age distribution in Trinidad and Tobago

Year group	Percentage of total population	Males	Females
0–14 years	19.5%	105,994	100,156
16–64 years	71.6%	397,699	358,755
65 years +	8.9%	51,965	42,039

Source: Central Intelligence Agency (CIA) World Factbook (2007)

Table 3.2. Further demographic statistics for Trinidad and Tobago

Demographic indicators	Trinidad and Tobago (est. for 2007)
Population growth rate	–0.883%
Net migration rate	–11.13 migrants/1000 of the population
Life expectancy (at birth)	Males: 65.87 years; Females: 67.87 years
Literacy	98.6%

Source: CIA World Factbook (2007)

Table 3.3. Selected economic indicators for Trinidad and Tobago in 2006

Economic indicators	Trinidad and Tobago (2006)
GDP per capita	US$19,700
GDP real growth rate	12.6%
Unemployment rate	7%
Industrial production growth rate	17%

Source: CIA World Factbook (2007)

The country is a member of the Caribbean Community (CARICOM), a 15-nation group of independent Caribbean countries (all English speaking) forming a regional bloc – mainly for economic and fiscal co-operation, but the role has extended to collaboration in human and social development, legal and judicial affairs, culture and communications among others. The Caribbean Examinations Council (CXC) is the recognised examination body for the CARICOM region at the secondary level.

Trinidad and Tobago is one of the most affluent societies in the Caribbean, with a buoyant economy very much dependent on oil, gas and petrochemicals. It is also one where crime has been on the rise, largely a result of the narcotics trade and gun running. Young men, in particular those who have not been successful at school, are implicated in murders, kidnappings, pedalling and smuggling of drugs and ammunition and robberies. There is widespread acknowledgement in society that young men are not benefitting as they should from their education, especially in terms of social responsibility. That these young men are mainly of African descent is a sensitive issue for an ethnically charged society. However, the problem extends to both males and females who have left school without or with minimal qualifications – chances are that they will be exploited on the labour market, will not be able to maintain an adequate standard of living and will become a potentially destabilising force in society.

Exploring the Bias: Gender & Stereotyping in Secondary Schools

Education

From emancipation (1834) there was pressure to provide education for the previously enslaved in a bid to Anglicise the colony. This was called 'elementary' education and was supposed to provide 'the elements' only to enable the populace to take up their place as free men and women. As a result, universal primary education has long been a reality in Trinidad and Tobago. Before and since independence (1962) there was a demand for universal secondary education and since 2000 that goal has been achieved. Tertiary education is now free as well for those who qualify. Although there are almost total participation rates at the primary and secondary levels, there is continued concern about chronic underachievement.

In Tobago, poor performance at the secondary level has been linked to the fact that too many students leave the primary system without basic literacy and numeracy skills. Overall, the administration and management of education, the poor distribution of resources, as well as teacher absenteeism and few professional development opportunities have been identified as the more important reasons impacting on both primary and secondary education on the island (Trinidad and Tobago, 2001).

The education structure in Trinidad and Tobago (Figure 3.1) comprises:

- two years of early childhood care and education (ECCE),

- seven years of universal primary schooling, two at the infant and five at the standard levels, for the 5–11 age group,

- five years of universal secondary education, and

- two further years in sixth form for those who qualify.

For the nation as a whole, in 2004 there were 27,462 pre-schoolers who attended early childhood care and education centres. There are 484 public primary schools (denominational and government) with a total enrolment of 147,328-75,299 males and 72,029 females (CSO, 2005). There were 2,067 male teachers and 5,857 female teachers in the primary system (CSO, 2005). At age 11, primary students sit the exam known as the SEA (Secondary Education Assessment), their performance determining their placement at a secondary school. Using the SEA as a placement device makes it a high stakes examination, and this has been much criticised because it is felt that not all groups have an equal chance of passing. Exam performance seems to favour those of higher-income groups, which also means that certain ethnic groups are privileged.

The traditional grammar secondary schools are in high demand. The 'alternative' sector comprises junior secondary schools, senior comprehensives, composite schools and senior secondaries, which have all been built by the state since 1970 on the comprehensive model. They were meant to increase equity in the system – more school places which could be accessed by those unable to find a place in the traditional grammar schools, with a wide variety of curricula choice providing academic, technical and vocational subjects. Today the alternative sector has the most children in the secondary system, a large majority of whom belong to lower-income groups. Many of these schools are plagued by a high incidence of indiscipline and lawlessness, as well as by chronic underachievement, particularly of boys.

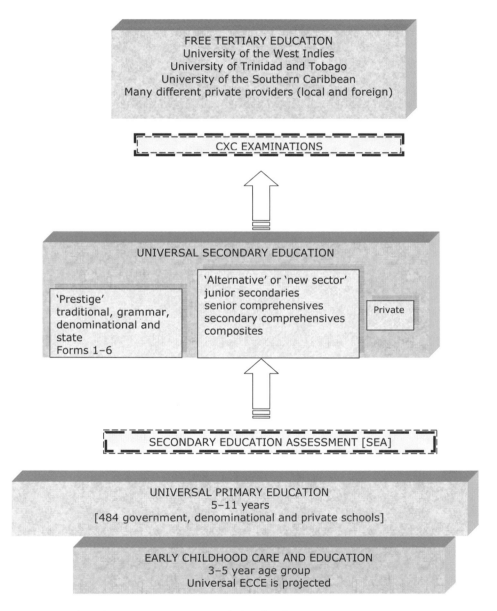

Figure 3.1. The education system in Trinidad and Tobago

Exploring the Bias: Gender & Stereotyping in Secondary Schools

Gender differentials in education

The research literature on educational achievement in Trinidad and Tobago and the Caribbean generally pinpoints a case of poorer academic achievement among boys. However, there are complex patterns based on ethnicity, residence, socio-economic status, learning environments, as well as ability levels, which lead one to ask 'Which boys and girls are underperforming?' On the whole, there seems to be more attention focused on the issue of male underachievement, while we still have much to learn about the inequities that girls suffer in the education system. A summary of the most relevant trends and research findings is listed below.

Primary system

- Males more than females tend to be held back a grade in greater numbers at all primary grade levels, except standards 5 and 6 – the years of transition to secondary school (Worrell, 2006).

- From 1993 to 1997, males were dropping out of school more than females (UNDP, 2001) and according to Brown (2006) that trend has continued.

- Among the 7–9 age group (standards 1, 2 and 3) overall girls scored higher in mathematics than boys, and a significantly greater proportion of boys were in the lower tail of the distribution (Brown, 2005).

- While scores seemed to favour females generally in the SEA, more boys were placed in schools of their first choice. Selection practices based on the number of school places for boys in certain geographical areas disadvantaged girls (De Lisle and Smith, 2004).

- Females scored higher than males generally, and larger differentials favouring females were more likely among students below the 50th percentile; these tended to be students of lower ability, in lower achieving urban schools and in rural areas (De Lisle and Smith 2004; De Lisle, Smith and Jules, 2005).

- There is a concern that the design of the SEA does not ensure gender fairness – the composite score is heavily weighted towards linguistic-verbal competence, which seemingly disadvantages boys (De Lisle, 2006).

Secondary

More boys are placed in junior secondary schools than other types of secondary school (Mustapha, 2002; Worrell, 2006). These are, generally speaking, lower achieving schools and from there they go on to the senior secondary schools where the majority choose the technical–vocational area. More males drop out of school than females. A review of 2000, 2001 and 2002 CXC data for Trinidad and Tobago shows girls generally outperforming boys, except in mathematics. In science, technical drawing and information technology more girls received higher grades (De Lisle, 2006).

In 2002, the pass rate for males in English language was 57.3 per cent and for females 69.5 per cent. Both genders had a pass rate of about 50 per cent in mathematics, the girls just a little behind (Niherst, 2003, p.v).

Stereotypical curriculum choices continue (Morris, 2002) and locate females, especially in the 'alternative sector', towards lower paying jobs as office and store clerks or in the food preparation or garment making industries. Qualitative studies suggest that gender is mediated by context, particularly low expectations for student success, and that girls do better than boys in such contexts (Worrell and Morris, 2007). Postmodern studies show a range of masculinities and femininities. A 'hard core' masculinity seeks to subvert the conformist behaviours associated with school success. School is a place where boys learned to be men, while girls have a more instrumental view of schooling – as insurance for life after school (Mohammed and Keller, 2007).

Explanations for gender differentials in achievement in the Caribbean

There has not been as much work done on interrogating the nature of female underperformance, as it has been masked by the generally better academic performance of some girls. Male underperformance in Caribbean education systems has been theorised in the following ways. The male marginalisation thesis states that men in certain low-income groups have been deliberately obstructed in their quest for education and higher-status jobs by men with power in society, while women have not been so disadvantaged (Miller, 1992, 1994).

Family socialisation, particularly gender socialisation in the Caribbean tends to privilege boys relative to girls. They are dealt with more leniently, have fewer chores to do and enjoy more freedom. Consequently, the formal, sedentary nature of most classrooms irks and irritates boys and they are not disposed to exert much energy in highly abstract and theoretical exercises (Figueroa, 1996; Chevannes, 2001). At the same time, images and stereotypes of masculinity emphasise sports, outdoor activities, fun and games, hanging out with friends and even risky behaviours associated with violence and crime – and the processes of schooling tend to emphasise quite the opposite, for example, reading – so schooling seems to be anti-masculine (Parry, 2000; Chevannes, 2001). Caribbean societies tend to be homophobic, so that any suggestion of the feminine in a male's behaviour is to be avoided. The peer group becomes an effective policing mechanism ensuring that boys do as little school work as possible and are engaged in manly pursuits – only certain sports and certain curriculum areas (Plummer, 2005). Nor does the feminisation of the teaching profession provide boys with role models that can rival the attributes of the dominant masculinities that most boys adopt.

More qualitative-type studies are necessary to flesh out the trends and patterns described above. For example, while males are not doing as well as females generally, they are performing creditably well. However, both males and females in the lower ability levels, in lower performing schools and in rural areas, particularly Tobago, seem to be at risk. The home socialisation experiences of girls tend to work with the ethos of the school to produce competent students, but this also means that girls tend to be compliant and obedient in classrooms. If this is the case, then to a large extent they may not be developing to their full potential. The ideologies associated with a hegemonic type of masculinity seem to be working to boys' disadvantage and this serves to further exacerbate the cumulative disadvantage accruing from poverty, attendance at low performing schools and a rural location.

The role of government

The overarching national policy framework is the Government's Vision 2020, which seeks to attain developed country status for Trinidad and Tobago by 2020. Gender was identified as integral to that process and a subcommittee on gender was established so that gender would be a part of the deliberations on development. The government has shown commitment to gender equality by amply providing resources to all schools from ECCE centres to the secondary level, where curriculum has been expanded to include the visual and performing arts, science, information technology and physical education and, at both primary and secondary levels, the technology available in schools has been upscaled for computers and internet access. In 2005 and 2006, education received a major share of the government's budget in an effort to create a seamless education system from early childhood through to the tertiary level. A seamless education system is one where all people can have access to all levels and stages of education – the emphasis being that no one is excluded.

The Ministry of Education has some specific policy guidelines about gender inclusion, for example –

- Equal numbers of boys and girls are chosen in allocating students to secondary schools for entry into form 1.

- All newly established state schools are co-educational.

- All subject areas, even those that are stereotypically gendered, have places for each gender.

- Young pregnant girls are allowed to continue their education – while pregnant or come back to school after delivery and resume their education.

- In certain secondary schools where there are large numbers of children who did not 'pass' the SEA, students are given a choice of leaving and going off to a skills-oriented programme such as the Adolescent Development Programme or to remain in their school. Both boys and girls are given this choice; formerly it would have been an option only for boys.

- A competency-based qualification, the Caribbean Vocational Qualifications (CVQ), has been created to comply with CARICOM Approved Occupational Standards in agriculture, business, communication, construction and other areas. It offers an alternative route to higher education, which will allow recognised and portable qualification into countries participating in the CARICOM Single Market and Economy (CSME) – an attempt to widen the certification opportunities open to both males and females.

The country has also benefited from two extensive reform movements in education as well. The Fourth Basic Education Project (1995–2002) targeted primary and lower secondary education, seeking to improve provision, access, curricula and professional development capability. The ongoing (1999–2007) Secondary Education Modernization Programme (SEMP) is also engaged in similar areas of school improvement.

However, there is no explicit gender policy guiding efforts towards gender equality and equity. There is a commitment to ensure equality at the policy level, evidenced by the government's ratification of a number of regional and international agreements. Despite these initiatives, a Draft Gender Policy, which was developed based on widespread national consultation, was rejected by the government and is now in the process of reformulation. There were some controversial issues that tested the government's willingness to fully accept the principle of gender equality. Not having a national gender policy is a matter of some concern, because some generalised commitments only operate in the breach.

The Research

Despite attempts at establishing gender equality in schools, gender stereotypes and gender discrimination continue because they are for the most part 'invisible' – that is, the dominant beliefs, perceptions and practices that guide how males and females relate to one another and among themselves are largely taken for granted. The focus of the inquiry, therefore, was on the processes in schools that helped to create, re-create or transform stereotypes related to gender.

Gender equity is focused on fairness or justice. Unequal outcomes, for example the underachievement of boys relative to girls, present a signal that schooling does not treat boys fairly. Equity is a more processual indicator than equality and more difficult to determine by quantitative measures. For example, interactions and relationships might adversely affect only certain categories of males, or girls may be achieving but there are many who are not. In addition, students' own ideas of their gender identities may be conspiring to (re)produce unequal outcomes. Thus, if one wants to understand the outcomes of education it becomes necessary to try to identify and examine the actual processes involved. Equality tends to be related to access and outcomes and does not penetrate the 'black box' of schooling.

The inquiry focused on the following:

• What are the processes in classrooms, schools and the education system that promote or compromise gender equality and gender equity?

- What gender stereotypes exist in school interactions and how do they impact on gender equality and gender equity?

- Are gender stereotypes being maintained or questioned by the processes of schooling?

The Sample

Five secondary schools were selected in Northern Trinidad. The research procedures employed were the same for all the countries involved in this project and are discussed in the early chapters of this book. The schools selected are listed below, followed by brief case studies –

- School A: all-girls, traditional, grammar-type school, denominational, urban (female principal)

- School B: all-boys, traditional, grammar-type school, denominational, urban (male principal)

- School C: co-educational, comprehensive-type state school, urban (female principal)

- School D: co-educational, comprehensive-type state school, rural (male vice-principal)

- School E: co-educational, traditional, grammar-type state school, urban (male principal)

School A

This is an all-girls traditional grammar school controlled by a denominational board (Christian), but as is the practice, the government pays salaries and contributes to the school's upkeep. Established in the early 1950s, the school is a prestigious institution accepting some of the top performers in the SEA (the placement examination that primary students sit at the end of standard 5). It offers secondary education from forms 1 to 6.

At 800 students, this is a medium-sized school in Trinidad and Tobago. Although the grounds are spacious, the buildings tend to be overcrowded, though the whole place is kept clean and attractive. There are fields for hockey, football, volleyball and a netball court. The auditorium doubles as a gymnasium, but there is a general lack of sports equipment. However, the recent addition of physical education as an examinable subject at CXC is prompting the purchase of new equipment.

Other than the principal's room and general office, there are two staff lounges, one washroom (now 'unisex', as the school has begun to take on male teachers), 21 classrooms and the large multi-purpose hall or auditorium. There are also two computer labs, one language lab, one audio-visual room, one music room, one art room,

Table 3.4. Distribution of teachers by sex and subject area at school A

Subject	Males	Females
Mathematics/IT	1	8
Sciences/IT	2	9
Modern studies	2	5
English		7
Business studies		4
Foreign languages	1	6

one geography lab, seven science labs (one for general science, two each for physics, chemistry and biology) and a library.

The teaching staff numbered 45 (six male and 39 female) at the time of the research. There were two female members who had been contracted through the On-the-Job-Training (OJT) programme for young, untrained, recently qualified people who would like to be teachers. There were no vacancies.

Most students are Christian and are Indian in ethnic origin. There are also smaller numbers of Hindus and Muslims, almost all being Indian as well, so that this school has a relatively large Indian population. Students belong to all socio-economic groups, but many are from the higher-income brackets.

School B

This is also a single-sex (boys only) denominational school of another Christian denomination to that of School A. Established in the 1950s, it is considered a prestigious institution. The school accepts those who scored in the 85th–95th percentile in the SEA and student enrolment is normally about 450 making it a 'small' secondary school. It offers the traditional grammar-type secondary education from forms 1 to 6.

The buildings have not been expanded since it was built, so that while the school is generally well kept, the classrooms tend to be overcrowded. In the grounds of the school, there is a football field and a basketball court. Other than the principal's and the vice-principal's offices, there are two deans' offices and one staffroom equipped with desks and chairs, storage cupboards and a mini-kitchen and dining area. There are 13 classrooms and three separate labs for physics, chemistry and biology, an audio-visual room and a small computer lab. Each classroom is equipped with basic supplies – blackboards, chalk and dusters – and school furniture such as desks and chairs for students are adequate and well kept. While there is no auditorium or hall, the chapel is large enough to have a monthly assembly. Every morning, worship is conducted over the public address (PA) system.

Table 3.5. Distribution of teachers by sex and subject area at school B

Subject	Males	Females
Mathematics	1	2
Sciences/IT	3	3
Modern studies		3
English	1	3
Business studies		2
Foreign languages		2
Physical education	1	

There were 21 members of the teaching staff – six male and 15 female – at the time of the research. There were no vacancies.

Students are predominantly Christian, with significant numbers of Hindus. All ethnic groups are represented with some whites and Chinese. All socio-economic groups are represented, but most boys belong to middle- and upper-income families.

School C

This is a co-educational school built by the government in the 1970s in a bid to expand provision and access to groups who were previously obstructed from secondary education. From its inception, the school was plagued by low achievement and episodes of lawlessness and violence. As a comprehensive school, it only accommodated forms 4 and 5 and at times the enrolment reached 1,500 students – a very large school. As such, its intake was mainly from the junior secondaries that accommodated students from forms 1 to 3. In the 1990s, it was converted to a seven-form school – with an intake at form 1, the usual but somewhat reduced intake at form 4 and a form 6 intake as well. It is thus a large and complex system to manage because now it has the trappings of a grammar school, and so its appeal has widened, while it also has the usual comprehensive offerings in technical–vocational subjects.

The school is situated on spacious grounds. There are different blocks of classrooms, labs and workshops. The grounds and the outer walls of buildings are kept clean and attractive, but inside classrooms the louvres have been vandalised, as have the electrical sockets and the loudspeakers for the public address system. There is a large playing field for football, and basketball, tennis, netball and badminton courts.

Other than the principal's and vice-principal's offices, there is a large staff room and a staff lounge, one room for deans and another office for security personnel, two washrooms, one each for male and female staff, 42 classrooms and a large multipurpose hall or auditorium. The school is also equipped with three computer labs, one language lab, one audio-visual room, one music room, one art room, two science labs each for chemistry, physics and biology, and a well-stocked library of reference materials, fiction and non-fiction items and a West Indian collection. In addition, there are separate workshops for the mechanical, construction and electrical subject areas as well as for home economics, beauty culture and agricultural science. There are separate toilets for boys and girls.

The teaching staff numbered 104 (45 males and 59 females) at the time of the research. There were three males who had been contracted for the remedial math programme, one female for remedial English and two teachers (female) on contract for the teaching of beauty culture and social studies.

Most students are Christian, but there are significant numbers of Hindus and Muslims. Ethnically, there are more students of African origin than those who are Indian or of mixed ethnicity. Some students come from the middle class, but the majority is from lower socio-economic groups.

School D

This is a co-educational, comprehensive school built by the government in the 1970s in a bid to provide access to secondary education in a remote part of the country. It is situated in northern Trinidad, in a rural belt where fishing and farming are the dominant occupations. The school has suffered from low achievement and it has to contend with a high turnover of staff. Its remote location makes it unattractive to teachers because of the long commute: few teachers live in the immediate vicinity. The school accommodates students from forms 1 to 6. Enrolment is just over 600, making it a medium-sized school. Unlike School C, it has mainly a grammar-type curriculum and includes a few technical–vocational subjects such as agricultural science.

Table 3.6. Distribution of teachers by subject area and sex at school C

Subject	Males	Females
Mathematics	5	8
Sciences	8	8
Modern studies	3	8
English	1	13
Business studies	6	14
Foreign languages		2
Visual and performing arts	2	4
Electrical construction	6	2
Building construction	6	
Mechanical construction	8	
Total	45	59

The playing fields are extensive, but not properly equipped with sports facilities. There are different blocks of classrooms, labs and workshops, but the buildings have not been renovated since the school was built. Consequently, there are major repairs to be done, such as long cracks in the walls and leaking roofs.

There is one room for the principal's office and one staff room. The classrooms are generally dilapidated, with inadequate desks and chairs that are in poor condition. Teachers find that for a school close to the sea it still suffers poor ventilation. There are science and computer labs and an up-to-date gymnasium that is well equipped. However, sports equipment and supplies are locked away and permission must be granted for use. Science and mathematics kits have been recently acquired and the library is well equipped with over 13,000 titles. There are separate toilets for boys and girls.

The teaching staff numbered 46 (24 males and 22 females) at the time of the research. There were four male teachers on contract and ten lab assistants, also on contract. There were vacancies for principles of business, English and agricultural science teachers. The school's population is overwhelmingly African in origin, with Christianity being the major religion. The enrolment as at September 2006 is given in Table 3.7.

School E

This is a government school built in the 1950s. It is a traditional, grammar-type school unique in that it is not denominational, not single-sex **and** it is generally highly regarded as one of the country's top achieving schools. The total student enrolment is normally about 700, making it a medium-sized secondary school. It offers secondary education from forms 1 to 6.

There has been some expansion over the years, but now it is an oddly arranged set of buildings with little space for further development unless more storeys are added. It is generally well kept, but the classrooms tend to be overcrowded and poorly ventilated. Next door to the school is a very large playground that is used for all sports.

Table 3.7. Distribution of students by sex and class level at school D

Classes	Males	Females	Total
Form 1	45	50	95
Form 2	49	66	115
Form 3	35	32	67
Form 4	75	74	149
Form 5	66	94	160
Form 6	12	21	33
			Total = 619

Other than the principal's office, there is a staffroom and lounge. There are 19 classrooms and separate labs for physics, chemistry and biology, and a well-stocked library. Each classroom is equipped with basic supplies – blackboards, chalk and dusters – and school furniture, such as desks and chairs for students, is generally adequate. There were 45 members of the teaching staff – 14 male and 31 female – at the time of the research. The 2007 enrolment is 313 boys and 347 girls, the total being 660 students. Students come from all socio-economic and ethnic backgrounds.

Portraying Gender Processes in Schooling

The following sections report and analyse statements made by school administrators, principals, teachers and students about gender relations in schooling. Also included are observations of students in classrooms, as well as in physical education sessions outdoors and analysis of texts used in classrooms. Attention is paid to how gender is constructed and reconstructed in the normal processes of schooling through the perceptions and stereotypes that different groups have for one another, as well as how they regard one another within the group. At times ways of breaking the stereotypes that threaten gender equality and equity are discussed.

Normalising sex equity as gender equity

In the schools under consideration, there is an apparent misunderstanding about gender and gender relations that shape and influence the typical stereotypes that educational administrators, principals and teachers adopt towards the education of boys and girls. To a great extent, this misunderstanding is also perpetrated in the government's stance on gender, where in the absence of an explicit gender policy there is only a general commitment towards equality. As a result, it is expected that boys and girls will be treated equally (this is not questioned even amidst the much debated educational phenomenon of male underperformance). It is difficult for most people to take the issue seriously, because it appears as if both boys and girls are being treated similarly. They tend to locate the problem away from school – family dynamics, say, or gender socialisation – or see it as an effect of having mainly female teachers.

The fundamental misunderstanding seems to lie in confusing 'sex equity' as being 'gender equity'. When people think they are discussing gender, they are really speaking about sex. 'Sex' refers to the biological differences between boys and girls and differentiates them as a group. 'Gender', on the other hand, emphasises a relationship or relationships based on social constructions of what it means to be male or female. How boys and girls tend to choose subjects based on how they self identify would qualify as a gender issue. When the government allocates funds for schools, when principals and staff deploy and translate these resources into equipment, facilities, curricular arrangements and activities, there is the collective understanding that boys and girls would benefit and participate equally, thus sex equity.

Such a disposition might also mask a deeper intention (either conscious or not) to stay away from controversy. Gender as a social issue presents all kinds of problems and strong feelings for adults who seem to view it negatively. If it can be dealt with in schooling in an 'objective' and removed way, such as in the equitable supply and distribution of resources, then that is the policy most people will endorse. The single-sex schools stated that the issue was irrelevant, since they dealt only with males or females. This represents an even deeper misunderstanding than that which confused sex and gender. This attempts to sanitise the relationships that students may develop or are already developing by steadfastly ignoring those of the opposite gender. The determination to stay away from controversy becomes tantamount to gender prejudice, as stereotypes of the other gender go largely unexamined by the young people. We are beginning to see emerging something about how schools are organised that prohibits the development of healthy relations.

Such a view is really a contradictory position as the teaching staffs are mixed: males are present at the girls' school and females actually outnumber male teachers at the boys' school. Yet at the girls' school the principal was adamant, 'This is a female school' and 'I don't think that we are ready for either male teachers or deans' – even though they have a few. At one co-educational school where they couldn't use the same argument, a male teacher tried to play down the issue and said that if gender awareness must be introduced in schools it had to be done cautiously. One gets the impression that teachers and others feel that to raise the issue of gender is to stir up a hornet's nest. So it may not be just a simple misunderstanding of sex and gender, but a deliberate mindset to ignore the gendered ways that structure school experience – because therein lies controversy. The contexts of schooling – their academic focus, the top-down nature of social relations – do little to question the stereotypes of the wider society.

Just as sex equity is mistaken for gender equity, discussions that raise the issue of gender seem to be reduced by participants into a discussion of boys as separate and distinct from girls (sex). This becomes problematic, as the following excerpt shows. On being asked about gender issues at her school, this principal spoke innocently enough about a perceived problem:

> '... the children coming from the junior secondary schools, the females tend to choose this school to a large extent. Our school is not noted particularly for any sporting activity and so males tend to choose other schools ...'.

Several consequences stem from this initial premise. It says about the boys who do come to the school that they may not be sports-oriented. Would this then be the reason why a more vibrant sporting programme has not been introduced? Yet what about the girls? Surely sports are for everyone? Gendered ideas that sports are largely for the sports-conscious, the highly talented – mostly males – disadvantage the varieties of femininities and masculinities present in the school. Sports in this view are seen as a male preserve.

Gender surfaces elsewhere as well. In the rural co-educational school, the vice-principal spoke passionately about keeping boys and girls separate – in a co-educational school! They tried an intervention with an intake of 'good boys' (higher-achieving boys than those who would normally have been allocated to this school) and decided to keep them all in one form 1 class and all the girls in another class. For various reasons things went awry, and he now describes them 'as a class of miscreants'. Any policy based on keeping boys and girls separate in a co-educational school where they have both male and female teachers, is creating an unnatural and artificial set of conditions, trying to force boys and girls not to interact too closely.

In all fairness to the participants and perhaps more puzzling yet, as the discourse intensifies a better-developed sense of gender emerges. For example, the principal who spoke of sports earlier in terms of gender stereotypes, is able to see the issue in terms of relationships – and even of getting input from the young men themselves – when asked about the curriculum:

Interviewer: 'Should gender play a part in developing the curriculum?'

Response: 'Certainly. In developing themes and schemes of work, I would think that one would take gender into consideration. I always say teachers teach how they were taught, so again it would call for some discussion ... and really to be guided by the young men themselves ... [A]s adults we can think of so many things that may benefit boys, but indeed we really have to get a consensus from the boys that these things are beneficial ... so that there must be some input from the students themselves ...'.

When she speaks of the school as a space or site, for example, to which students choose to come or not, she does not focus on gender, but speaks of boys in stereotypical terms as being different to girls. But, in speaking about the curriculum, she begins to talk about the relationships forged via teaching and learning, between teachers and the boys, recognising varieties and different interests. She also recognises that opportunities and entitlements develop through a better understanding of one another (students and teachers, males and females). This contradictory stance may also be evident in how others approach the issue: when confronted with a problem about the place or site generally (for example, male underachievement at this school), people tend to talk in terms of boys or girls (sex). When pressed about solutions to the problem, there is a change of focus to seeing the people in the place as having to discuss and relate healthily to one another. While this is encouraging, it is apparent that such discussions or insights only happen by chance or because of the particular context of an issue being discussed – in the normal manners in which schools are organised, there is little 'space' for such relations to surface. Nonetheless, it does signal to us that school change may be easier to bring about if the focus is initially on instruction.

Gender equity seems to be an elusive goal, especially if interpreted as sex equity. Stakeholders revealed stereotypical conceptions of gender, all based on a belief that gender was a topic fraught with controversy. This belief is probably mired in the confusion of 'gender' as 'sex', which pits boys against girls and men against women, fuelling the idea that the whole issue is volatile and controversial. If gender was properly understood as being about the relationships between the sexes, then it is quite likely that gender equity would seem a laudable goal for young people. Thus, the most pernicious stereotype is the one that prejudges gender as a harbinger of discord – by emphasising sex it succeeds in confusing and obfuscating the path towards gender equity.

Male underachievement: who is to blame?

Perhaps more than any other issue, arguments about male underperformance in the education system focus on the notion of 'sex' rather than 'gender'. In this discourse either girls or women are blamed for the underachievement of boys, and this is based on stereotypes of the interactions between male students and female teachers or boys and their mothers. Some further apportion blame to men, fathers or even male teachers. Others blame the boys themselves. Few individuals saw the school as being deeply implicated in the processes associated with male underachievement. All these arguments based on identifying some group that is culpable are sexist arguments: they assign some totalising characteristics to a group because of their sex and most important all ignore relationships with girls or between girls.

One principal felt that since Trinidad and Tobago was dominantly a '... matriarchal society ...', we have a situation where it is '... women who rule and manage homes'. He elaborated that girls are taught 'care giving values', while boys are largely left to fend for themselves. In school, he sees the problem being compounded by female teachers. With two-thirds of the staff being female, the more experienced among them are '... genuinely interested in raising the level of consciousness of the boys ...', but because of the boys' home socialisation and the female teachers' 'soft' (or motherly) approach, this becomes difficult. He goes on to show that the younger teachers who are unsure of themselves may try tactics that do not work, in other words they do not know how to '... approach the male of the species'. Thus, in his view, women do not know how to deal with boys – not mothers or experienced or inexperienced female teachers. The overabundance of female teachers in this all-boys school is likely to entrench the problem of males' underperforming. However, he does say that the female teachers on staff work much harder than the men. Yet that is in line with his thesis that women are taught to care and to nurture, so that they labour more than the men on staff.

This is a hard and deterministic view that sees the problem of male delinquency and underachievement as resulting from the dominant influences of females in their lives. As a result, there is little room for intervention because home and society play the major roles in shaping gender identities. Gender socialisation is reinforced in schools, because it is largely a female teaching profession. However well elaborated this principal's thesis may be, it is really a set of stereotypes that he invokes to explain relationships between boys and women. Moreover, under his headship nothing will be done to nurture ideas about gender equality or sensitising boys on gender issues, because he feels that they have already been wired a certain way.

Another view is again underscoring home socialisation and the influences of the wider society in explaining why boys underachieve. It does not lay blame on women, but on the boys themselves and their 'openness' to these influences.

> Response: 'My personal feeling about influencing the male is that it is very difficult now as a teacher, because [of] the outside influences, the world, having become a very materialistic world – I call the present generation a Nescafé generation – everything is now for now. They need instant satisfaction. And so when I try to put across to them the old values that we might have been accustomed to, it seems to have no relevance to them. Still what I try to do is to always keep pointing out to them and looking at present day occurrences in the society, crime for example – look at the young men – what have they achieved? Victims and perpetrators of crime. What have they achieved in their short lives? You keep asking them – "Do you think you will ever reach ... an age where you will be able to look back and say, 'Ah... this is something I have done in life'?".'

This is a male teacher at one of the co-educational schools presenting his position regarding boys and being 'at risk' in the school environment. His point is that the school can hardly make an impact on the influences from the home and wider society because they are so all-pervasive. All a teacher could do is appeal to 'conscience' or the 'inner person'. This is a fatalistic view that seems to put young men even more at risk, because nothing seems possible by way of a classroom or school effort to address the issue. The most damning stereotype at work here is the belief that boys' socialisation via the mass media and youth culture is so totalising that there are no 'spaces' or potential left for teachers to work with. The organisation of schooling seems above the social issues affecting students; the emphasis continues to be on academic issues.

A seemingly more-balanced view is put forward by a female teacher who teaches mainly boys. She indicts the school generally and teachers in particular in dealing with students from the lower socio-economic classes. She probably comes closest to seeing the school as being poorly organised to encourage healthy relations.

> Response: 'What I am saying is that the cultural difference between a teacher and most of students coming out from working-class homes and what we perceive as a difficult environment. It is so different that when a teacher looks at that child, their body language, the manner in which they speak, ... their whole persona ... they [will] show their own disapproval. And the children [will] see it. And the chances are that that child has been experiencing that from the time they entered the system in primary school. I think that students react because they are accustomed to people always

being on the attack. And they have to find their [own] way to survive and to feel safe. And that's the only way they know.'

She feels that it is not necessarily a gender issue, but one of social class. The teachers at her school were mainly middle class, while most of the students came from lower socio-economic environments where poverty and hardship permeated their lives. Boys in particular were at risk, and much more of a pastoral programme was necessary to rescue them. The stereotypes then that imbue schooling and put boys at risk stem, in her view, largely from an inability on the part of teachers to deal with cultural diversity. The milieu of the comprehensive school, where there is the largest number of students from low socio-economic groups, presents to teachers problems of relating to the 'other'.

Male underperformance therefore elicits strong views from principals and teachers, each in some way perpetuating gender stereotypes that frame the problem as being insurmountable. What may be instrumental in helping to perpetuate these stereotypes is the 'traditional' nature of schooling – the pressure for academic rather than more affective goals, the uniform nature in which learning is understood and the social distance that separates teacher and student. These are the 'normal' processes of schooling and they do not encourage discussion, critical reflection or even something as elementary as feedback. It may be instructive for us to think about relationships in schools as being the heart of what children learn – and in terms of remedying problems, whether gender based or not, relationships may be the key.

Rendering the female invisible

In the discussions and arguments that surround contemporary schooling in Trinidad and Tobago, there is an implicit understanding that girls are 'non-problematic', are 'okay', but there is also the position that girls' success may be continuing to disadvantage boys. A strong theme coming from male teachers at school B and elaborated by others is that boys need to be 'rescued' so that their education is of utmost importance. As one teacher puts it, '... it is still a man's world out there and boys have to be groomed to take over the mantle'. Another male teacher added, '... women have just taken over their place, so boys have to show their mettle'.

In the eyes of the vice-principal of the rural school, we again see 'gender' as a relational concept being misunderstood. He sees it as referring to 'male' and 'female', yet in his discussion he never sees girls as experiencing any disadvantage. He says, 'the females are dominating education ...' and female teachers '... want to get rid of the boys, instead of dealing with the boys in a class situation ... and relating to them'. He is almost saying that the balance should be shifted, so that the boys are on top once more. He reveals this more clearly in discussing sports.

'In sports now, the males have become the dominant gender and our school is a top sports school. In the past, the females were the top sports gender. So the males have taken that

role! ... That's what we need to do with the males – build their self-esteem... We tend to pull them down and take away their manhood.'

This ignores girls and how they might feel; he even sees boys as only being affirmed when they have beaten girls at something.

Another teacher echoes such sentiments, showing well thought out positions about boys but failing to see that girls are equally implicated. This female teacher noted that boys lived mostly with mothers, grandmothers and aunts, and so what they learned about modelling, life and interaction would come mainly from females – and she didn't see this as healthy. Yet, she thought it 'normal' for girls. These assumptions tend to be widespread in society in Trinidad and Tobago – that the absence or occasional presence of a 'father figure' in a girl's life doesn't affect her; it only affects boys. Yet learning to be female is not confined to only learning things about women. To a lot of people gender issues are seen in binary terms and what policies they suggest are mired in a separatist philosophy of boy versus girls.

In addition, male teachers readily admit that they treat girls differently to boys, and their perceptions of girls actually minimised their contact with girl students as opposed to boys. They tended to be very lenient with girls, seeing them as 'dainty', and were quite at a loss in having to deal with aggression in girls. Most of the time they would speak to them about their wrongdoing and in rare cases sent them to the office – usually when they couldn't help it because the girls had been involved in a fight. With boys they felt more secure, giving them harsher punishments – such as using sarcastic language to condemn their actions, making fun of them in front of the class, putting them outside the class or sending them to the dean. Both male and female teachers expected girls to be 'ladylike', and as a result excused boys for certain behaviours but took the girls to task for the same behaviours.

'Normalising sex equity as gender equity' leads to a number of problematic ways in dealing with the issues of male underachievement in schools. It confuses exactly what the discourse is about, so that stereotypes and gender prejudice prevail and masquerade as genuine arguments. At the same time, it tends to render females invisible while the gendered processes of schooling seek to sideline girls, making even their seeming success a reason to ignore them.

Legitimising a hegemonic masculinity

This section focuses on how schools seem to play a major role in the construction and reconstruction of masculinities. It may be that it is certain conceptions of masculinity that actually jeopardise the achievement potential of boys.

Sports: a metaphor for the masculine

Earlier we saw that one principal saw sports only in terms of boys' participation. At the same time, a vice-principal felt vindicated when boys as sporting heroes triumphed over the girls' record. While some girls are involved in sports, more boys either play or elicit a deep interest in sports, mainly football. The only exceptions were at the all-girls school, where a vigorous sports programme is pursued, and the co-educational grammar school, where the all-girls football team is more successful than their all-boys team.

In the rural, co-educational comprehensive school, the girls in the observed class formed two netball teams while boys played free football in a nearby field. One small boy was included in the netball team: a boy looking on called him 'gay' and a girl called him a 'faggot'. Both boys and girls stood on the sidelines and commented freely. The (male) teacher's focus remained on the students playing netball and when a male student made remarks to him about one player's bottom, he made no comment.

In this brief scenario, we see certain aspects of how sports are gendered. Boys watching netball are more inclined to speak of the female form rather than the skills displayed. Boys never play netball; if they do, they are not 'true' males. In this case, onlookers – both male and female – call into question the nature of the masculinity of the lone boy netball player. So, females too find that it traverses the drawn gender lines for a boy to allow himself to play netball. The reverse is apparently not the case with the all-girls' football team from the co-educational, grammar school, where girls receive acclaim for their success. Perhaps it is only when girls excel at a heavily dominated 'male' sport that they are regarded seriously.

While girls engage in sports for physical exercise and to develop their skills and talents generally, boys seem to gravitate towards sports as a means of continuing to construct their image of themselves, their masculinity. The sporting arena is the one place, not the classroom, which hails a hegemonic, 'hard' kind of masculinity. In the classroom, the innocent enough events that are discerned through the eyes of constructing gender may seem ridiculous, but they show the continued urge and drive to always be interpreting a boy's own and others' behaviour in terms of developing masculinity. For example, in the all-boys school during a biology lesson on heating and cooling of the body, one boy responding to the teacher said that you could stand in front of a fan to cool off and was reprimanded by his fellow students with, 'You gay or something?' By contrast, the playing field construed as an opportunity for demonstrating 'maleness' also made it the venue where all sorts of typically gendered statements and stereotypes could go unchallenged. There is much scope in addressing how sporting stereotypes has separated the sexes. Encouraging sports that are not as heavily gendered (swimming, lawn tennis, cricket, badminton) and games (chess, scrabble, draughts) could provide spaces where boys and girls may interact equally and freely.

Male as protector

Heavily gendered images in a traditional mould tend to characterise boys' and girls' aspirations for themselves – though with girls there were some contradictory signals.

Despite all the talk about male marginalisation and boys' underperformance, boys believe they are the future breadwinners and will be the 'head' of the family. They spoke of protecting their wives and felt that they would not like their wives to work. In their homes, they did not have any substantial domestic responsibilities compared to their sisters. Consequently, they were growing up in home environments that did not challenge the usual stereotypes of gendered family responsibilities or the spheres of interaction, where males were more active in the public domain and females in the private domain of home, family and other relatives. The spectre of male underperformance did not seem to impinge on what their future scenarios might be like.

Girls on the other hand showed more diverse and contradictory interpretations. For example, they did not mention getting married and having a family in any specific way. At the all-girls school, they spoke with some distaste about the details and indignities of pregnancy and childbirth. All spoke of their desire for 'independence', which translated into 'making their own money'. Yet at the same time they co-operated with traditional gendered notions of body image. While agreeing on the principle of gender equality, girls felt that hard manual labour, being dirty and sweaty, was generally not a 'respectable' image for a 'lady'. That boys held this view as well could explain why girls shied away from thinking of careers in some technical–vocational areas. Their attraction to the opposite sex plays a major role in how girls think of themselves – so that choice of career may depend a lot on what is considered 'ladylike'.

Gendered stereotypes about what is considered feminine and masculine in terms of careers, interactions and negotiation with the opposite sex, and what goes on in families, are largely unchallenged in the normal course of schooling, family life and preparing for choosing a career. These gendered images and stereotypes continue to perpetuate ideas about male superiority and female inferiority. Among other scenarios, they do not help females deal with the very real possibility of having partners who cannot match them in terms of earning power; while for males it means that their notions of masculinity may be not be flexible enough to accommodate a partner who may be contributing as a head of a household or main 'breadwinner'.

This is a social issue that schools ignore. The heavy emphasis on the academic curriculum circumscribes the full development potential of young people. There are spaces, contradictions and opposition to the traditional stereotypes, but without some recognition and discussion they remain as 'outliers', and even though they may become more and more commonplace, in people's minds they tend to remain as 'outliers'. The exploits of the girls' football team, the resolve of some girls to 'follow the money' rather than be 'ladylike', the lone boy playing netball, the incidence of girls fighting over boys, could all form the basis of some vigorous discussions about gender relations. The fact that it seems to be more and more girls who are traversing the gender-drawn lines of what is acceptable is also something to be openly discussed.

Reinforcing masculinity

Boys spoke of having to do heavy lifting like moving tables, which they did not necessarily mind. What they grumbled about was being expected to bring a chair for a girl who did not appear to be incapacitated in any way and when the chair was within arm's reach. Sometimes they said teachers asked them to clean up the class-room, while the girls stood outside 'looking nice'. However, it seemed to be good-natured grumbling, because one principal said that he witnessed occasions when boys insisted on carrying the girls' chairs. Boys and girls seemed to enjoy the encoun-ters where boys showed some form of gallantry and girls enjoyed the attention. In co-educational schools, therefore, boys and girls found something enabling in the contact between the sexes. Boys in school B, on the other hand, felt unanimously that girls should not be allowed to come to their school (they would be too much of a distrac-tion). Boys in co-educational schools believed that the presence of girls gave them more opportunities to practice masculinity, while boys in the single-sex school felt that a place apart from girls gave them the opportunity to continue to build mascu-linity without the threats that girls might provoke. Traditional ideas such as the pervasive masculine roles of provider, aggressor and protector, and of females as the 'second sex', all seemed to be routinely inscribed into their daily interactions at school.

Boys' interactions with male teachers were underscored by notions of preserving the masculine sphere. With some of the male teachers, there would be sexist remarks if they saw boys working closely or sitting together. This was not regarded as a form of sexual harassment. In both co-educational and the all-boys school, male teachers treated boys as if they were 'partners' with a great deal of joking and sexual innuendo. Such behaviour on the part of male teachers hints at a certain kind of 'boy–boy' relationship designed to maintain if not a hardcore masculinity, then one that is commonly accepted as masculine. On the whole, men and boys display a sharper and better-defined sensitivity to masculinity than femininity. Females are not so preoccu-pied with observing and commenting on boys' masculinities as boys themselves. At the same time, females have a lot of leeway in their interactions with other females, as a matter of fact much of this interaction goes unnoticed and without comment.

Boys said that they could speak freely to male teachers and felt more camaraderie with them than female teachers, though they admitted that male teachers seemed to have less patience than female teachers. They felt that the bond they shared with the male teachers had its origins in the fact that they had both experienced 'growing up male'. However, they were quick to point out that in interacting with a male teacher, however close the bonding, there was a limit to what would be tolerated, whereas with girls the male teacher could be far more caring and sympathetic (although girls disagree about this). Male teachers, then, do not allow too close a contact with male students, because such contact is opposed to a masculinity that should be strong and autonomous. It seems then that male teachers play a pivotal role in the gendered processes of schooling – shoring up traditional masculinity and femininity by draw-ing lines about how much emotional involvement to invest in students.

Boys, especially in the all-boys school, felt that the normal relations of peer pressure could get out of control and could affect their ability to get on with their work. Boys are often challenged when attempting to do school work and called names such as 'nerdy' or 'girly'. To a large extent, boys among themselves establish norms of behaviour that emphasise rough play and controlled aggression. To be able to tolerate and take part in the building of this type of masculine interaction is seen as a form of strength. Those who cannot do so are seen as weak and become susceptible to repeated acts of bullying. This common mock-aggression becomes transformed into something more sinister if it is suspected that the weakness being shown stems from a feminine masculinity. Schools are not safe places for boys who do not subscribe to the rough and tumble norms for male behaviour; this is especially the case for those who seem to display an alternative sexual orientation.

Boys in school E spoke of the worrying issue of a boy who seemed of a different kind of masculinity: they felt that he didn't belong there and he made them uncomfort-able. To them this kind of masculinity is a 'weakness', and so it brought a sense of uneasiness because they felt that to condone it would mean that the whole place, the school, would acquire an image of being a 'soft' or a 'queer' place.

Boy:	'This boy does actually say he like boys and girls beat him up ... because he is always saying to the girls to get out of here ... and he is overdo it, he is always saying like "yuh want to be meh friend" ... and ... he is retarded!'
Interviewer:	'The boy wants to be your friend – that's not retarded.'
Boy:	'Miss, something wrong with him. Something mentally wrong with him.'
Interviewer:	'What if he has a deficiency as you all claim ... so just talking to him wouldn't help because he has a deficiency, right? ...'
Boy:	'Yes, but if he was so deficient, he not supposed to be in a school like this!'

Schooling is characterised by processes that legitimise a hegemonic masculinity. Other masculinities, such as the one described above and those that do not revel in sports or emphasise academic success, are sidelined and subject to different levels of ridicule in order to induce conformity. Femininity is not a dominant or even readily visible gender identity – only when a range of femininities arises is there outrage or even bewilderment at 'unladylike' behaviours.

Masculinities, femininities and learning

Overwhelmingly teachers agreed that boys are more 'action oriented' when it came to learning compared to girls and they seemed to enjoy project work, visual aids, technological input and were quite able to brainstorm ideas for design and critique models, inventions and artefacts. 'The whole idea of going home and studying for a test, somehow they don't respond too well'. Boys, it was agreed, tended to shy away from the 'reading subjects'. Those in the all-boys school and the co-educational schools agreed that teaching and classrooms in general did not cater to these characteristics, and so it was only in specific subjects that some boys could have more enabling learning experiences – technical drawing, physical education, computer science, music, art, technical–vocational subjects and science. They saw boys' liking for mathematics in terms of their penchant for problem solving.

Teachers spoke of having to go at a slower pace with boys and being more 'teacher centred' in their interaction with male students. They felt that girls had a greater capacity for independent work and seated work. Most teachers admitted that they did not use separate strategies consistently and tended to fall back on whole class approaches that relied mainly on traditional, didactic interaction. Undoubtedly, then, one of the reasons why males may underachieve is because schooling and class work is construed as 'feminine' and teachers themselves, accustomed to stable portrayals of the traditional classroom, are reluctant to invest in a more active pedagogy.

All students have aspirations of completing their secondary education successfully and going on to the tertiary level. Their career choices were very similar – law, medicine, accountancy, business. Only boys chose to be engineers or pilots, while one boy wanted to be a chef. It is a matter of concern that students, whether in high-achieving or low-achieving, schools spoke of careers that demanded many years of tertiary education such as medicine or the law. Boys and girls who were low achieving said that they had no reason to feel that they would not achieve their goals, even those who came from low-income families. Ten years ago, I conducted research in one of these schools on career aspirations and the findings were remarkably similar. However, I found that by the time they had reached form 5 and their internal examination marks could not be ignored, they had begun to 'downgrade' their aspirations from 'accountant' to 'working in an office' and from 'owning a business' to 'store clerk'. It is something that we should note – that schooling and examinations serve to sort and allocate students to different rungs on the labour market, and for the majority of these students there is a certain loss of self-esteem in relinquishing cherished ideas and having to settle for 'lesser' jobs (Mohammed, 1996).

No girl or boy felt pressured to choose a career because of the wishes of their parents. They all felt that their parents wanted them to be successful at whatever career they chose, and felt that they would receive support and encouragement. Although the boy who wanted to be a chef stated that his mother was not too happy with his choice, his sister is a chef, while another boy said he was expected to go into the family's business. The limited influence of parents on the career choices of their children today probably stems from the wide range of careers that now exist, of which they may know little or nothing at all. As a result, parents are more open to the career choices of their children.

Boys felt that their parents liked them because of their humour and because they could be relied on to do heavy chores and run important errands when the need arose. Girls on the other hand could not say whether their parents liked any specific characteristic, but liked them to be 'good girls'. One girl at school A said, 'I'm really, really limited and restricted. I'm not allowed to talk to boys or anything. Not any kind of contact with boys and I really don't like it. That is really my only problem with my parents'. The anxieties that parents suffer in particular about their 'girl children' are so complex that adolescents tend to be impatient with the limits imposed. A typical worry of parents of high-achieving girls is that they may become involved with a boy who is not academically inclined and will thus derail the girl from achieving her full potential. Gender relations for the girls are a normal part of life; for their parents it becomes a frightening prospect.

Girls and boys learn in both the classrooms and at home that there are different expectations for each. While there is a semblance of democracy in homes, girls are heavily sheltered and constrained. In classrooms they learn how to put 'being lady-like' or 'invisible' to work for them – whether classes are boring or not – as they seem to be continually aspiring towards 'independence'. The obstacle course that families put in their way, and which they encounter in schools as 'expectations for young ladies', predisposes them to always be thinking of strategies, scenarios, implications and consequences as a matter of course. It is difficult to ignore the conclusion that they learn how to come to terms in a practical way with the situations that schooling and family life present. Boys, on the other hand, expressed their liking for being a boy by equating the status with 'freedom' from the restrictions that usually related to girls, and with people looking to them to take charge. The expectations that popular stereotypes equate with young manhood disadvantage boys – most boys aspire to but cannot fully realise the dominant forms of masculinity. In addition, while femininities can run the gamut (even amidst notions of 'being ladylike'), masculinities are only acceptable within a narrow range of behaviours and dispositions. Boys learn from early on that they have to go through the rites and rituals of aggressive masculinity, and whether they can 'manage' or not becomes a daily and unending mode of being. In a way, boys are 'trapped', while enjoying their 'freedom'. These gendered life courses determine to a large extent what boys and girls learn.

Gender as text: portraying relationships

Textbooks were the main resources used in classrooms in the schools studied. To some extent, the analysis of each text reveals an effort on the part of authors and publishers to portray men and women authentically, mindful of the varieties that can occur.

English. There are many photographs and drawings of males and females, though the ratio is approximately 3:1 and the images tend to depict women in traditional roles as mothers or out shopping and men socialising, outdoors or in scenes of violence. Both men and women are portrayed in positions of power in the workplace, but men more than women. The extracts used, such as poems and literary works, are almost totally derived from men – Emerson, Naipaul, Lawrence. There is liberal use of 'he' and 'his' and thus more attention to males in the text.

Social studies. The text attempts to portray men and women equally and they are shown in a variety of roles, traditional and non-traditional. Both males and females are depicted as having power and authority or being passive. While there seems to be a conscious attempt at gender balance, it can be noted that portrayals of negative activity seem to emphasise males. All instances related to juvenile delinquency and street children feature males. Particular attention is paid throughout the text to ensure that both males and females of different ages, ethnicities and socio-economic statuses are shown in a variety of roles.

Mathematics. Diagrams and tables comprise the bulk of the illustrations and tend to be abstract, and so do not portray any social situations where gender is a consideration. Mathematical problems show attempts to portray men and women equally as motorists and in business. However, people are usually referred to as doctors, scientists, teachers, students and athletes, and in such cases the reader's own stereotypes may be invoked. The learning approaches and assumptions of the texts seem to succeed in getting students to examine their practices, because real-life situations are depicted for problem-solving exercises. These help in nurturing reflection, which may transfer to other areas of their experience.

Information technology. Drawings are limited to flow charts and computer screens and there are no illustrations of people. The text deals with theories and concepts that relate to programming and hardware. There is no content depicting the contributions of men and women. The language tends to be impersonal, often using 'you'. The learning approach of the text does not allow for reflection, communication and negotiation, rather exercises require clinical statements of facts and practical applications of theory. Certainly the use of computers is not a simple and straightforward matter, there being a whole psychology of use question which may be gendered to some extent. Therefore, only content that may be examinable is treated in this text, and not the social situations that impact on information technologies and how they are perceived. Texts like these give subjects like information technology a male bias.

Biology. The illustrations do not reveal any bias towards males or females. However, in the captions to diagrams and in the chapter titles the author uses the term 'man' frequently to refer to men and women – 'The sense organs of man', 'The skeleton of man'. This is counteracted to some extent in the actual text, where 'human' is more often used to refer to males and females.

Home economics. The illustrations in this text represent males and females in a variety of situations, traditional and non-traditional and they seem to be shown equally. In the section on sexuality and puberty, cartoons are used which seem to downplay the issue of gender and lends an air of gender neutrality to the illustrations. This could have been a deliberate decision to reduce the kind of attraction that photographs and conventional diagrams seem to have for the adolescent when human reproduction is being studied. While this could be a specific technique for this issue, nevertheless it succeeds in making females invisible, even though the topic is their own biology.

The analysis of textual materials used for instruction shows that the issue of gender equality is one with which authors and writers continue to struggle. The equal distribution of illustrations and the variety of ways of depicting males and females seems to be easier to do than to make the actual text gender fair. Subjects like science, information technology and mathematics continue to present a gender-neutral stance, while they are heavily gendered in appeal.

Conclusion and Implications for Policy

This study highlighted the nature of prejudice and stereotypes that impacted on gender equality and equity in schools. It is evident that there is no urgency or pressure to examine 'taken for granted' assumptions about males and females. Some people have well thought out views and elaborate theories based on their personal convictions about gender. Thus, it becomes quite easy for a male principal to blame women for the plight of boys.

These unexamined beliefs and convictions are the source of the problem, and they solidify into stereotypes that guide and fashion the nature of the educational experience, not only for boys and girls but also for male and female principals, teachers and supervisors. When the topic of gender is raised, the participants in this study tended to think of 'sex' – whether one is male or female, and the so-called traits associated with each. This male–female dichotomy confounds any meaningful discourse on 'gender'. At the level of the nation, 'gender equality' is enshrined in law and the Ministry of Education allocates resources and entitlements equally to males and females. Yet what results is merely 'sex equity' – that boys and girls are treated in the same way, they are both given the same kinds of resources and opportunities. 'Gender awareness', however, which few people discussed, involved an understanding of differences and relationships and therefore that 'same' did not necessarily mean 'equal'. This is where stereotypes and prejudices come in: monies are allocated to schools, for example, for a sports programme (the assumption being that it is spent equally on boys and girls) and the facilities may be provided; however, because of prevailing norms and stereotypes girls do not take up the opportunity. This kind of discussion grasps the nature of 'gender'.

When there is a clear understanding of what 'gender' entails, inevitably teachers and principals will begin to question curricular norms and routines, and will begin to interrogate their own practice. When one understands gender, it does not make sense to say that gender issues are not highly relevant in an all-girls school because of its single-sex status. In fact, it has been found that in many all-girls schools there is a pronounced 'male' orientation to curriculum using males as the model for performance and development of knowledge (Schmuck, Brody and Nagel, 2002). In this study, most people were either at the point of unexamined biases or they had an understanding of gender equality as 'sex equity' (Schmuck, Brody and Nagel, 2002). The most pressing concern that emerges from the study is for people to understand what they are talking about. For this to happen, really deep-seated policy changes need to take place, going beyond the usual recommendations to interrogate the very assumptions we have about the school as an organisation.

The study of classroom, school and system processes clearly reveals a number of stereotypes that serve to engender schooling in Trinidad and Tobago and seem to a large extent to be going unquestioned. These stereotypes are summarised below:

- **Gender equality is a controversial issue and should be ignored in schooling or only introduced in a limited way.** This attitude does not appreciate a deeper exploration of social life. It is also symptomatic of the school's curriculum – ignoring controversial issues, yet consistently advocating critical thinking. It speaks to a one-sided view of the curriculum – the academic over the affective.

- **Since there is a general principle of equality for all enshrined in the institutions of the land, and since there are few glaring examples of unequal practices, then gender equality must be a reality in schools.** Such pre-judgements tend to be based, like the first point, on a notion of social life that is ordered and harmonious and questions like these seem to have the potential to create disturbance.

- **Gender is about the separate characteristics of men and women.** This view tends to reify and reinforce the traits associated with conventional notions of masculinity and femininity. It stereotypes males and females in terms of these characteristics and does not recognise the varieties of masculinities and femininities that exist.

- **The education of boys is a much more urgent and critical problem than the education of girls.** This stereotypes all boys as doing badly and all girls as doing well. It ignores the fact that high-achieving boys do as well as high-achieving girls, and that underperformance of both boys and girls is an urgent issue – particularly for certain categories of students: those from low-income families, in low-achieving schools and in rural areas.

- **Girls' schools or boys' schools have little to do with issues of gender.** This is as a result of the stereotype that sees males and females as binaries – yet gender by definition is about the relationships between boys, men, girls and women. This relational aspect was almost absent from the views expressed by participants in this study. Schools do little to focus on the relational aspects of students and staff.

- **The issue of boys' underachievement and underperformance results from the influence of females.** This view indicts female teachers as not knowing how to deal with boys. It sees the relative success of girls as creating low self-esteem in boys and that females cannot be appropriate role models for boys. These are all stereotypes based on a notion of boys' and girls' affairs, interests and schooling as separate and distinct processes.

- **Boys need male role models to improve performance.** This ignores the notion that girls, too, may well need both males and females to better understand themselves as people.

- **Sports are an avenue through which boys can find themselves.** This portrays females as less inclined to be athletic and more oriented to the home and 'lady-like' pursuits. It militates against the all-round schooling and development of girls and 'non-athletic' boys.

- **Teacher-directed learning and pedagogy is the best way to 'do' education.** This stereotype exists even though research shows (and teachers acknowledge) that the conventional classroom does not enable or interest boys to a large extent. Again, we see emphasis on the academic curriculum without serious consideration being given to learning styles or students' needs.

- **Males are strong and females are the weaker sex.** These stereotypes, while being eroded in the wider society, are still held firmly by boys, and girls. Adults today are less inclined to make such bald and bold claims. Students, especially those who do not read widely, need a learning experience that will challenge these stereotypes.

- **Sexual harassment is 'much ado about nothing'.** This targets behaviours that boys consider 'normal' for men in Caribbean societies. Schools do very little to help override the strong pressures to keep silent about acts of harassment or to challenge the mindset of the perpetrators.

- **The masculine self becomes 'stronger' through sports.** To this may be added, the sciences, aggression, being non-serious and minimal participation in activities that may seem to be 'girlish'.

- **Heterosexuality is normal.** Other sexual orientations are deviant and people who display them should be marginalised.

- **Gender exists as a robust variable.** Boys' underperformance can be explained solely in relation to what happens to boys or their own dispositions. Such stereotypes fail to take into account how social class and ethnicity at least serve to disaggregate boys into very different sub-groupings.

There was little evidence that the processes of schooling were helping students and teachers to question the stereotypes that prevented the full expression of gender equality and equity in schools. The research however showed that:

- giving boys and girls both the opportunity to take the same sleight of subjects from forms 1 to 3 laid the foundations for less gendered subject choices in later years,

- physical education as an examinable subject at CXC might introduce a wider group of students, girls and boys, to sports in the near future,

- the visual and performing arts for CXC is an avenue for non-traditional interactions between boys and girls, such as opportunities for more expressive communication,

- subjects like social studies had the potential to be a platform to begin a dialogue about these issues; social studies texts tended to be more sensitive to gender issues in terms of how illustrations and the actual text depicted social life and the relationships between the genders,

- most schools had a well-stocked library, which could be also be a platform to mount a more vigorous debate about these issues,

- some girls were assuming leadership positions along with boys, and

- some girls were not inclined to be quiet and submissive as the prevailing gender norms seem to suggest, but were quite outspoken and openly challenged boys.

The policy implications include the need to address:

- an explicit recognition on the part of educational authorities that gender equality and gender equity are not being realised in schools, even when resources appear to be distributed equally,

- more widespread attention to the fact that 'gender' issues are really treated as 'sex' issues where boys and girls are seen as separate entities – a biological perspective that reduces 'gender' to essentialist views of males and females; gender has to be seen on the part of decision-makers in a more relational way and in education not as if males and females lived in separate worlds,

- a determined thrust to build gender sensitisation and awareness sessions into teacher education programmes, into the professional development activities of schools, into parent–teacher associations and into the school's curriculum,

- homophobia, bullying and racism as institutionalised aspects of social relations,

- the production of materials that could be used in gender-sensitisation workshops for all categories of education personnel – supervisors, principals, teachers and students,

- the creation of a research agenda by the Ministry of Education to collect both quantitative and qualitative data in schools, so that more can be learned about gender issues and schooling – especially about low-achieving girls, rural populations and Tobago among others, and pedagogy that could enable both boys and girls to improve achievement, and

- the institutionalisation of a national gender policy to provide a rational set of guidelines for the education sector about raising awareness of gender, gender equality and gender equity

A final word

Taking on gender as a relational concept necessitates that all groups in the school interrogate their interactions and the assumptions guiding their interactions. Schools are not set up this way. Instruction, at the heart of all the relationships in the school, continues to be about **teaching**. If schools focused on **learning** they would have to come to grips with knowing more about their students in all their dimensions, bringing to the fore all the biases, perceptions and stereotypes that groups have about themselves and one another. Schools, even after experiencing wave after wave of reform, still stabilise around images where the Ministry of Education tells principals what needs to be done, principals transmit these dictates to teachers, who tell students as a substitute for instruction. In a milieu where sedimented practices are stronger than any reform, standard operating practices lie in obedience, conformity and maintaining the status quo. The tremendous emphasis on the academic curriculum sidelines any viable attempt to address the affective, the emotional and the relational in the lives of all stakeholders at the school.

Studies like this one show the need for schools to be redesigned, allowing the ideas guiding instruction to emerge from the school's dialogue and debate with itself about a more humane experience. Gender sensitivity awareness sessions can only be successful in fracturing stereotypes if they feed into a process of school-wide re-thinking and research about the norms governing schooling. To attempt to fracture stereotypes while the entire organisation remains firmly entrenched in an authoritarian, masculinist, achievement-oriented paradigm just echoes the futility of the spate of reforms that the education system has been undergoing since the early 1990s. Tinkering with the system may result at best in the semblance of change. Our challenge (and gender is only one ingredient in this agenda) is to begin to see the main project of the school, instruction, in a more relational way – one that it includes all stakeholders interacting in collaborative and collegial ways. Collaboration and collegiality about what matters continue to be given only lip service in schools today.

CHAPTER 4

Making Gender Sense in Malaysian Secondary Schools

Maria Chin Abdullah
Persatuan Kesedaran Komuniti, Selangor (Empower)

Introduction

'I hate having to do the dishes that my brothers leave in the sink, while they go out with their friends.' **15-year-old girl**

'My mother supports me (in her studies) ...hmm... but I have to stay home to do housework. Itu biasa [that's normal].' **15-year-old girl**

'I want to work as soon as I leave school.' **15-year-old boy**

'I have to follow my father to sea to help him fish ... I do miss school sometimes.' **15-year-old-boy**

In 2007, when the Education Section, Social Transformation Programmes Division of the Commonwealth Secretariat commissioned its regional study, Malaysia was selected because of boys' low academic participation in education. This chapter sets out to discuss, document and evaluate whether the education system has contributed towards the advancement and development of gender rights and equality given the present context of a rapidly changing society in Malaysia. While it will interrogate some of the underlying reasons for boys' under participation at schools, the study will try to make gender sense and evaluate whether girls' improved performance and participation in education means that gender equality is being achieved.

The Sixth Malaysia Plan (6MP) (1991–1995) and the Seventh Malaysia Plan (7MP) (1996–2000) recognised equal opportunity and access for boys and girls to education as national policies and are being implemented. In 1995, the Malaysian government made a further commitment to gender equality by signing the Convention on All Forms of Discrimination Against Women (CEDAW). In its report to CEDAW, Malaysia acknowledges in article 5 the existence of 'widespread stereotyping of women as followers and supporters rather than leaders or equal partners in Malaysian society', and 'various cultural and institutional factors, which are predicated on restrictive notions of a woman's role in society' and 'often intersect to form barriers to the advancement of women's career and upward mobility in an organisation'.[1] Female enrolment into public universities increased significantly from 57.8 per cent in 2001 to 61.7 per cent in 2007 (Ministry of Women, Family and Community Development (MWFCD), 2008:23) indicating a lower participation of boys at tertiary levels. Despite their progress, however, women in Malaysia still occupy a secondary position in the public and private spaces. The position of men as heads of household and decision-makers is still upheld in Malaysia. Boys are taught from a young age to be aggressive, not to cry or show their emotions, to be independent and to be a provider/protector. Girls are taught to be housebound, submissive, caring and self-sacrificing.

The socialisation process is deeply entrenched in the thinking of Malaysian society. In a survey on gender-based violence (Abdullah, 2006), 61.22 per cent (out of 2,055 respondents) of males and females strongly agreed that 'if a woman wants to visit her friends or relatives, she needs her husband's permission to go'. On the contrary, when another question was posed, 'A female has the right to express her opinion even if she disagrees with her boyfriend', 86.28 per cent of the respondents agreed with the statement. Certainly, the young respondents had separated their social behaviours between being single and married. They do not see the contradictions, and accept that when married, women take on certain socialised roles. Institutions, such as the media, government and religious departments, have also reinforced stereotyped behaviour and some of them have taken on a biased, moral policing role.

Women, in particular, are bombarded with contradictory messages about what is desirable, expected and acceptable of them. Holding hands in public, women's dressing and wearing make-up are now contentious issues as over-zealous religious authorities and politicians propose fines and possibly jail terms for alleged offenders. Malaysian women are at crossroads. They are encouraged to contribute towards the national economy and yet when they do, they are pulled back, reminded of their family role and blamed for the social ills that youth are engaged in. Women are constantly reminded that their sole responsibility is still to care for the head of household and family. Government policies fortify such prejudices. In the 2008 budget, the government announced that working women in the public sector might take up to five years of maternity leave to allow them to take care of children. Such a move further confined women's contribution and identified it as being supplementary. Unfortunately, this choice is not offered to males, because they are expected to be the economic contributors of the family and not homemakers. Such double standards need to be contested.

When women ask for equality, it is often misunderstood as women wanting to be the same as men; this is not the case. They are asking for their basic human rights to be recognised. The roles of women and men are socially constructed by society, without recognising that they have differences in needs, competence and opportunities. This has resulted in women's worth or the contributions that women make to become devalued and, consequently, has led to discrimination and inequality. Advancing substantive equality means recognising the diversity and differences in the varied needs and roles played by women and men; it also means shaping, promoting and empowering women, and men as well, to claim their rights to achieve equality, justice and non-discrimination. Institutions, such as those of the education sector, can either be the antithesis that brings about prejudices and discrimination or they can be the agents of change to advance equal opportunities and results for girls and boys.

Education policy and the government's commitment

Malaysian education policy

Children in Malaysia begin primary schooling at the age of seven for a period of six years. There are two major types of government-operated or government-assisted primary schools. They are the national schools (*Sekolah Kebangsaan*), which use Malay as the medium of instruction, and the national-type schools (*Sekolah Jenis Kebangsaan*) which use either Chinese or Tamil as the medium of instruction. In 2003, science and mathematics were taught in English, starting with new entries into the primary 1 level.

Secondary education in government secondary schools last for five years. Government secondary schools use Bahasa Malaysia (formerly known as Malay language) as the main medium of instruction, but since 2006, selected subjects are taught in English, i.e. mathematics and science. The education system is exam-oriented. Students in year 6 are required to sit for the *Ujian Pencapaian Sekolah Rendah (UPSR)* or Primary School Assessment Examination, before they can proceed to the secondary school level. In the third year, or form 3, students sit for the *Penilaian Menengah Rendah (PMR)*, Lower Secondary Assessment. At form 5, students sit for the *Sijil Pelajaran Malaysia (SPM)*, Malaysian Certificate of Education, which is equivalent to the British Ordinary or 'O' Levels (now GCSEs – General Certificate of Secondary Education).

Malaysia's primary and secondary schools follow the National Integrated Curriculum (NIC), which has been set by the Ministry of Education since 1983. There are vernacular schools that teach Chinese and Tamil and follow the NIC. In post-secondary and higher-level education, curricula are varied and depend on the educational institutions offering the courses. Colleges and universities are now under a separate ministry, i.e. the Ministry of Higher Education. Private schools do exist: those that offer the National Integrated Curriculum and those offering international syllabi.

The Ministry of Education develops and monitors the progress of the national school system and curriculum. It is guided by National Education Policy and its implementation includes the following areas:

- An education programme which encompasses all disciplines of knowledge, skills, norms, values, cultural elements and beliefs to assist in the full and holistic development of individuals physically, spiritually, mentally and emotionally, as well as to inculcate and enhance desirable moral values and to impart knowledge (Government of Malaysia, National Education Policy, 2005:4).

- Implementation of various policies, as follows:

  o **1960–1970s.** Under the New Economic Policy, efforts were made to integrate the three major races and to eradicate poverty in Malaysia. Access and opportunities to physical facilities and infrastructure improved in rural areas with the introduction of double-session schools, a school health programme, a 'textbook-on-loan' scheme, a supplementary food programme, raising universal education up to the age of 11 years and with the building of hostels to increase participation by rural children.

  o **1991–2000.** In line with Vision 2020, the role of education on human resource development was emphasised to accelerate the country's economic growth and competitiveness. The education sector was liberalised, which led to the growth of private higher learning institutions to fill the gap in local universities' intake. In addition, programmes were introduced to cater for children with special needs. A special degree programme was initiated to upgrade the qualifications of non-graduate teachers. The Smart Schools[2] pilot project was launched in 1999.

  o **2001–2010.** Over and above its policy on 'Education For All', primary levels 1–6 were finally made compulsory in 2003 with an amendment to the Education Act. Plans were made to extend the Smart Schools project in 2004. The Education Development Master Plan 2006–2010 was launched in 2007 to further develop primary and secondary education.

  o The Ministry of Women, Family and Community Development, together with the Ministry of Education is developing a manual on sex education for schools. The manual aims to promote responsible and safe lifestyles and to encourage parents and teachers to participate.

  o In the recent 2008 budget, the prime minister made a long-awaited announcement to abolish school fees and to distribute free school textbooks to students at both primary and secondary levels.

Accountability processes

The Malaysian education system, guided by the Educational Development Plan (EDP) 2001–2010, follows a set of processes and procedures. As stated in the EDP, there are four tiers in the education management system (Government of Malaysia, EDP, 2003:7–2) The Ministry of Education (MOE) is where 'all activities concerning policy formulation development planning, curriculum development, public examination administration, and financing are managed and co-ordinated at the ministry level. It monitors educational programmes, with support from the state and district education departments' (Government of Malaysia, EDP, 2003:7–1). The State Education Department (SED) is in charge of school management, monitoring and inspection of educational policies and implementation of programmes. The District Education

Department (DED) assists the state in its tasks, while the school management runs the day-to-day business of the school.

The management of the curriculum and assessment is carried out by several departments/divisions, such as the Curriculum Development Centre (CDC), Technical Education Department (TECED), Malaysian Examination Syndicate (MES), Malaysian Examination Council (MEC), Special Education Department (SpED) and the Islamic and Moral Education Department (IMED) (Government of Malaysia, EDP, 2003:7–3).

The monitoring and evaluation of the implementation of the education policy, programmes and finances is carried out by three key bodies at various levels, namely, the Educational Planning and Research Division (EPRD), the Federal Inspectorate of Schools (FIS), and the Schools Audit Division and Internal Audit.

For sure the MOE has laid down its vision, action plans and institutions to ensure 'Education for All' is achieved. However, there are a number of issues and challenges that need to be addresses.

Issues and challenges

Literacy rate

While there is almost equal access and opportunities offered to both girls and boys, statistics from the Ministry of Women, Family and Community Development (MWFCD, 2008) show that while Malaysia's female adult literacy rate for those aged 15 years and older increased from 86.6 per cent to 89.5 per cent in 2007, the rate is higher for the males – increasing from 93.8 per cent in 2000 to 95.1 per cent 9n 2007 (ibid., 2008:22).

Gender stratification

Table 4.1 shows that in 2007 girls and boys had almost equal participation at primary and secondary levels. It was only at the matriculation and tertiary levels

Table 4.1. Literacy and enrolment rate by level of education, 2000–2006

Literacy	2000		2002		2004		2006	
rate 10 +	93.8%		94.0%		95.1%		Not available	
	Female	Male	Female	Male	Female	Male	Female	Male
Primary	1,425,889 (48.6%)	1,507,988	1,454,338 (48.7%)	1,534,946	1,517,386 (48.6%)	1,603,500	1,539,387 (48.6%)	1,628,388
Secondary	985,692 (50.5%)	965,054	993,176 (50.4%)	977,947	1,013,702 (50.1%)	1,010,186	1,065,416 (49.8%)	1,074,879
Post secondary	45,071 (66.4%)	22,759	70,783 (66.7%)	35,382	104,492 (66.4%)	52,781	86,180 (65.1%)	46,115

Source: Ministry of Women, Family and Community Development (MWFCD) 2008:22

that boys' participation dropped to 34.9 per cent as compared to the girls at 65.1 per cent.

Female enrolment into public universities continues to increase from 57.8 per cent in 2001 to 61.7 per cent in 2007 (MWFCD 2008:23). However, it must also be noted that in 2005, participation rates for postgraduate levels showed that female students accounted for 52.9 per cent for the master's level but dropped to 38.1 per cent at the doctorate level (see Table 4.2).

Ironically, even though more women continue to enter the tertiary level, the labour force participation rate has remain stagnant, registering an average of 46.4 per cent in 2005, as compared to male participation, which averaged 79.5 per cent (see Table 4.3).

Women's lower participation was further confirmed when the 2007/08 Human Development Report (HDR) ranked Malaysia in 63 out of 177 countries under its gender empowerment measurement (UNDP, 2008). The formal equality for girls may have been achieved through their entry into education, but substantive equality in terms of women's labour force participation still requires attention.

Table 4.2. Percentage of enrolment by level of study and sex, 2003–2006

Levels of Study	2003/4		2004/5		2005/6	
	Male	Female	Male	Female	Male	Female
Diploma	40.6	59.4	41.2	58.8	41.8	58.2
First degree	36.6	63.4	35.9	64.1	38.1	61.9
Postgraduate diploma	45.1	54.9	NA	NA	35.2	64.8
Master's	51.2	48.8	46.3	53.7	47.1	52.9
PhD	64.3	35.7	61.4	38.6	61.9	38.1

Source: MWFCD, 2008:27

Table 4.3. Percentage labour force participation rate by gender, 1990–2005

Gender	1990	2000	2002	2003	2004	2005
Male	85.3	83.1	81.5	82.1	80.9	79.5
Female	47.8	47.2	46.7	47.7	47.3	46.4
Overall labour participation rate	66.5	64.7	65.4	64.4	64.4	63.2

Source: MWFCD online, 2006:7

Exploring the Bias: Gender & Stereotyping in Secondary Schools

Students' dropout rates

Despite efforts to make education more accessible to students, there are still students who do not complete the 11 years of basic education. Table 4.4 shows a higher dropout rate among male students and this trend starts at the primary school level.

The UNESCO EFA report in 2001 also indicated that in 1995, 11.9 per cent of the students in form 3 (lower secondary level) did not continue their education into form 4 (upper secondary level) in 1996. For both levels of schooling, male dropout rate was higher, registering 16.53 per cent in 1995 as compared to females' dropout rate of 7.48 per cent (UNESCO, 2001:3).

Quality of management and teachers

Most school personnel are graduate and non-graduate teachers or education administrators from the education service, while other administrative and support staff make up the non-education personnel. In 2006, female teachers in primary schools formed 67.4 per cent of teaching staff and 64.4 per cent in secondary schools (MWFCD online, 2006).

The ratio of officers in the education service with a diploma (non-graduate teachers) is 12:1 (Government of Malaysia, EDP, 2003:7-5). The promotion of education service officers occurs in three ways: selection for a promotional post, time-based promotion and selection of master/excellent teachers. However, there is not much incentive when it comes to promotion for graduate teachers as opportunities

Table 4.4. Dropout rates in public schools at primary level, 1992–2003

	1992		1995		2000		2003	
	Female	*Male*	*Female*	*Male*	*Female*	*Male*	*Female*	*Male*
Year 1	(−1.91%)	(−3.22%)	NA	NA	NA	NA	NA	NA
Year 2	−1,882	−1,933	−799	−1,685	533	26	−4,101	−5,111
	(−0.84%)	(−0.84%)	(−0.35%)	(−0.69%)	(0.22%)	(0.01%)	(−1.63%)	(−1.93%)
Year 3	−1,082	−1,061	−390	−389	−638	906	745	925
	(−0.51%)	(−0.48%)	(−0.17%)	(−0.16%)	(−0.27%)	(0.36%)	(0.30%)	(0.36%)
Year 4	−1,161	−1,275	−605	−211	−4,770	−3,113	115	−26
	(−0.55%)	(−0.57%)	(−0.26%)	(−0.09%)	(−2.04%)	(−1.26%)	(0.05%)	(0.01%)
Year 5	−2,281	−2,539	−1,146	−1,381	2,271	1,357	−795	−366
	(−1.11%)	(−1.17%)	(−0.52%)	(−0.59%)	(1.05%)	(0.59%)	(−0.33%)	(−0.14%)
Year 6	−2,798	−3,537	−2,561	−3,199	−2,123	−3,267	−1,143	−1,595
	(−1.44%)	(−1.72%)	(−1.23%)	(−1.46%)	(0.9%)	(−1.31%)	(−0.49%)	(−0.66%)
Total Loss (%)	NA	NA	NA	NA	−2.73	−3.46	−4.13	−4.21

Source: SUHAKAM, 2006:12

are limited, coupled with long waiting periods (Government of Malaysia, EDP, 2003:7–5).

The average class size for students has not significantly changed over the years. In 1990, average class size was 33.6 for secondary schools and in 2005 it was 32.5. This is high when compared to the OECD countries, where the average class size is 23.9. The teacher to student ratio has also remained almost the same: in 1990 it was 1:18.9 and in 2005 1:16.3. The OECD countries' average is 1:13.6. This continues to add stress to teachers, as they face difficulty coping with their many tasks: preparing and teaching, attending to students' academic problems, examinations, overseeing students' co-curriculum (extracurricular) activities and upgrading their skills as and when required (Arifin, 2004:5–7).

Approach to school discipline

In the last two to three years, there has been much debate on the disciplinary approaches taken by teachers, as some teachers still practice the traditional disciplinary approach which comes with public caning, slapping and/or public humiliation of students. Increasingly, there is pressure for a much more equitable and respectful approach towards misbehaving students. Some of the following incidents of public discipline being used by teachers have come under public scrutiny and criticism:

- A teacher from a primary school forced 120 girl students to lift up their skirts to see who was menstruating, as a sanitary pad was found in the toilet.[3]

- A teacher in a rural school tore the baju kurung (an item of Malay female attire) off 13 schoolgirls because she found their attire to be too short.[4]

- A teacher from a secondary school forced nearly 200 girls to soak in a fishpond as a punishment because the school's toilet bowls were repeatedly blocked by sanitary pads.[5]

While these reported cases may be few, it is important to note that the approach taken by teachers to resolve problems is through harsh punishment. Girls' sexuality is controlled through the use of punishment. Menstruation and 'indecent' dressing are viewed as 'dirty' and shameful. These are the kind of informal 'moral' teachings used to repress girls' sexuality. Such punishments are arbitrary, unwritten and are totally at the discretion of the school teachers or heads. There are competing interests, where on the one hand the government is committed to the greater participation of women, yet on the ground such values are not held by all teachers. Stereotypes are reinforced and challenge any attempts by girls to exert their rights and to foster a more equitable relationship. The government has called 'to raise the capacity for knowledge and innovation and nurture [a] "first class mentality"' (Government of Malaysia, NMP:30). Humiliating punishment will not bring about a non-violent environment, but will only serve to suppress critical minds and reinforce skewed sexuality.

The Malaysian Study

In the 1970s and 1980s, the Malaysian government had to deal with girls' under-achievement and participation at all levels and, in particular, in male-dominated subjects like science and mathematics. At that time, boys seemed to be performing well in these subjects. However, since 1990s, the trend shows a slow decline in boys' enrolment at schools after form 3.

In Malaysia, most studies refer to the underachievement of boys when referring to the overall progress of education in the country. The Malaysia report for UNESCO on Education for All (2001); the UNDP Malaysia Report on the MDGs (2005), and the SUHAKAM Report on the Human Rights Approach to the MDG Goal 2 on Achieving Universal Primary Education (2006) have described the trends affecting education and students and highlighted the statistics on the academic under-participation of boys. However, these studies and papers have not provided an in-depth analysis to understand why boys underachieve and what does this mean. The national statistic tends to relate the underachievement of boys to their low enrolment rate rather than performance.

Selection of schools

Four secondary schools in the state of Kedah (north of Peninsular Malaysia) were selected. The selected schools represent a contrast between the urban and fast-growing economy of Sungai Petani and two nearby, stagnating rural towns.

The state of Kedah is well known as the 'Rice-bowl of Malaysia' and is responsible for between 40–50 per cent of the country's rice crop. Economic progress has taken place in leaps and bounds the urban centres of Sungai Petani is now classified as one of the fast growing towns in Peninsular Malaysia. In contrast, economic progress seems to have remained the same in nearby rural towns, where residents' main sources of income are farming and fishing. In 2005, the town of Kuala Muda was hit by the tsunami (which caused vast destruction in Aceh and some South Asian countries) and this drastically changed the economic purchasing power of its residents. The average monthly income of fishermen in Kuala Muda is about US$167–US$257 per month, depending on the catch or harvest. Poverty in these areas borders Kedah's

Table 4.5. Types and location of the selected schools, 2007

Schools	Types and location of schools	Gender
School A:	National secondary school (urban)	All girls
School B:	National secondary school (rural)	Mixed girls and boys
School C:	National secondary school (rural)	Mixed girls and boys
School D:	National secondary science school (urban residential)	2/3 majority boys with 1/3 girls

rural poverty line of 655 ringgit (RM) for 2005 (Government of Malaysia, NMP, 2006:329).

Respondents

The students selected for the classroom observation and the focus group discussions were aged 16 years. It was not possible to expand the age group. One of the conditions from the Ministry of Education was that the study should not disturb those students of ages 15 and 17 years old as they were preparing for their major public examinations. Other respondents included principals, teachers, administrative staff and officials from the District Education Department.

Profiles of schools

The four schools that were involved with the study were as follows:

School A: national secondary school (urban, all-girls school)

School A is located in an urban centre and is a top school, awarded with a 4.5 star for its students' academic performance. For the past ten years, the pass rate of students averaged 98 per cent for the final form 5 examinations. School A started as a missionary school and was later transformed into a national government-run school.

At the time of the study, school A had a total of 770 students, which comprised 409 (53.1 per cent) Malays, 54 (7.0 per cent) Chinese, 297 (38.6 per cent) Indians and 10 (1.3 per cent) others (usually caucasian and foreign students). Form 4 had a total of 144 students. In school A, 12 female students, five teachers (with one male teacher), the headmistress and a female administrator were interviewed. The students were from a mix of ethnic backgrounds. The working language of the teachers and students is Bahasa Malaysia, but most of them speak English and occasionally a student will use their vernacular language.

School B: national secondary school (rural and mixed school)

School B was set up by the government as a national school. The classes offered are from forms 1–5, lower and upper form 6 ('A' Levels). At the time of the study, the pass rate of students averaged 78 per cent for the final form 5 examinations. School B had a total of 1,059 students, which comprised 1,054 (99.8 per cent) Malays. Form 4 had a total of 290 students.

In school B, the people interviewed comprised ten female and eight male students, along with five teachers (two of whom were male). The headmistress was busy and not available, even though three attempts were made to establish an interview. The working and spoken language of the teachers and students is Bahasa Malaysia.

Exploring the Bias: Gender & Stereotyping in Secondary Schools

School C: national secondary school (rural and mixed school)

School C, also set up by the government as a national school, had an average pass rate of 80 per cent per cent for the final form 5 examinations at the time of the study. This school had a total of 1,045 students, which comprised 1004 (96 per cent) Malays, 26 (2.5 per cent) Chinese and 15 (1.4 per cent) Indians. Form 4 had a total of 154 students.

In school C, the people interviewed comprised 12 male and 12 female students, six teachers (two male teachers), the headmistress and one assistant head, who was in charge of students' affairs. The working and spoken language of the teachers and students is Bahasa Malaysia.

School D: national secondary science school (urban with 2/3 boys majority)

School D is an elite boys' residential school, located in an urban centre. The school was established by Kedah royalty and has greater access to finance as compared to the other three schools. The school boasts a 100 per cent pass rate for the final form 5 examinations. Entry into the school is through a selection process and students are selected based on their having above-average results. School D had a total of 661 students at the time of the study, which comprised 94.9 per cent Malays, 0.45 per cent Chinese, 2.7 per cent Indians and 1.2 per cent others. Form 4 had a total of 135 students.

In school D, the total number of people interviewed was nine male students, six teachers (three women and men respectively) and a senior administrator. The working and spoken language of the teachers and students is Bahasa Malaysia.

Vision and mission

The schools all shared a similar vision to achieve excellence in their performance. School B added that it aimed to be among the top ten best schools in the state of Kedah, while school D gave a timeframe of 2010 to achieve its vision. The mission statements set by the four schools had common principles:

- to consolidate the management unit so as to lead, manage and administer with efficiency and effectiveness,
- to nurture their students with love, positive values and thinking,
- to ensure a conducive and safe school environment for teaching and studying,
- to consolidate the maturity and discipline of the school to be effective and sustainable,
- to give attention to the welfare of students, in terms of finances, motivation, social support and counselling.

Schools B and C put special emphasis on fostering a good relationship with the community. This reflected their position as rural schools situated near to villages.

School management

The school managements in schools A, C and D were dominated by female teachers (Table 4.6). Not all teachers were degree holders, except for school D, which claimed that all its teachers held a degree. Teachers' skills in management and teaching are upgraded through courses offered by the MOE.

On closer look, Table 4.7 shows an interesting gender representation with three schools out of the four having female heads. This female-dominated representation matches national statistics, where female teachers made up 64.4 per cent of teaching staffs in 2006.

In school D, males held the top four positions at the time of the study, while in school B, key positions were all held by males, except for the female head teacher. In school C, fewer males dominate, but they were placed in charge of students' affairs (i.e. mainly discipline), science and mathematics and technical and vocational subject areas.

In terms of the ratio of teachers to students, Table 4.8 shows an average of about 1:18 teacher: student ratio. This ratio was higher than the Malaysian national statistics of 1:16 for year 2005.

Table 4.6. Teachers' population by gender

Employment	Gender	School A	School B	School C	School D	Total
No. of posts	Female	39	36	37	41	153
sanctioned	Male	7	43	21	26	97
Total		46	79	58	67	350
No. of teachers	Female	39	36	37	41	153
in position	Male	7	43	21	26	97
	Total	46	79	58	67	260
No. of permanent	Female	39	36	35	41	151
teachers	Male	6	43	21	26	96
	Total	45	79	56	67	247
Contract/part-time	Female	0	0	2	0	2
	Male	1	0	0	0	1
	Total	1	0	2	0	3

Table 4.7. Schools' hierarchy by gender, 2007

Posts	School A		School B		School C		School D	
	F	M	F	M	F	M	F	M
Principal/head	1		1		1			1
Senior assistant	1			1	1			1
Senior assistant (students affairs)	1			1		1		1
Senior assistant (co-curriculum)				1	1			
Afternoon school supervisor	1						1	
Senior teacher (co-curriculum)	1							1
Senior teacher (language)	1			1	1		1	
Senior teacher (science and maths)		1	1			1	1	
Senior teacher (humanities)	1			1	1		1	
Senior teacher (technical and vocational)	1		1			1	1	
Counsellor	1		1	1	1	1	1	1
Total	**9**	**1**	**4**	**6**	**6**	**4**	**6**	**5**

Table 4.8. Ratio of teachers to students, 2007

	School A	School B	School C	School D
Total no. of teachers	46	79	57	67
Total no. of students	770	1,596	1,045	661
Teacher–student ratio	1:17	1:20	1:18	1:10

Enrolment and academic achievement

The study team made repeated attempts to obtain the enrolment for the year 2007. Unfortunately, two of the schools were unable to provide this as their records were not in order or were not held with the school. Table 4.9 confirms that girls'

Table 4.9. Enrolment of students in surveyed schools, 2006/07

	Total	Total male	Total female
Form 1	826	384	442
Form 2	893	395	498
Form 3	860	405	455
Form 4	723	291	432
Form 5	662	256	406
Total	3,964	1,731	2,233

enrolment is higher compared to boys. It also indicates that from form 1 to form 3, boys stayed on but their numbers reduced as they reached forms 4 and 5. In contrast, the number of girls enrolled from form 1 to 5 remained almost the same.

Although the gender composition of all four schools was not of equal, some observations can be made. Table 4.10 shows a comparison of schools A and D and indicated that girls tend to do well in language and art subjects (e.g., moral studies, history, commerce and accounting). In school D, boys showed better results in science and engineering subjects such as physics, chemistry, additional mathematics and engineering technology and drawing. Girls also do well in science subjects, but mainly in general science, mathematics and chemistry. Boys in schools B and C had much lower results. One possible reason could be that boys when placed in a more disciplined environment, as in the case of school D, could perform better.

Availability and accessibility of facilities

All four schools are well equipped with more than basic facilities, which is in line with the government's push to build competitive and information communications

Table 4.10. Total results for the form 5 examination taken in 2006

SCHOOLS	A		B		C		D	A	B		C		D	
GENDER	F	M	F	M	F	M	F	F	M	F	M	F	M	F
SUBJECTS/GRADES	1A	1A	1A	1A	1A	1A	1A	8E	8E	8E	8E	8E	8E	8E
Bahasa Malaysia	60	2	24	3	17	12	20	0	5	2	14	3	0	0
English	54	1	8		1	8	11	6	19	37	13	12	0	0
Islamic studies	13	3	22	1	3	42	44	0	5	5	11	1	0	0
Moral studies	28	0	0	1	2	0	0	1	0	0	0	0	0	0
History	40	0	10	0	0	35	21	4	16	20	14	7	0	0
Commerce	0	0	0	1	3	0	0	4	0	0	0	0	0	0
Principles of accounting	53	0	0	0	3	0	0	2	0	0	2	4	0	0
Home economics	0	0	0	0	0	0	0	1	0	0	0	6	0	0
Art	15	0	0	0	2	0	0	0	0	0	9	5	0	0
Mathematics	69	5	29	3	8	71	46	0	24	37	19	10	0	0
Additional math.	14	0	7	0	0	24	18	12	6	5	0	0	2	2
Engineering technology	0	0	0	0	0	2	0	0	0	0	0	0	0	0
Engineering drawing	0	0	0	0	0	1	0	0	0	0	0	0	0	0
Science	3	0	0	1	2	0	0	0	0	0	21	7	0	0
Physics	5	0	0	0	0	12	5	7	0	2	7	7	0	0
Chemistry	10	0	2	0	0	18	13	5	2	2	7	9	0	0
Biology	7	0	0	0	0	8	8	6	3	1	7	5	0	0
Jumlah	371	11	102	10	41	233	186	48	80	111	124	76	2	2

Note: 1A and 2A are top scores while 8E denotes failure.

technology- (ICT-) based human resources. Schools are equipped not only with the basic facilities of electricity, water and telecommunications equipment, but most teachers (especially those teaching science and mathematics subjects) are equipped with a liquid crystal display (LCD) projector and laptop for presentations.

School building

Schools B, C and D are owned and administered under the MOE. However, school A, a Catholic Missionary turned national school, does not own its land or school building, which are owned by various church groups (all Catholic) and a token monthly rental of RM200 is paid for the hire of the teachers' room. The disparity in land and facilities between school A (the all-girls school) and the other schools was apparent. School D, being a boarding school, not only has two halls and more land space, but is also more financially sound. Even schools B and C have better facilities and more land.

Facilities for management and teachers

All four schools are well equipped and have special offices for their principals with a large administration room next door. School D, being resource rich, has better facilities in terms of rooms, equipment and the school is kept clean as it has the funds to pay for its upkeep. Its computers are sited in a special room, adjacent to the staffroom, and are only used by teachers. A corner has been set aside for reading and interaction purposes. Table 4.11 shows the kind of equipment and facilities available to the teachers at the four schools.

Table 4.11. Equipment and facilities in all four schools, 2007

	Equipment and facilities for teachers	Tables and chairs	Air conditioners, lights and fans	Refrigerators, sofa sets	ICT equipment, e.g. computers, scanners and printers	Toilets – teachers	Amenities For students	Classrooms	Science laboratories	Computer laboratories	Counselling rooms	Living skills	Sick bays	Art rooms	Library	No. of library books	Indoor halls	Toilets with 7–11 cubicles – students
School A		92	14	–	3	1		22	4	2	1	2	1	2	1	14,862	–	3
School B		90	19	–	2	2		31	4	2	2	6	1	–	2	16,200	1	4
School C		80	18	2	3	2		24	5	2	1	3	1	–	1	15,000	1	8
School D		92	32	2	15	2		22	9	2	1	3	2	2	1	18,000	1	5

Facilities for students

The number of classrooms range between 22 and 31; they are well ventilated with adequate lighting, and have three to four ceiling fans per classroom. Table 4.11 indicates that a wide range of equipment and facilities is made available for the students. Some of the classes had LCD projectors and white screens, but these were only available for teachers. However, the following observations were made on the kind of gender bias that exists in the provision and utilisation of the facilities.

Living skills. Living skills refer to domestic science, carpentry and other skills that students, boys and girls, learn besides mainstream subjects. Students have to sit for examinations in living skills. However, the kind of skills offered to girls and boys depend on the schools. School **D** had better facilities than the other schools, as it had three rooms available for sewing, cooking and a well-equipped mechanical workshop. School **A** only had two classrooms for cooking and sewing, with no other options offered. The teachers themselves did not question this and accepted the classes as fixed. Two of them said: 'It has always been like that – from day one'. Others offered the excuse that there were insufficient classrooms to conduct more technical classes.

Schools B and C had rooms for sewing and cooking classes, but more rooms for electrical and plumbing lessons. In school B, it was pointed out that boys' dropout rates were high and such lessons would equip the boys before they left school. In 2006, only 16 male students from school B made it to form 6 out of 116 males who studied form 5. Those who did not pursue form 6 may have enrolled in vocational or private schools or joined the labour market. Statistics for the other three schools were not available, so comparison was not possible.

When asked if the teachers expect girls to respond better (than boys) to 'domesticated' living skills, most teachers did not think so. However, the living skills lessons offered by the schools reinforce this perception.

Libraries. The procurement of reading materials in schools B, C and D indicated bias towards boys' interest. School D had 18,000 books with most shelves on science, mathematics, computers, engineering and sports (e.g., rugby and football). School C had 16,000 books and school B had 15,000, mainly on engineering and technology. This suggests that more emphasis is being placed on boys' interests. In comparison, school A had only 14,862 books on art subjects as well as fiction in diverse languages, Bahasa Malaysia, Chinese and Tamil, and more books on philosophy and general sciences.

Art. School A had an art and a music room with a piano for the students' choir group. School D has a big art studio, which was popular among the students. School B allocated a corner, under the staircase, for art classes and school C had no specific art room. Little effort was made to encourage art classes, even though more girls were interested.

Toilets. Separate toilets were allocated for girls and boys, with private cubicles, common sinks and mirrors. Hygiene and cleanliness of the toilets was far from satisfactory, except for in school D. Waste disposal was not provided for properly, as small waste paper baskets become full quickly. Inadequate disposal facilities may be one of the reasons why sanitary pads were not disposed of properly, as in the case with the schools in Melaka and Sarawak.

Sports and games. School A offered women-oriented games in school, such as netball, basketball, hockey and volleyball, but other games were played outside the school – as will be discussed later. Schools B, C and D encouraged male-dominated games, such as, football, hockey, cricket, softball and *sepak takraw* (a game where you kick a shuttle using one's ankle). Girls in these schools were only offered netball, hockey and volleyball. Girls and boys in schools B, C and D do not play games together. The segregation of girls and boys was an unwritten policy carried out by the schools.

Science and ICT facilities. Compared to its living skills facilities, school D placed greater emphasis on science and technology. It had nine laboratories – three general science laboratories for forms 1 to 3 and two laboratories for physics, chemistry and biology for form 4 and 5 students. School A had two laboratories, one for lower secondary students (13 to 15 years old) and a separate laboratory for physics, chemistry and biology that was utilised by upper secondary students (16 and 17 years old). Schools B and C placed less emphasis on science – they only had one general science laboratory each.

Limitations of the study

The study had some limitations. As all the interviews and focus group discussions were conducted in Bahasa Malaysia, it was difficult to observe any grammatical gender bias – the language itself makes no such distinction, as compared to the English language. For example, the word 'dia' is a generic word used to refer to both male and female and there is no 'he' or 'she' in Bahasa Malaysia. Bias can only appear when names of people, denoting their gender, or pictures are used to illustrate a situation or action.

The study only covered four schools and a small geographical area. It was not able to compare its findings with other factors that affect performance and participation, such as, ethnicity, religion and income levels. Schools such as those with *orang asli* majority and vernacular schools were not covered, and these perhaps may have given a different perspective to the analysis. The study was limited to only using gender relations as a factor to analyse girls' and boys' performance and participation.

Findings of the study

Education system processes and practices

District Education Department (DED) hierarchy

The Sungai Petani District Education Department (DED) had 12 women and 29 men holding positions in the hierarchy at the time of the study, out of which seven women were in the Administrative and Finance Department. The head District Education Officer (DEO) was a woman and she had two female and seven male assistant DEOs. Unfortunately, the study team was unable to speak to the DEO head as she was busy. An interview was conducted with senior personnel at the Education Department at Sungai Petani.

The senior DEO confirmed that the infrastructure of all schools in Kedah was being upgraded and teaching aids were supplied to enhance teaching. He also confirmed that different training workshops were held and offered to those teachers who were involved in that particular subject, but there were none on the concept of gender.

As for the subjects such as sewing and cooking, the DED had left it to the discretion of the schools to select their own curriculum activities. There were no guidelines on how schools select such activities for females and males. He stressed that there was no gender discrimination when it came to employment of school heads and teachers. Two-thirds of the teachers were females and one-third males. He did not think that gender bias happened in the allocation of teachers' school tasks as the criteria were based on competence and experience. This point of view was confirmed by the principals and teachers from the schools, as discrimination in promotion was based on perceived factors, such as favouritism.

Understanding gender

The senior DEO had heard of the word 'gender' when attending seminars organised by the Ministry of Women, Family and Community Development and read it in the papers. However, he did not really understand the meaning of the word. Upon clarification, he agreed that girls and boys do behave differently. Girls do better in science, mathematics and art subjects, as they are more conscientious and dedicated to their goals, while boys tend not to be such high achievers. Having said that, he pointed out that statistics also indicate that boys do better when they are in standard 6 and form 3, but their results decline when they reach form 5. He felt that the problem was the attitudes of the boys, as those from the rural areas are more carefree and do not show much interest in their studies, while boys in urban areas perform better.

Tackling violence against women

In cases of violence, a system has been set up by the DED. The school has to make the initial report – written or by phone and followed by written (in case of

Exploring the Bias: Gender & Stereotyping in Secondary Schools

emergency) – and only then does the DED step in. A police report will then be made if the case warrants police investigation. For example, there was a case where a girl was pregnant; the DED in consultation with the school management relocated the girl to another school, the reason being that the girl did not want to continue her studies in the same school, and there was the concern about the stigma that she may suffer if she remained. Unfortunately, the usual response is still to transfer girls in such cases to another school without dealing with the psychological impact she has face.

Sex education

When the sex education curriculum was mentioned, the senior DEO was supportive of its introduction. He felt that sex education had to go beyond physical or biological understanding. It was important to inculcate values of non-violence and respect to both girls and boys.

Discipline

Disciplinary actions are taken at the school level. State / district education departments are informed of cases and they give their advice on the course of action, depending on the severity of the case.

School management

Girls and boys face different social issues and management handle them differently. These issues are outlined below.

Bullying and violence against women

The school management deals with issues such as bullying and forming gangs among the girls. There is a system to resolve these issues, which are usually handled by the principal and the senior assistant. Bullying does occur in the girls' school: the principal of school A discussed how she usually talks to each member of the gang individually, before bringing them together for a group discussion. She felt this method was able to bring a more amicable resolution to the problem.

Three of the schools reported cases of violence against women. They were as follows:

- In 2006, a girl became pregnant by her boyfriend. She stopped coming to school because her parents no longer allowed her to go.

- In 2003/4, there was a case of incest and this was brought up to the DED level. An investigation was conducted and eventually the perpetrator was caught.

- Sexual harassment by 'flashers' does occur outside the school gates. However, when incidents have been reported to the State Education Department and police have patrolled the area, no further incidents have been reported.

In school A, discussions on violence against women tend to happen after the event. In other schools, there were no such discussions. School D emphasised that violence against women does not occurred in the school and this was confirmed by the teachers.

One of the girls from school A expressed that she expected the school to be able to provide protection for students. Information on violence and crime was only disseminated to the students whenever 'big' incidents occurred, but according to her by that time 'it's too late'.

Discipline

School A emphasised that it followed an unwritten school motto: to forgive (wrong doers), perhaps due to its strong missionary influence. However, the principal explained that this does not mean there is no penalty for wrong doers or that the problem is not dealt with. A student who has misbehaved does get punished or suspended for a temporary period. When she returns to school, conditions are set for the student to improve herself: she has to work hard to get back her merit points within the year and her work and behaviour is monitored by her class teacher. Support is given to her to regain her confidence and to help her work towards increasing her merit points. If she improves, she will be given additional merit points so that she is encouraged to be better. The manner in which the school handles students' issues appears to be encouraging as opposed to the traditional disciplinary punishment, such as public caning and disgrace.

In schools B and C, the teachers did not want to comment on their disciplinary measures. In the classroom observation, it was noticed that teachers in the mixed and all-boys school seemed to be more lenient in their discipline with boys. For example:

- Boys were observed to wander in and out of the lessons.

- Boys were chatting among themselves while lessons were in progress.

- In a language class, eight boys were late and another two entered ten minutes later.

On none of these occasions were the students reprimanded or asked for an explanation. The difference in the disciplinary actions taken against boys may reflect an acceptance by the teachers that boys are irresponsible and there is nothing they can do about their behaviour. This may further reinforce the boys' attitude that there is no penalty, or simply that they receive a lighter reprimand (than girls would) for their bad behaviour. In contrast, no such expectation is directed to the girls, as they are expected to be obedient and responsible.

School D, on the other hand, has strict disciplinary rules which students are aware of. They include no television, no going out of the school premise unless within specific times, not being allowed to wear fashionable trousers and students not being permitted to visit the toilet for too long. Students' time was managed with homework sessions, group study sessions and games.

School textbooks

The study reviewed the form 4 textbooks to analyse if there was any gender bias in the contents. The findings are outlined below.

History. There was no mention of women heroes and the contribution that women have made, be it internationally or nationally. Pictures used as illustrations depict mainly men who were in power, in leadership and as inventors, e.g., Julius Caesar, Socrates, Plato, Aristotle, King Alaudin Riayat Syah (Melaka ruler) and so forth.

Biology. There was little bias detected except when it came to inventors. All male inventors were highlighted in the introduction to photosynthesis, such as Joseph Priestley and Jean Baptiste van Helmont.

Bahasa Malaysia. Gender bias was located in the pictures, e.g., *rukun tetangga* (residents' association), which depicted all males, and male runners in sports with girls cheering on.

English. On many occasions, the pictures in the textbooks portrayed men in leadership positions, e.g., when introducing the concept of greetings, a male was portrayed as the speaker while the majority of the audience were women.

The findings indicate strong gender bias in the portrayal of men's and women's roles and a lack of recognition for women's contributions in Malaysia. Women are under-represented and when they did contribute, they are not mentioned. Biased gender language is used by teachers to describe the roles of women, which further reinforces the idea that women are subordinate to men.

Principals and teachers

Changing attitudes is a long process and one of the quickest and most efficient channels is through education. Gender stereotyping and discriminatory attitudes are learned and can be changed. The education system can play a role to bring about a more gender-sensitised attitude among young Malaysians. Teachers can play this role and, therefore, what and how teachers think and what they value becomes crucial in promoting gender equality and non-discrimination. Their perceptions and the roles they play in and outside the school environment will help shape the behaviour and thinking of students. Below summarises the expectations and perceptions of the school personnel who were interviewed.

Expectations

Students' performance

Students' performance in schools A and D were higher than in schools B and C. Teachers from these two schools put in extra effort to maintain their high academic records. In school A, teachers experiment with various teaching methods to upgrade the learning curve of students. School D seems confident that its students will maintain its all-time record of 100 per cent pass rate in the form 5 examination. As put forward by the senior administrator, 'it's a matter of how many A's the students score'. Evidently, teachers place high expectations on the students. Most of the teachers expressed that the trend was for boys to do well in mathematics, additional mathematics, physics and engineering subjects while girls were better in languages and art subjects, but were catching up with the boys in science subjects. This opinion was also verified by schools B and C.

Students' participation

Boys' participation in other non-academic subjects and parts of the school curriculum left much to be desired. A male teacher from school C lamented:

> 'We have tried every way to involve the boys ... when it came to volunteering, they pretend to look away. In class, we try to think of ways to involve them, but most of them don't seem interested. Ah! when it's sports, they become alive! ... but unfortunately they are only interested [in] play[ing] the games but not [in] do[ing] the hard work of organising.'

Another female teacher from School B said:

> 'I am happy to work with the girls ... you get better feedback.'

Boys did not seem to want to volunteer to do any work, e.g., in preparation for sports day, and seemed to have no interests in school clubs. They tended to be only interested in male-dominated games, such as football, rugby and *sepak takraw*.

Outside school activities seemed to attract boys more. A number of the boys were involved with '*mat rempit*' (motorbike racing), black metal, hanging out at cybercafés and shopping malls. A male teacher from School B said:

> 'One day, we tracked these students (those who played truant) and found most of them at an urban shopping mall. I am not joking ... they prefer to lepak (loiter) there and not go to school.'

Central Square in Sungai Petani was identified as the mall most frequented by the young. Raids have been carried out, but they have had no effect on those who regularly played truant. Such activities were less observed among female students.

The reasons for boys truanting tend to differ. Truants in the urban schools included students from high-income households, or students who were neglected by their parents. Those from rural areas were boys with parents who fish or farm for their living and from lower-income brackets. These parents need the boys to help out in their work, which results in them missing school. According to a teacher:

> '... there is a pattern – they tend to miss school during Sundays and Thursdays. When we look for the students, we are told by their parents that they are at sea.'

In certain states, like Kedah, Sundays and Thursdays are work and school days as they follow the Muslim calendar. Efforts were made by the teachers, especially in schools B and C, to organise motivation camps for the boys, conduct talks on local radio stations on students' education and also to offer parenting classes for the community. However, the parents' turn out was very poor.

In contrast, boy students from School D had little chance to play truant as they are in a residential school with very strict rules and regulations. Nonetheless, the boys were also found to be unenthusiastic in their attitudes towards helping out and volunteering their assistance. A teacher said:

> 'Even though they do get good results, some boys tend not to want to help out in organising school activities and they leave it to the girls.'

Different expectations are placed on boys, as their parents, and to a large extent society, expect them to be the breadwinners, while girls' roles are supplementary and domestic in nature. From an early age, boys begin to learn that they are the head of family and the breadwinner – and because of such expectations, in many ways society excuses boys when they behave irresponsibly.

Perceptions

Understanding gender

None of the teachers in the schools understood the meaning of 'gender'. Two male teachers said that they had read about gender in the media when it was mentioned by the MWFCD. Two female teachers had read the word 'gender' when it was used in government forms. Besides that, they did not understand what gender meant. Only the principal of school A and another teacher from school D had heard and understood gender as being socially constructed by society and as such is something that can be changed.

The study team carried out an exercise with the teachers and asked them to state the positive and negative characteristics of a woman and a man. Table 4.12 summarises their responses. Most of them presented stereotypical perceptions of both females and males. When the concept was further discussed with them, some female teachers (six) from school A felt that even when women do not play the traditional roles, opportunities were limited and discrimination existed. A female teacher said:

'More women are going out to work. However, they still need to prove that they are able to excel well in their work. There are more opportunities open for men.'

Table 4.12. Gender roles as perceived by teachers in the four schools

Female		Male	
Positive	Negative	Positive	Negative
Have mothering skills/ homemakers	Men have more employment choices than women	Strong	Lazy
Serious about their work		Can share housework	
Responsible for their children		Clever	
Able to handle problems well		Leaders	
Patient		Hardworking	
Suitable as educators for their children		Take care of the family and able to work at the same time	
Perform better than the males			
Biological differences			
Shy			
Weaker			
Emotional			
Better in time management			

Reflecting on their personal lives, most of the teachers (six) from school A said they shared out the housework among their children – regardless of gender – and encouraged and supported their children in their studies and the choices that they make. When asked further, some of them admitted that they do differentiate the kind of work that they ask boys to do, especially for work that required more energy. They were stricter with their female children's mobility, and are reluctant to allow them to go out too late at night. A male teacher responded that he felt that men as well as women are educators, and such responsibility should be shared as parents are role models for their children. He felt that as a male he felt more responsible towards the family, especially for their safety.

Expression of stereotypical ideas

During the focus group discussions, it was observed that there was some gender-biased language being used. Expressions such as women 'are good at being mothers', that they have 'soft' skills, are 'mature and able to look after the house well', they are 'more hardworking, more honest than boys', 'women are more patient', they are suitable 'as educators' and 'homemakers' were used to describe a woman and her role. Teachers themselves classified how girls and boys should behave and what their social roles were. They also put boundaries on what girls and boys can and cannot do. A male teacher said:

> 'Girls need to be protected and be cautious when mixing with boys. I will make sure my girls (referring to his children) do not go out of the house.'

Another teacher said:

'*Boys are boys and girls are girls.* Itu biasa *(it's normal).*'

In the discussions, it was also observed that female teachers tend not to speak up when their male colleagues dominate the discussion. They whisper among themselves to exchange opinions. The exception was school A, where the female teachers were more outspoken and held strong opinions. However, in this case there was only one male teacher present.

Yet as teachers utter these biased ideas and unconsciously display gender stereotypes in their attitudes and behaviours, they do realise that times have changed and that girls are not only performing well academically, but are able to build successful careers if they want to.

Gender-sensitive training

No gender training programmes were offered to the teachers, nor were gender concepts incorporated into any teacher training courses.

Sex education

The teachers were informed by the study team that the MWFCD had intentions to introduce sex education and a manual was being drafted. All respondents, both principals and teachers, were unaware of this document, except for one teacher who had read about it in a newspaper. Nor was there any consultation of school personnel, even though consultations were carried out with non-governmental organisations.

On a more positive note, all the teachers agreed that it was necessary to introduce sex education at the school level, as it was not covered in the curriculum. Six of the teachers stressed that it was important that social relationships between boys and girls be introduced. One male teacher said:

'*...it's not enough to talk about it in biology classes; it does not touch on values and morals.*'

Another teacher said:

'*We can't avoid this subject when the students are becoming more aware.*'

At the time of writing, the issue of introducing sex education or education on sexuality was still in the early stages at the Women's Ministry.

Students

Aspirations and motivation

At all the focus group discussions with female students, they showed high motivation to excel and to further their studies. In school A, 90 per cent of the females wanted to study for a degree, master's and some of them aspired to obtain PhDs. Some of the girls (three) expressed that they would prefer to go into employment after form 5. Male students did not exhibit such a high academic drive, except for those in school D. Some of the boys (18) said they would prefer to start work after completing their secondary education; some (five) were contented with having a diploma, while the others wanted to continue up to form 6. Only boys (six) from school D were motivated to go on to obtain a PhD (see Table 4.13).

Expectations

There was a strong expectation from the student respondents that they would have support and guidance from their parents, especially in helping them plan their studies. Most of the girls showed confidence in their parents' support, e.g., 'they are happy when we get good results'. For the boys in schools B and C, their parents

Table 4.13. Aspirations of girls and boys, 2007

School/Gender	Aspirations	Female	Male	Total
School A	Architect	3		
Art designer		1		
Engineer		2		
Hotel manager		1		
Lawyer		1		
Medical doctor		3		
University lecturer		1	12	
School B	Medical doctor	3		
Manager		2		
Pilot		1		
Soldier			4	
Teacher		5	3	18
School C	Accountant	1		
Architect			1	
Firefighter			2	
Lawyer		2	1	
Medical doctor		6	1	
Police			2	
Soldier			4	
Teacher		3	1	24
School D	Business person	2	4	
Medical doctor		4	6	
Surgeon			4	
Teacher		6	1	27
Total		46	35	81

expected them to help in the padi (rice) fields, to be hard working, help in the shop and vegetable farms, but placed less emphasis on studies. The male students from school D did not have to manage their schoolwork along with helping their families, as they were in a boarding school. They expressed the view that there were high expectations from teachers and parents for them to excel in and further their studies.

Most of the students said that they would like to have better communications with their parents. About 85 per cent of the girls said that they preferred to talk to their mothers rather than their fathers, as the latter did not seem to have time or showed lack of understanding. Some of their responses included:

'there's nothing to talk about....'

'[I'm] scared to talk to him.'

Among the girls, there was high expectation for them to do housework after or before completion of school homework. About 20 of the girls said they had to do a lot of housework. They all said it almost in unison:

'... sweeping, looking after [our] younger brothers and sisters, washing the plates left in the sink by [our] brothers – we hate that!'

The girls were resentful that there was so much favouritism of their brothers. They all seemed to refer to males as 'lelaki' (the boys) even though they were their brothers.

'... the boys... they seem to get everything they want.'

'... the boys get more than me.'

Only two girls who had no male sibling said that they were not discriminated against. Five girls were of the opinion that if they do get married, they will teach their sons to be more responsible and make them do housework. However, most of the girls accepted the 'state of affairs' as given, as these domestic roles were 'girls' work'. Even though they were unhappy, they did not raise them with their parents. It appears that they have accepted that such chores and relationships cannot be changed. It was observed that these girls were, therefore, brought up to accept a stereotypical domestic role, even if they perform well in their studies.

Most of the boys replied that they do not do much housework. Some of the boys giggled and said:

'... itu kerja wanita (it's girls' work).'

Others said:

'... my mother does all the work.'

Only two boys in school B said that they did help to wash plates, clean shoes and ironed their own clothes. In school D, some of the boys said that they do housework, but sheepishly admitted that they only do it occasionally. In general, the boys leave housework and serving to their sisters and mothers.

Perceptions

Understanding of gender

In common with the teachers, the students did not understand the meaning of the word 'gender', nor did they indicate that they had heard of it from their teachers or the courses they attend. When asked to name the positive and negative characteristics of a woman and man, they listed the usual stereotyped roles that they ascribe to males and females (see Table 4.14).

Table 4.14. Gender roles as perceived by students in the four schools

Female		Male	
Positive	*Negative*	*Positive*	*Negative*
Women do win in the 'Fear Factor' (a cable TV series)	Have to take care of their reputation	Strong	Easily influenced by 'bad factors' (drugs, smoking)
Can do the same work as males	Menstrual flow becomes cumbersome during camping trips	Energetic in sports	Immature
More mature and able to be rational	Forced to do housework	Clever	Don't seem to be able to think about their actions
They are able to think through things before acting	Always bullied by boys as they give girl work to do	Able to socialise freely and make friends easily	Not responsible
Mentally stronger	Emotional	Open to positive aspects	Don't need to do housework
More alert	Dependant	Are leaders	Have too many distractions
Not easily influenced by 'bad factors' (referring to drugs and smoking)	Discriminated against in academic choices	Creative	No direction in their lives
Possess 'soft' skills		Critical	
Able to look after the house		Innovative	
Good homemakers and able to take care of the family		Have high aspirations	
More hardworking		Have more opportunities	
More honest			
Don't need to do heavy work			
Careful			
Receive a lot of praise			
Ambitious			
Need to dress up			

Girls from schools A and B felt that women do have limited choices in terms of occupations. Some jobs are already slated for boys while girls are excluded –as, for example, in the political arena and in top corporate positions. Opportunities for boys were viewed with resentment. For example, if a boy obtains average marks, why is it that he can get into IPTA (Public Institute for Higher Learning) while a girl with a similar grade cannot? They expressed that women were discriminated against in some jobs because corporate companies tend to use the excuse that when women get pregnant they have to leave their jobs or they have to give women maternity leave. So, preference is given to men as they do not have such responsibilities.

The findings indicate that while girls are able to realise their potential, especially in academic achievement, they feel discriminated against as they watch boys sailing through applications that girls have to work twice as hard for in order to be consider as candidates. Discrimination was also felt at home when household chores were burdens placed only on girls and yet parents expect them to complete their school-work in time. While boys had no such burden, they can do what they want and had the freedom of movement.

Low participation of boys

Different responses on boys' underachievement were recorded. A majority of the girls felt that boys were more relaxed with schoolwork, were lazy, that they liked to go out riding their bikes, wasted money on shopping, lacked the drive to study and that their parents did not seem to be able to control them. Few of the boys disagreed with the girls' point of view. However, no boy expressed the need to change.

Students in decision-making processes

School prefects are appointed by the principle and senior teachers. Any complaints are made directly to the class teacher or students' affairs officer, but not through the prefects.

In schools B, C and D, all the students accepted that the two key positions – head prefect and class monitor – should be occupied by a male and not a female. No one appeared to want to question this process. There were female prefects, but their roles were viewed as being supportive. In terms of gender balance, all three schools had almost equal numbers of girls and boys acting as prefects.

Merit as the basis for selection was not used as a yardstick, as appointment was based on sex – as long as you are a male you are a leader. Girls, despite of their academic performance, were placed subordinate to males. Giving such privileges to boys had unconsciously created discrimination between the girls and boys.

Sex education

Some girls expressed that they would welcome sex education, even though they did not understand what it meant. Upon further explanation from the study team, most of them felt that the sex education offered by sanitary towels companies was insufficient. When sex was taught in biology classes, it was on reproductive issues only and not on relationships. None of the girls said that they shared issues regarding boyfriends with their teachers. They prefer to share their problems with their friends. The boys also shared this view.

Expressions of stereotypical ideas

Gender bias was often reflected in the language used when the students described the roles of women: 'good as mothers', 'having soft skills', 'mature', 'able to look after the house well', 'more hardworking', 'more honest than boys', and 'girls are weak' (see Table 4.14).

Gender-biased behaviour was observed among the group. In a mixed group discussion, the girls tended to be quieter and needed a lot of encouragement before they gave their opinions. It was difficult to get them to participate in the discussion. The girls tended to listen when the boys spoke and they seldom contradicted the boys' opinions. When they were separated, it was easier to get responses from the girls.

In school D, gender-biased ideas were expressed as one of the boys said:

'I expect to find a good wife and [to] be able to look after my parents.'

This aspiration was echoed by his friends. Boys from the school were more vocal (than boys for the other schools), more directed in their goals and confident. In school A, three of the girls showed confidence and they were unwilling to accept existing stereotyped roles as prescribed by society. One of them cried out:

'... why should I change ... I like being a girl.'

But what does 'being a girl' mean? The respondent seemed confident that she would be able to assert herself and make her own choices.

Classroom and outside classroom processes

Classroom engagement

During the Malaysian study, a total of 21 classes were observed and 626 students, both males and females, were involved in the classroom observations. Table 4.15 shows the breakdown of the students in the various classes.

In school A, there was good rapport between the teachers and the students. For example, when a student does not understand a particular issue, the teacher takes time to explain. Efforts were taken to help the weaker students. In school A, the teachers who were observed expected students to develop their own notes in the

Table 4.15. Classes observed and number of female and male students, form 4

	Classes	Teachers and subjects	Girls	Boys
School A	Form 4 (1)	Male teacher, chemistry	33	
	Form 4 (2)	Female teacher, history	21	
	Form 4 (3)	Female teacher, physical education	25	
	Form 4 (1)	Female teacher, English	24	
	Form 4 (2)	Female teacher, moral education	37	
	Form 4 (1)	Female teacher, Islamic studies	21	
School B	Form 4 (1)	Female teacher, mathematics	16	17
	Form 4 (2)	Male teacher, Islamic studies	13	5
	Form 4 (3)	Male teacher, Malay literature	10	18
	Form 4 (1)	Male teacher, English	24	12
School C	Form 4 (1)	Male teacher, physical education	8	28
	Form 4 (2)	Male teacher, additional mathematics	22	4
	Form 4 (3)	Male teacher, English	21	4
	Form 4 (4)	Female teacher, Islamic studies	15	19
	Form 4 (5)	Male teacher, history	8	12
School D	Form 4 (1)	Male teacher, chemistry	10	33
	Form 4 (2)	Female teacher, history	6	21
	Form 4 (3)	Female teacher, physical education	6	25
	Form 4 (4)	Female teacher, English	10	24
	Form 4 (5)	Female teacher, moral education	1	37
	Form 4 (6)	Female teacher, Islamic studies	15	21
		TOTAL	346	280

class, and guided them with questions related to the subject. This worked well, as observed in the history class where a roster for teams of four to five students was set up. Each team was expected to present (on large pieces of white paper) their summary notes on the relevant subject. Every student had a turn to do a presentation. According to the history teacher, this had helped them to learn with understanding. Questions were asked and the student or her team were expected to answer.

Another instance of this good rapport was when the students wanted to go home early, they were able to approach and discuss the matter with their English teacher. While this could be due to school A being an all-girls school, which resulted in less inhibition, the friendly environment in the school played an important part in breaking down barriers as well.

In schools B, C and D, the relationship between the teachers and students did not appear to be close and there was a stricter teacher–student relationship. The teaching method used was a top-down approach, whereby the teacher teaches and the student responds. Seating arrangements separated the girls from the boys, and those who were weaker in ability were placed in the front seats. Again, such segregation was an unwritten rule set by the schools. Boys usually occupy either the side or the back rows, while girls are in the front rows or side rows. Generally, there was less response and participation by boys, but in some instances boys tended to be more active learners. When this happened, girls tended to retreat, keep quiet or talk among themselves.

In school B, in the Malay literature class when the boys were vocal and responsive to questions posed by the teacher, girls tended to giggle and speak softly among themselves in response to the questions. In school C, girls were more diffident. During the history class, the girls tended not to ask questions during lesson, but preferred to do so after class. When solving a mathematic problem, the girls discussed in small groups among themselves, while the boys solved it individually. In contrast, in an additional mathematics class, the teacher had to repeatedly engage the boys to answer her questions while the girls were more responsive. In school D, the boys were vocal, asked a lot of questions and responding politely to the teachers. The girls were quieter and always allowed the boys to speak first. The teachers did not seem to make much effort to encourage girls to speak in such instances.

Gendered practice in language

Gender bias was observed in the way language was used to maintain and reinforce norms about how girls or boys, men or women should act and speak.

Gender stereotypes used in sentences by a teacher:

Example 1

- 'He inherited money from his family.'
- 'Assuntha cooked and looked after Wilson.'

Male (but no female) inventors used in examples:

Example 2

- 'John Loud introduced the first ballpoint.'
- 'Hungarian brothers improved on the pen introduced by Loud.'
- 'Alexander Graham Bell invented the telephone.'

Gender stereotypes used in sentences by students:

Example 3

Two girls were selected by the English teacher to construct active and passive sentences. The girls wrote the following sentences, which reflect gender stereotyping:

- 'Ahmad kicks a ball. The ball was kicked by Ahmad.'

- 'Salmah looks after her younger sisters and brothers. The younger sisters and brothers were looked after by Salmah.'

Gender-biased ideas

In school C, during a biology class on balanced diets for teenagers, a special mention was made to the girls about the dietary needs of pregnant women. No reference was made about boys' nutritional needs. The teacher assumed that the girls would all become pregnant eventually.

The above examples show that both teachers and students hold stereotyped ideas on the roles of boys and girls.

Outside classroom engagement

In school A, while the sports facilities offered to the girls were limited, an interest in sport was still encouraged by the teachers. In a hockey lesson, the teacher was joking with the girls and encouraging them to try, even though some of them kept missing the ball. The teacher showed patience and the students were able to reciprocate. There were also sufficient hockey sticks for everyone to have a go at the game. School A's head confirmed that the students were active in games and sports and that they had won many awards for the school, e.g., in hockey and tennis. They had also won three times in a *pantun* (poem) competition.

As mentioned earlier, schools B, C and D emphasised boys' sports more (than girls'). There was a tendency for the teachers in these schools to be more interactive, patient and engaging with male students when it came to games and sports activities.

Conclusions

Arguably from the above findings, schools and teachers work on an already-tested model for good teaching and resource management. From the study, teachers do know their purpose and subject matter well, and in some cases demonstrated excellent interpersonal skills, especially in mediating the learning processes and students' behaviour. The learning environment was also well equipped in all four schools to aid the learning and teaching process of both students and teachers. There were no issues concerning lack of basic facilities, therefore.

However, one cannot assume that having efficient and well-organised teaching methods, a well-equipped environment and trained teachers will automatically help to promote gender equality. The study found evidence of gender bias and this surfaced at almost all levels: in the classroom, school textbooks, interaction between students, in the attitudes and thinking of principals, teachers and state education personnel, in the use and construction of language and in the gendered behaviour of students and teachers. Below are some summarised points and conclusions drawn from the study in Malaysia.

The feminised nature of teaching profession

In all four schools, women dominate the teaching profession. This contrasts with the 1960s and 1970s when teachers were mainly men. In school D, male teachers were placed in the school's top four positions and in school B, men were put in charge of important areas, such as students' affairs, science, mathematics and technical and vocational subjects, despite both schools registering more female teachers.

Provision and access to facilities

In schools B, C and D, there was little gender-sensitivity in the provision of facilities such as sports and games and library materials, as most of these catered for boys' interests. Girls' interests were not seen to be important and their opinions were not sought on whether or not they wanted other options.

Classroom engagement

Both boys and girls tend to respond well to a learning environment that encourages their interests and commitment and has a strong learning culture. However, boys tend to perform well in a more guided system that emphasises good behaviour, inspires high standards of achievement and gives rewards when certain goals/standards are met (as in school D). Girls, on the other hand, tend to prefer an environment that provides them with encouragement and a close bond with teachers (as in school A). For example, where weaker students are provided with more encouragment.

Boys tend to do better in pure science, additional mathematics and technical subjects, while girls are better in language and art subjects. Both do well in general science and mathematics.

Teachers' gender perceptions

Stereotyped ideas are held by teachers, females and males alike, and some of these ideas are transferred to students in their teaching. Gendered practice can be observed in the language used, which tends to maintain and reinforce norms about how girls and boys, men and women should act and speak. This appeared in the way sentences were constructed, examples used to illustrate concepts, and in making gender assumptions about girls' and boys' sexuality.

Teachers accept the stereotypical roles of girls and boys. Examples include boys being made head prefects, being considered less responsive and less responsible, and the view that they cannot be controlled, falling back on the myth that 'boys are boys'. As for girls, they are considered intrinsically well behaved, responsible and that they will do well in exams. Such acceptance gives the impression that changing gender roles is not possible.

At the same time, the interests of girls were not always taken into consideration by teachers – as in schools B, C and D, where sports and games were geared more towards boys' needs. Issues of violence against women/girls were only addressed when such incidents occurred. There did not seem to be any efforts made to equip girls and boys to deal with violence. The long-awaited introduction of sex education does not seem to be a priority for schools.

Students' aspirations

Boys from rural schools have lower aspirations as compared to those from urban centres. At an early age, boys from low-income families are expected to work and bring an income to the family. Their position as leaders is reinforced in the family structure, which may give boys the impression that they have special privileges and are superior to girls.

Most girls are consistent in their aspirations to do well acadmically, even though they may be average students. Despite the high performance and participation of girls, they are still taught to accept stereotyped 'women's' roles, even though they are unhappy with those roles, and such teaching further discriminates against girls and depicts them as being supportive and subordinate to males. Girls tend to feel that they are less important than boys.

It is impressive that the four schools studied were all provided with proper and adequate facilities and equipment, as these help to create a good learning environment for students, allow them to explore and seek information. By taking on a gender-neutral approach to Education For All, the government has assumed that the system will cater to the needs and concerns of both girls and boys and, therefore, the question of discrimination will not arise. However, the study has shown that there are other factors at play: these limit certain students in their development, while at the same time providing special privileges to others and creating a false assumption that such privileges are their right.

The disparity and differences in girls and boys development is closely related to highly stereotyped thinking, values and unwritten policies that are carried out or held by district heads, school heads, teachers, parents and also by the students themselves. These have restricted girls to demure, passive and non-critical roles. A hidden and subliminal form of consciousness that teaches girls and boys to accept inequalities and discrimination as being unchangeable is contributed to by factors such as: being insensitive to the interests of girls in sports and elective subjects; girls and female teachers not speaking or feeling constrained to speak their opinions in front of males; segregation of girls and boys in classes and sports; gender-biased language used in lessons and in school textbooks; and accepting that girls have to do housework and serve their brothers. On the other hand, catering to boys' interests in sport, accepting that boys will not volunteer for social tasks, ensuring that only boys hold key decision-making positions like prefects and class monitors, have made boys to assume and expect themselves to lead and girls to follow. The special privileges given to boys have created discrimination, as they have resulted in the trend shown by Malaysia's national statistics, whereby women's participation in the labour force has remained the same for more than two decades. The assumption is that women's work is supplementary and when 'push come to shove', they are meant to stay at home to care and to serve, despite of their high academic achievements.

There are numerous cross-cutting challenges, including ethnicity, poverty and accessibility to schools, which are not discussed in this chapter. The task of delivering and strengthening the values of gender equality is only true if there is a realisation that equality and justice are the norms and not the exceptions.

Suggestions for the Ministry of Education

Below are some suggestions for Malaysia's Ministry of Education to advance gender equality:

- Conduct a nationwide study to ascertain the key factors influencing the participation and performance of both girls and boys, so that appropriate measures can be taken.

- Re-educate and gender sensitise teachers to recognise women's contributions to society so that their approach to students is more inclusive, responsive, humanistic and so that they are able to teach girls and boys to become comfortable as equal partners.

- Compile and provide up-to-date sex disaggregated data on students' performance and mobility, dropout rates and truancy, so that a holistic analysis can be achieved.

- Enforce and implement sex education in all schools, starting from primary to tertiary levels, so as to inculcate values of respect, equality and non-violence.

- Involve parents and the community by having sessions with parents so that they understand the long-term value of education for their children, as opposed to placing importance on their immediate economic contribution.

Notes

1. Ministry of Women, Family and Community Development (MWFCD), Malaysia Report to the United Nations Committee on the Elimination against Women (First and Second Report) (2004), para: 89 and 90. Malaysia.

2. The Malaysian Smart Schools, set up in July 1977, were meant to promote best practices in technology-enabled teaching, learning and school management. Website: www.moe.gov.my [accessed 7 May 2009]

3. New Straits Times (2007) Shocking Punishment: Cold, dirty penalty over sanitary pad. 22 July 2007. Malaysia.

4. The Star Online (2007) Teacher tears 'too short' baju kurung uniforms. 19 August 2007. Malaysia. Available: http://thestar.com.my/news/story.asp?file=/2007/8/19/nation/18636963andsec=nation.

5. The Star Online (2007) 200 schoolgirls to soak in a fishpond, 23 July 2007. Malaysia.

CHAPTER 5

Education, Gender and Fa'aSamoa: 'the Samoan Way of Doing Things'

Gatoloai Ms Tilianamua Afamasaga
Oloamanu Centre for Professional Development and Continuing Education,
National University of Samoa

Setting the Scene: Samoa Country Profile

The Independent State of Samoa is in the Pacific Ocean, northeast of Australia and New Zealand, between latitudes 13 degrees and 15 degrees south and longitudes 168 degrees and 173 degrees west. Its population of 179,186, with 51.9 per cent males, represents a 1.4 per cent natural increase between the censuses of 2001 and 2006. Like many developing countries, Samoa has a very young population: according to the 2001 Census, 50.6 per cent of the total population were 19 years old and below, while 35.9 per cent were of school ages 5–19 years.

The economy of Samoa relies on a narrow resource base that is limited to agriculture, tourism, small-scale manufacturing and fisheries. GDP per capita doubled over the ten years 1995–2005 to US$2,000 with sectoral competition standing at 14, 23 and 63 for agriculture, industry and services (Samoa National Human Development Report, 2006). Samoa's macro-economic performance is extremely vulnerable to external factors such as commodity prices, crop diseases, the demands of tourism and natural disasters, especially cyclones. The 2001 Census showed that foreign aid, government overseas borrowings and foreign remittances by Samoans overseas were the main resources that fuelled the local economy.

Ninety-one per cent of the population identify themselves as Samoans – who are Christians with a distinct culture and language, which are an important part of the core school curriculum at both primary and secondary levels. Access to schools in Samoa is virtually universal, with a primary school in each of the 160 villages and a secondary school in every school district (a collection of about 16 to 17 villages). Big districts often have two secondary schools. Thirteen secondary schools are located in urban areas.

Traditionally, schooling and education have been held in high regard in Samoa. In recent years, however, people's perceptions have changed slightly and it appears that this high regard for education is starting to erode (GoS–Asian Development Bank [ADB] Education Sector Review, 2004).

Socio-cultural context

Fa'aSamoa: 'the Samoan way of doing things'

All areas of Samoan life, including village, district and national government political systems are based on *fa'aSamoa*: 'the Samoan way of doing things'. *Fa'aSamoa* emphasises the importance of the extended family (*aiga*) and the village (*nu'u*) and the place of love (*alofa*), respect (*fa'aaloaloalo*) and obedience (Tuia, 1999).

Samoan social structure rests on kinship values, with the village (*nu'u*) and the family (*aiga*) at the centre. It is believed that the welfare of the individual will flow out of the wellbeing of the village and family (Faibairn-Dunlop, 1999; Meleisea, 1987a). Each family within a village is represented by a holder of a chiefly title (*matai*) at the village council or general assembly (*fono a matai*). This council, consisting of all the titled people of the village (*matai*) and led by the high chief, governs the village and has responsibility and say over family members and land. The *fono a matai* is the forum by which matters are debated and decisions made: all *matai* have an equal say in its proceedings and decisions (Meleisea, 1987b).

Within *fa'aSamoa*, expectations and roles of individuals and groups within families and villages are determined by factors including locality, holder of title (*matai*), age and gender. The important relationships within the family and village that govern the protocols, roles, activities and behaviour include the special relationship between brother and sister (*feagaiga*) and that between different groups of the village (*va*); untitled men of the village, married and unmarried (*both aumaga*); unmarried 'daughters' of the village (*aualuma*); and both men (*fai avâ*) and women (*nofo tane*) who marry into the village.

Men and women of the village have higher status than those who marry into it. Notwithstanding origin, however, both men and women are able to ascend to the position of *matai* within their own families and take up positions of respect and responsibility within the village hierarchy.

Status is relative and linked to space, location and context. A daughter of her village has a very high status, higher than that of her brothers. When she marries and lives in her husband's village, however, her status automatically becomes much lower than that of her husband and her sisters-in-law. Locality is a leading factor in determining roles and responsibilities of individuals and groups. When a spouse is attending a gathering/ceremony at their partners' village/family, they have a specific role to perform that would be different if the gathering was occurring at their own family or village setting. Tasks are determined by other factors such as age and gender: both men and woman have different roles and relationships in different environments, not solely determined by gender. For example, regardless of gender, a wife or husband may be required to carry out menial tasks and take a passive role in decision-making in their spouse's family/village affairs. The roles are reversed within their own family/village affairs.

Age is another important factor in *fa'aSamoa*. The age of an individual has a great deal of influence in roles and relationships within families and society: if measured against the gender issue, it is probably more significant. A younger person knows that he or she will not be served by an older person: it is protocol for the youngest person present to perform serving duties and it would be shameful if such roles were not fulfilled.

Children are born into Samoan society as sons and daughters of a family/village in which their rights and status are those of a distinct group. Boys and girls are socialised into their activities as '*tamaiti*' (children) according to their age with minimal gender differentiation. Gender becomes important as children grow into adolescence and adulthood, however, and expectations and tasks become differentiated. Gender becomes important when youths enter adulthood and acquire the status of 'sons of the village' (*aumaga*) or 'daughters of the village' (*aualuma*): **status and roles** immediately change.

New roles are linked to the gendered division of labour within the village setting. Tasks seen as being physically more demanding, including plantation work, building houses and some forms of cooking, are considered to be young male domains, whereas the creation of artefacts (*fai oloa*) for traditional exchanges (for example, weaving and *siapo-* [cloth-] making) are perceived to be the domain of young women. Where men and women carry out similar activities, there may also be also gendered differentiation within the activities. For example, both men and women may fish, but women fish in lagoons and men in the open sea.

Samoa commitment to traditional customs and new approaches is exemplified in a change in the type of objects associated with customary gift-giving ceremonies. The giving of tapa cloth (*siapo*) has been replaced with the giving of cotton material; coconut oil replaced with a can of coke; a whole roasted pig replaced with boxes of canned fish and barrels of beef; taro is replaced with boxes of biscuits. In some instances, the giving of money replaces the giving of fine woven mats (*ie toga*) (Fairbairn-Dunlop, 1991).

The church and the school

The arrival in Samoa of the missionaries in the 1830s saw the introduction of new hierarchies in village and family life (Meleisea, 1987b). The church minister was given the importance and respect previously afforded to the high chief. This is of particular significance as the position of church minister was and remains reserved for men: women are not permitted to be appointed as ministers or pastors.

With the acceptance of Christianity by the Samoan population, the position of the church minister has been given high status in all areas of family and village life. The wife of the church minister is given status and respect within the family and village, but not on the same level as that of her husband.

The arrival of the missionaries also saw the introduction of western style education. Pastor schools (*aoga faifeau*) were established very quickly throughout Samoa and reading and writing was introduced to the Samoan people. Missionaries developed the Samoan alphabet and together with Samoans, translated the bible into the Samoan language (Petana-Ioka, 1995).

The church has profoundly influenced Samoan life, society and culture to such an extent that it has become completely integrated; this is not the same for school. The school's place within village and family life is considered to be the place where European (*palagi*) ways are taught: traditionally, the school is not considered the place to teach children about Samoa or its culture. Today's educators have to struggle to incorporate Samoan and things Samoan into the curriculum. Even with the introduction of Samoan issues into the curriculum, the perception is still held by many that the school is a place of foreign knowledge and ideas. In this regard, the school and education have not been integrated into the culture as the church has. By extension, the status of the teacher in the village is inferior to that of the church pastor.

The location of many of schools may illustrate the fact that they do not have the same influence or standing as the churches. Many school buildings are constructed on land that is not suitable for anything else (e.g. houses or plantations), or not wanted by anyone, e.g. school buildings being built on old cemeteries or schools positioned at the back of the village close to the sea. Nor is it expected that the school will be the place to challenge cultural protocols in regards to roles and relationships.

The area of enquiry used for this study was the school. However, as outlined above, the church has a much larger influence on Samoan life and culture. In fact, the church has changed gender relationships within the *fa'aSamoa* where the school system has had little influence.

Education

Gender and educational policies and strategies

In 2006, the Government of Samoa (GoS) and the Ministry of Education, Sports and Culture (MESC) launched its second Strategic Policy and Plan for the ten years from 2006-2015. Like the first set of policies from 1995-2005, the policy framework is articulated by a set of principles and key concepts, which include equity, quality, relevancy, efficiency and sustainability. The concept of equity in particular calls for the system to 'treat all individuals fairly and justly in the provision of services and opportunities' (GoS–MESC, 2006). It further states that:

'... policies, strategies and practices will be identified and articulated appropriately to avoid treatment that may disadvantage any social group. Those which address existing inequalities in access, treatment and outcome, will be promoted.' (GoS–MESC Strategic Policies and Plan 2006–2015, 2006)

The policies recognise that 'education is a basic human right and no child should be left out of the system'. Samoa is also committed to the Education For All (EFA) initiative, the achievement of the Millennium Development Goals (MDGs), the Forum Basic Education Action Plan (FBEAP), the Pacific Plan and other regional initiatives that promote education for all people. These are the basic policies into which gender polices must be integrated.

Co-educational or single-sex schools

The missionaries set up the first schools in Samoa: typically single-sex schools and mostly for boys. When the German administration (1900) and the New Zealand administration (1914) gradually took over more control of the education system, more co-educational primary schools were established. It was a similar history for the set up of secondary schools. Single-sex girls' schools were set up to cultivate 'young ladies' after the fashion of similar schools in the missionaries' home country, which in the 19th century was usually England. At the attainment of political independence in 1962, Samoa had 11 single-sex schools and 24 co-educational ones, as outlined in Table 5.1 below.

The single-sex schools included six boys' and five girls' schools: nine of these were church schools. The Catholic mission had only single-sex secondary schools while the London Missionary Society (LMS) had two single-sex schools and two co-educational ones. The Methodist mission had one girls' school and one co-educational school, while the Mormons and Seventh Day schools had only co-educational schools. The government had two single-sex schools for boys and several co-educational schools.

Table 5.1. Secondary schools by governance, 1962

Governance of school	Boys-only school	Girls-only school	Co-educational
Catholic	3	3	0
LMS (London Missionary Society)	1	1	2
Methodist	0	1	1
Mormon	0	0	1
Seventh Day Adventist	0	0	2
Government	2	0	18
Total	6	5	24

Source: (Western Samoa) Department of Education Annual Report (1962)

The picture is very different today. There are no all-boys secondary schools remaining in the country, while there are only two all-girls schools both of which are mission schools, one Catholic and one Congregational. Indications are that one is still running well while the other (the study school) has an uncertain future according to all the signs.

School participation rates

National school participation rates in Samoa are relatively high, especially at primary level – as the tables below show. While these figures are not disaggregated by gender, they are of particular interest because they illustrate the high participation rates at the primary school age level.

From Table 5.2, it is immediately apparent that participation rates at primary level are much better than those at secondary level. The trends were quite similar in the nine years from 1998–2006, as shown in Figure 5.1 below. It should be noted that some students who would be at secondary level (12–14 years old) are included in the 5–14 age cohort, generally identified as the primary cohort.

Table 5.2. National school participation rates

Year	1998	1999	2000	2001	2002	2003	2004	2005	2006
Ages 5–14	91%	89%	91%	92%	96%	95%	97%	96%	95%
Ages 15–19	44%	46%	42%	44%	43%	48%	45%	45%	45%

Source: MESC Statistical Digest (2006): part 2 p. 5

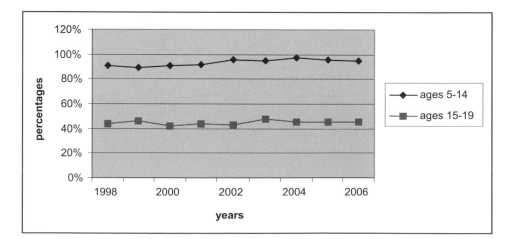

Figure 5.1. National school participation rates
Source: Samoa MESC Statistical Digest (2006): part 2 p. 5

Exploring the Bias: Gender & Stereotyping in Secondary Schools

Of significance is the fact that participation in secondary schools is so low, particularly as there are schools in all districts and in theory access to secondary schools for all children. According to a government study conducted in 2004, the reasons for this might include the reduced value given to education, particularly in the rural areas, a sense of the irrelevance of education to real life and an inability to pay for the actual and/or opportunity costs of schooling (GoS–ADB, 2004). Table 5.3 lists the number of secondary and combined primary and secondary schools in Samoa.

Samoa has 25 government secondary (or combined primary and secondary) schools, 17 mission schools and two private schools. About 60 per cent of secondary school enrolments are in government schools.

Data in Table 5.4 below shows that in 2006, boys outnumbered girls at the primary level: there were 1,539 more boys than girls enrolled. Girls then outnumber boys at the secondary level, with 789 more girls than boys enrolled.

Table 5.5 shows that, in the years between 2000 and 2006, the average enrolment by boys in from classes 9 to 12 was about 47 per cent. In all but one instance, boys' percentage of total enrolment has decreased with each year of schooling.

Table 5.3. Secondary schools in Samoa, 2006

	Secondary	Primary and secondary
Government	24	1
Missions	12	5
Private	1	1
Total	37	7

Source: MESC Statistical Digest (2006)

Table 5.4. School enrolments by level, gender and status, 2006

	Male	Female	Total
Primary	20,654	19,115	39,769
Secondary	7,165	7,954	15,119
Total	27,819	27,069	54,888

Source: Samoa MESC Statistical Digest (2006)

Table 5.5. Percentage male enrolments, all secondary schools 2000–2006

Year/class	9	10	11	12
2000	49.9	48.8	45.9	5.5
2001	49.5	48.5	46.5	47
2002	50.9	48.9	46.9	3.5
2003	49.2	48.5	46.4	43.6
2004	50.1	47.6	46.7	43.7
2005	51.3	49.5	46.3	45.9
2006	49.8	49	46.3	42.1
Average	**50.1**	**48.7**	**46.4**	**44.4**

Source: MESC Statistical Digest (2006)

Boys' average percentage of class 9 enrolment was 50.1 per cent, reducing to 48.7 per cent at grade 10, 46.4 per cent at grade 11, and 44.4 per cent at grade 12. This is a significant annual drop, with consequences for the number of boys achieving final examination passes.

School curriculum and gendered achievement

The Samoan national curriculum requires all students to take the same subjects from year 9: English, Samoa, maths, social studies, and science. Other subjects such as food and textile technology (FTT), business studies, computer studies and visual arts are considered option subjects whereby they may be timetabled together and the students choose one. Health and physical education and music are not considered as subjects that students choose, but are treated as whole-school activities for two hours per week. All the subjects have official curriculum documents with visual arts, computer studies, health and physical education and music introduced in 2005 (even though the actual subjects have been present in secondary schools for many years).

A 2005 study by the Commonwealth Secretariat (Jha and Kelleher, 2006) points to the rising trend of girls outperforming boys at secondary level, starting since the mid-1990s. The results for all three subjects, English, Samoan and numeracy (ibid.: 107) showed that more boys than girls were at risk at the end of years 4 and 6. Similarly, for the Year 8 National Examination for the years 2001, 2002 and 2004, boys' mean scores were below 50 per cent, while girls were around 54 per cent. In the years from 2004 to 2006, girls took 51 per cent, 65 per cent and 66 per cent of the top places in the Year 8 National Examination respectively. This examination is used for secondary school selection; Table 5.6 shows the gender balance of selection for the top three Samoan secondary schools: Samoa, Avele and Vaipouli.

Table 5.6. Year 8 selection for government colleges by gender, 2004–2006

	2004			2005			2006		
	Samoa	Avele	Vaipouli	Samoa	Avele	Vaipouli	Samoa	Avele	Vaipouli
Boys	62	66	47	47	33	30	39	41	33
Girls	78	45	58	85	60	62	86	65	66

Source: MESC Assessment Division (2007)

The National School Certificate Examination (NSCE) is taken at the end of secondary schooling. Table 5.7 lists the national gender split for students who sat this examination in 2004, 2005 and in 2006.

The gender differences are quite substantial: girls outnumbered boys by 377 in 2004, 516 in 2005 and 353 in 2006.

The Research in Samoa

Approach

The study was carried out during May and June 2007. A team of four was assembled, with the team leader managing the ethics and administration of the research and three team members carrying out the data collection within four schools. The research process used a collaborative approach, with each researcher carrying out their data collection within their allocated school and writing up a case study report. The final report comprised a collection of the work done by the researchers individually and together in a collaborative manner. This chapter was finalised by the principal researcher in line with prescribed processes and procedures.

The central questions of the study were (i) to what extent do students, teachers, the school management and processes, and the education system and management challenge or reinforce dominant gendered notions, stereotypes, identities and relationships, and (ii) if they do or do not, how do we make sense of it all?

Table 5.7. Gender split for school certificate examinations

	Females	Males	Total
2004	1,442	1,065	2,507
2005	1,550	1,034	2,584
2006	1,325	972	2,297

Source: MESC Assessment Division (2007)

Data was collected from students, teachers, principal and administration staff, lesson proceedings, observations of extra-curricular activities, student–teacher interactions during recess times and classroom interactions. The data collection was carried out using interviews, group discussions, observation of staff meetings and detailed observations of lessons.

Lesson observations included focus on the physical nature of the class: the position of teacher's desk, arrangement of students' desks, and location of blackboards, windows and doors. It also focused on interaction, language and activities of the lesson: specifically teacher time and attention to the details of lessons and student needs; use of instructional language and quality of questions; and student-to-student interaction.

The procedure carried out in each school involved following a class during the school day as they went through their lessons, as it was hoped to collect data from a range of different subject lessons such as language, arts, maths/science and practical lessons (outside the normal classroom). Each researcher developed a relationship with the school principal(s) and teachers as a result of their time at the school, and was able to collect a wide variety of data both formally through interviews and lesson observations, and informally, though exposure to school procedures and management practices.

Analysis of the lesson observation data used a mixture of quantitative and qualitative approaches. The lesson observation schedules (Tools 1, 2, and 3) recorded the number of incidences within a set time frame. Interactions, language and activities were noted down for the different types of lessons in different classes. This data allowed the different classes to be compared and contrasted with each other, such as between the language and maths lessons, or lessons conducted by female and male teachers.

Capability, space and location

Theoretical frameworks

The two dimensions of enquiry used in this study are the 'capability framework' and notions of the 'space and location framework'. The capability framework, illustrated in Figure 5.2 below, emphasises entitlement, opportunities and capabilities. The assumption is that the possibility of gender equality will be enhanced if all elements exist for all children.

With respect to the first domain, that of 'entitlements', the entitlements of Samoan students and teachers in schools are very clear: they are stated in a variety of international, government and ministry policies and guidelines. The opportunities and capabilities of male and female students and teachers were assessed through the research. Students' experiences were analysed to assess if they had (i) the opportunity to achieve their fullest potential and (ii) the capability to make use of opportunities (the concept of capability includes the ability and power to make use of opportunities).

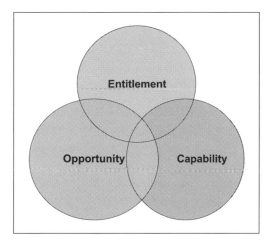

Figure 5.2. Capability framework

The second framework was that of space and location, as illustrated in Figure 5.3 below. Families and the home play an important role in creating social norms and capabilities. Society also plays a role in developing and maintaining or challenging gender roles and expectations. Two important institutions have the influence and capacity to influence both society (the macro level) and families (the micro level): these two institutions are the church and the school. The school is the focus of this study, but the school is not isolated from other societal institutions.

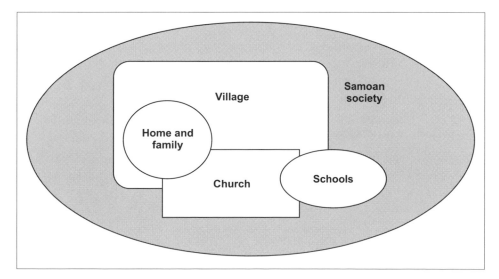

Figure 5.3. Space and location framework

Values and beliefs that are deep seated in religious orientations and in cultural perceptions of worthwhile learning impact on what goes on in the school systems. These needed to be considered in order to make gender sense of what goes on in schools. The spatial dimensions of schools and classrooms, the different locations of schools and relationship between the school and the church were significant focus areas for the study.

Foundations for the exploration

There is equal entitlement in Samoa society for both girls and boys to obtain formal education. There is nothing in Samoan culture that prevents either boys' or girls' entitlement to achieving status and leadership authority in village and family settings.

In terms of access to education and schooling, Samoa is well placed: every village has a primary school and every district (cluster of villages) has a secondary school, while some districts have two secondary schools – especially if the district is geographically large. Factors impacting on access or opportunity, however, include: the affordability of schooling (fees, contributions in kind, community contributions to school maintenance); distance from schools (transport costs, transport availability); immigration policies (depletion of family numbers/members); and other related issues. These areas need to be closely examined in an effort to make secondary schooling accessible to all.

The capability element is reflected in attitudes of teachers, students and parents and the importance they put on education. It also includes other factors, including parental capacity to pay school fees and lack of human resources, such as the critical shortage of teachers in the Samoan school system.

Locality and space are important and influential factors in what happens in a school and how it is managed and run. In comparison with schools, the church has a much more evident influence on Samoan society. As detailed above, the church has been completely integrated into Samoa's culture and customs, whereas the school is still considered a foreign or alien institution.

The schools and classes

The selection of schools was based on the stated requirements to included rural and urban schools, single-sex and co-educational schools. It was further decided to select year 9 and year 10 classes, as these were within the required age range of 15–16 years. (Where possible year 9 was chosen; if there were not four year 9 classes, year 10 classes were used). Table 5.8 lists details of the school studied.

The four schools in the study included two government schools, and two mission schools. The government schools were both rural and located at opposite ends of the

Table 5.8. Details of participant schools

School location	Gender of students	Governed by
Rural	Co-educational	Government of Samoa
Rural	Co-educational	Government of Samoa
Urban	Co-educational	Methodist Church
Urban	Single-sex, female	Congregational Christian Church of Samoa

island of Upolu, while the mission schools were an urban all-girls school and a semi-urban co-educational school.

The different profiles of the schools (government- or church-run, rural or urban, co-educational or single-sex) influenced the amount and type of resources available, responsibilities of students and subjects offered.

Ethics

Strict attention was placed on approaching and entering schools in the proper manner and following the correct procedure. Letters were first sent to the governing bodies of the schools selected. They were the Samoan Government Ministry of Education, Sports and Culture for the government schools and the Church School Boards for the Congregational and Methodist Mission School systems. Once permission had been provided by these bodies, a letter was sent to the specific schools informing them of the research. The researchers then co-ordinated with the schools through a series of initial meetings to set up the actual steps and procedure for the data collection.

Attention was also given to obtaining the correct informed consent from all participants. After the reasons for the research were explained in full to the participants, they were asked to sign a consent form if they then agreed to take part. Participants were given full opportunity to refuse to take part in the research study if they felt uncomfortable.

Constraints

Timing during the fieldwork was the main concern for all researchers. In addition to the late start, a further challenge was posed when one school had to be replaced by another, when it became obvious that it would not be possible to collect the required data from the first. Furthermore, several unavoidable incidences occurred that reduced the number of days available where lessons could be observed and group discussions convened. These occurrences were a school holiday break for two weeks, a large number of public holidays, an extra public holiday due to the state funeral of the Head of State, a church denomination annual international meeting, mid-year whole-school examinations, whole-school athletics days in preparation for the interschool competitions and whole-school culture days, with performances and singing competitions.

School-wide examinations also affected the type of lessons that were observed: they were either for revision or practicing exam questions. Three schools had school-wide athletics days within the data collection period. This was a good opportunity to observe school processes, but preparation for the event took away from classroom lesson time and content. At one school, the researcher included observations of a culture day programme, where the students had competitions in singing, dancing and cooking. The preparations for this special day affected many lessons prior to the event, with practices and rehearsals taking place instead of lessons. Even though these factors were seen as a constraint in one sense, they also provided an opportunity to observe the processes and procedures of school organisation.

The observation schedule, which involved counting teacher time and attention for 10-minute blocks, was also a limitation. There was actually very little interaction in the lessons observed, and a 10-minute block was too short to obtain meaningful data. In addition, the place within the lesson of the 10-minute block affected the results. If, for example, the 10-minute block was at the beginning of the lesson, which contained teacher instruction and explanation, there was a strong possibility of having no interaction to record.

The effect on the teachers and students of having the researcher present in the classroom was another constraint, although one common to all research undertakings. There was a high probability that the teacher and/or students may have altered their normal practice due to the researcher's presence. As the researcher spent more time at the school and attended more lessons, teachers and students became more accustomed to having an observer in the room.

Another constraint was the absence of interaction with parents and families: the study did not include interviews with parents, to have some insight into their expectations and aspirations for their children. During data analysis, there was a great deal of discussion about family life and students' experiences at home. Students described their home lives and teachers had a lot to say about their own perceptions of students' home lives and how family life impacted on their school performance, but this rich data was not triangulated with that from parents and families.

Using a team of researchers rather than one researcher has both advantages and disadvantages. One of the advantages was that the researchers were able to spend a good amount of time at their research school and develop relationships with the staff: this probably improved the quality of the data. Using the collaborative approach allowed group discussion of the data, issues were discussed where each team member expressed their point of view, leading to a thorough analysis of the data. While each school case study as written by the individual researcher had its own language and style, at the same time this variety added to the diversity of perspectives in interpreting the data collected.

Analysis and Discussion

Education system processes and practices

Government and mission schools

School systems exist in a context governed by economic, social and cultural factors. Two of the schools have important religious contexts: one is a co-educational Methodist college, while the other is a Congregational girls college. Both are governed by education boards, which are made up almost totally of male members who are part of the structure of administration of their church. The school boards are accountable to the church conferences, which meet annually: the Conference (*Koneferenisi*) for the Methodists and the General Meeting (*Fono Tele*) for the Congregationalists. Current church teaching about female and male roles follows the conservative perceptions of male and female as written in the Bible. There is still a tendency to regard females and things female to be of lesser importance than males and 'male' domains.

Church school administrators, therefore, do not have a perception of gender as an issue in the schools. The only female single-sex school run by the Methodists has been closed.

In contrast, the girls' school run by the Catholic Church is thriving. This may in part be due to the constant and vigorous support provided by the 'old girls' of the schools. The Old Girls' Association has been instrumental in changing the ethos of the school: current students have high aspirations to be leaders and to be effective members of their communities.

The government school system is, however, different. Government school control and administration is highly centralised in the Ministry of Education: it assigns teachers to schools, provides educational policy and practice, as well as systems of supervision and discipline. In Samoa, the schools' physical facilities are provided and owned by the community. Governance of the school is provided mainly by the local school committee, in which government agents – such as the school principal and the school review officer – are also represented. Local school committees are characteristically all-male, so that school governance tends to be dominated by male viewpoints and ways of doing things. In spite of this, boys are still underachieving: clearly there is no straightforward correlation between school governance in terms of male dominance and boys' achievement in schools.

Up to the early 1990s, 72 per cent of all primary teachers were women, but the corresponding figure for principals was only 48 per cent. In some schools, the only man on the staff would be the principal. By 2006, women constituted 73 per cent of primary principals and 39 per cent of principals in secondary schools.

Reflections

Church schools in Samoa are run by boards that are accountable to the church's highest council, while government schools are accountable to the Ministry of Education. Accountability structures are therefore different. However, the schools' core curriculum as provided by the government (the MESC) is adopted and used by all mission secondary schools. Recruitment to schools is either selection by exams or accepted as a matter of course.

School management processes and practice

Streaming practices

Schools use streaming practices to determine class composition. Table 5.9 illustrates the gender profile in the various streams of classes 9 and 10 in the three co-educational schools that were studied. The trend is clear: there are more girls than boys in school, girls dominate the top streams and are the minority in all but one lower stream. This is a stark illustration of the gender imbalance in the sample schools and the country more generally.

The research illustrated that girls outperform boys in the core subjects, even within those traditionally viewed as 'male': maths and science.

Table 5.9. Gender profile of streamed classes, co-educational schools

	School 1		*School 2*		*School 3*	
Year 9	**Boys**	**Girls**	**Boys**	**Girls**	**Boys**	**Girls**
Stream 1	10	22	16	18	10	21
Stream 2	9	19	18	26	19	17
Stream 3					20	16
Stream 4					24	10
Year 10	**Boys**	**Girls**	**Boys**	**Girls**	**Boys**	**Girls**
Stream 1	15	25	15	21	14	27
Stream 2	26	13	12	19	20	16
Stream 3					28	16

Gender attitudes

In all three co-educational schools, the principals were male and the deputies were female. One principal said he believed female teachers were more reliable and effective and tended to delegate more to female colleagues. Women were given more responsibility and more significant tasks in the running of the school. This was made even more apparent if there is an added qualification of age. Older female teachers took on the more prestigious tasks, such as being mistress of ceremony during the culture day or being the treasurer to receive the donations from the community during special events for the school. The younger female teachers tended to be given the more menial tasks of supervising students' cleaning up after an event.

One male principal had equal numbers of female and male teachers, with a high proportion of younger staff. There were two senior female teachers, who shared equal responsibility with two older male colleagues. Together they carried out all the significant tasks in the school, while the younger staff took on the more menial tasks.

Another principal had a much higher proportion of male staff than female. Most of these male teachers were ordained ministers, assigned as teachers for a contract period. Tasks were assigned in order of seniority and positions of responsibility; however, there were still clearly demarcated lines along male tasks e.g. managing rugby teams, organising boys for manual tasks, and female tasks such as coaching netball and inspection of girls' uniforms etc.

The only female principal in the study was in the single-sex (all-girls) school. She was an ex-student and 'product' of the school. She looks upon herself as a father and mother to her teachers and students. The one male teacher is an ordained pastor, and is accorded the usual respect accorded to religious ministers: apart from teaching, he did not carry out any additional management tasks.

Principals generally stated that girls and boys were treated equally in their schools, but with regards to tasks to be carried out there were gender-specific tasks to reflect what the students did at home. For example, girls performed lighter tasks such as serving the staff during mealtimes. Principals generally had the same perceptions as the teachers: that girls were achieving much more and were much better behaved than boys. In one recent case, some boys' bad behaviour and truancy had resulted in their expulsion. Generally misbehaviour or breaking the rules resulted in detention in all schools. Detention usually included weeding in the sun after school: this punishment is given to both boys and girls.

Teacher non-classroom tasks

Outside the classroom, younger female teachers supervised the girls while younger male teachers supervised the boys. Older teachers stayed in the staff room. In the two mission schools, teachers who were ordained ministers did not carry out any duties outside the classroom.

These observations carry an important message about the reciprocal relationships alluded to above. Relationships between people in Samoa are forged by the observation of what is termed the observations of *va* (a code of behaviour between people who are related, are strangers or are visitors to a community); *va tapuia* (relationships that are governed by strict [sacred] rules of behaviour because of some kinship affiliation e.g. brother and sister, father and son, mother and daughter); or *va fealoaloi* (relationships that are governed by respectable codes of behaviour e.g. *matai* and *matai*, villager and pastor, cabinet minister and prime minister etc). In the description given above, the supervision of girls by female teachers is *va tapuia*, while that between older and younger teachers is *va fealoaloi* and that of the deferment to the pastor is that of *va*.

Gender is thus an aspect of the forging of relationships in Samoan society in the same way that age and status are also important related concepts.

Reflections

Schools are open to all students who wish to attend school irrespective of where they live. Principals delegated tasks to senior teachers who were often female. Principals treated all students the same irrespective of gender, but punishments may be different for boys and girls.

Male principals profess a heavy reliance on their senior female staff, who were efficient and managed resources well. An equal number of female and male prefects were appointed every year, but it was impossible to obtain an equal gender ratio for the staff as women now dominate the teaching workforce.

Textbooks and other learning materials

The development of the current secondary curriculum in Samoa took great care to make all materials as gender neutral as possible. A gender specialist was employed during the writing stage to ensure that language was gender neutral and that there was a balance of focus on boys and girls in all reading, study and other resource materials. The implementation of the curriculum does not, however, reflect this.

Teachers

Gendered expectations

In the girls-only school, there was an expectation that schooling should develop girls holistically to (i) enable them to become fully literate and numerate, and (ii) develop their capacities in their roles as mothers and nurturers of family and community. According to these teachers, the girls in their school were underachievers in the academic sense and were in the school for a specific purpose: to be developed as good mothers and community members. Being a good mother included learning the vocational skills of cooking, sewing, weaving, embroidery, *siapo* (mulberry bark cloth-) making and other crafts. The girls are also taught typing and computing for those who might look for employment as office and clerical workers. There was clearly a belief that girls who were not academically able should be encouraged to be good mothers and home managers.

In the co-educational schools, teachers are aware of boys' underachievement. Their perceptions, however, were that the causes are rooted in the family and community. Teachers do not believe that they have a role to play in this problem. Their perceptions are that boys in rural areas are expected to help their fathers and family to carry out 'heavy' chores and other tasks after school such as fishing, plantation work, cooking and feeding the pigs. All these take up their time and prevent the boys from having time to rest or do their homework. Girls, on the other hand, tidy the house, iron, and rest and do their homework. Girls are therefore expected to achieve more because, according to the teachers, they have the opportunity to study and do their work for school. Teachers want their students to achieve well, irrespective of gender. They also see the relationship between having time to rest and being able to study and do homework as pivotal in school achievement. However, they do not see that they have a duty to change the role expectations of parents and bring about some behavioural change that might enable boys to have time to rest and do their homework while at home. They consider this to be the duty and prerogative of the parents.

When talking about their experiences in the classroom, teachers in two schools stated that girls do much better than the boys, they read better, they answer more questions, concentrate better, are quicker to understand and are generally more intelligent than boys. Some teachers stated that boys have shorter concentration spans, that they sit in the back, do not respond to questions, do not study hard, play around and talk a lot and are the last ones to hand in assignments.

Teachers in general could see that there were differences in the achievement of boys and girls, but they were not aware or convinced that they could do anything about it. Furthermore, they were not aware that their everyday practices might contribute to the boys' underachievement.

Language

Teachers' language use was differentiated by gender and age. In general, older female teachers tended to scold students. This practice is culturally understood to be 'counselling', but scolding does include the use of harsh language. Younger female teachers do not use that type of language and, it is perceived, would not have the 'mana' (or spiritual gift of wisdom) to use it. This could result in a perception by students that younger teachers are more relaxed. Older teachers, especially women, are expected to scold students as a means of discipline, while younger female teachers would respect their older female colleagues for providing such counselling to the students.

Reflections

Teachers expect girls to achieve better results than the boys, because they do not have to perform the heavy work that boys do, which takes up a lot time in the home. Girls are expected to have much more time to do schoolwork than boys. Teachers in co-educational schools perceive that they treat girls and boys the same, but girls still behaved differently from boys and they still achieved better results.

Teachers in the single-sex school did not consider gender an issue, as the schools mission was to prepare the girls for their future role as good mothers and members of their community.

Students

Aspirations

In rural schools, both boys and girls wanted to do well. They felt it would provide the pathways to a future with a good job, a better life, a family car and a good house. Both boys and girls based their choices on jobs that would provide financial security and sustainability of livelihood. Boys wanted to be police officers or become members of the *Manu Samoa* (the national rugby team). Boys regarded being a police officer as a good job for a man, respected in village communities. Girls wanted to be teachers, nurses, and bank officers, office workers or become the wife of a church minister.

Boys said that they respected girls in the classroom and in schools, because some were members of their village or church. Girls also respected the boys, but if they were cheeky then they called them names. In other words, the basis of respect of the opposite gender was different for boys who regarded village/community affiliation as important, while girls regarded good behaviour by the boys as more important. These perceptions seem to reinforce the socialisation processes within rural communities that place different expectations on boys and on girls. The observance of the 'brother–sister' covenant (*feagaiga*) of traditional society is stronger in rural schools (than in urban ones).

In the urban schools, particularly in the all-girls school, girls' expectations included being a good mother, living a good life and having the means to support their families. However, living in an urban area, particularly the youth culture that is apparent in the media, has had some influence and some of the girls now want to stay in town and be employed or maybe migrate overseas. In the semi-urban school, girls wanted to be lawyers, nurses, teachers, bank tellers and to be in the police force, while boys focused on the 'macho' jobs or what was considered masculine such as being a police officer, rugby player or computer operator. Some boys also wanted to work in a bank or office.

Interactions

Many boys felt that teachers favoured the girls, and that this was the reason why they did not participate as much as the girls. Some boys perceived teachers to be tougher on them, while some had self-perceptions that they were louder than the girls and maybe showed off at times. Girls seemed to favour male teachers, as they did not use harsh words with them. Female teachers are seen by girls as using harsher language, even though they do not use corporal punishment.

Student perceptions of each other, especially along gendered notions, are tempered by considerations of *va* the codes of appropriate behaviour that forge the relationship as perceived by the students. Hence girls looked upon boys as their 'brothers' and vice versa. Boys are expected by the girls to behave well around them and girls expect the boys to protect them. Boys expect the girls to treat them with respect. These expectations govern many of the interactions between students. Thus, in a co-educational science class it is often difficult for a teacher to discuss matters that pertain to sexual education: boys and girls in the same village may be in the same class, and it would be shameful if they were to be exposed to such taboo issues together.

Students in general are quite respectful of one another in the language they use. However, if boys misbehave, girls may use '*upu taufaifai*' or 'call them names'. Boys would consider a girl as '*le mafaufau*' (that she 'does not have a brain') if the girl used swear words around them.

Subject choice

The choice of students' most-liked subjects was not a significantly gendered factor: students did the same subjects from years 9 to 11 in most schools. For the optional choices of FTT, computer studies and business studies, it was found that **where** FTT was offered the girls choose FTT and both boys and girls choose business studies and computer studies. (The shortage of teachers in these areas has been a contributing factor to whether or not the subject is offered).

Reflections

All students want to do well in school. However, perceptions of future work are often mediated through gender roles and expectations of parents. These perceptions were seldom accompanied by any concept of gender equality or gender parity. This needs to become part of the curriculum if such a concept is considered to be worthwhile in the context of Samoa.

In general, it appears that students' expectations, aspirations and perceptions of what they want to be in the future and of the opposite sex are conceptualised along gendered notions of male/female roles, and what is considered to be the male or female domains, as they understand these from their homes and their communities. The notions of gender equality and gender parity need to be moderated through a curriculum and learning experiences that should rationalise a Samoan 'culture of change'.

Processes inside the classroom

This section discusses the activities observed inside the classroom, to identify if these processes reinforced or questioned dominant gendered notions, stereotypes, identities and relationships, how this happened, and what might be done to redress the situation.

Seating arrangements

The main teaching style adopted by all teachers was that of transmission, and in most classes, all children sit facing the teacher. Blackboards tended to be at the front of the room, the teacher's dominant work area: there were boards at the back, but they were used infrequently or for display purposes. In such environments, it is possible that the closer a learner sits to the teacher, the greater chance of being involved in meaningful interaction. Teachers stated that they let the students sit wherever they wanted to sit. They did not try to influence the seating arrangements in any way or use it as a tool to distribute their teaching and attention equitably around the classroom.

Generally girls sat together and boys sat together. Girls sat mostly at the front of the room while the boys sat at the back. A variation to this pattern was when girls all sit at one side of the room and the boys sit at the other. The sexes sit quite separately. Even when activities require group work on the floor, girls still tend to congregate together and likewise the boys. One of the advantages for the girls in sitting at or around the front of the classroom is that they are then able to dominate and claim the teacher's attention. This meant that boys (sitting at the back) were often left out of lessons. This was especially evident in classrooms that were crowded and the teacher had limited room to move around.

Some of the sample schools did not have chairs or tables, so the activities all took place on the floor. However, girls still sat towards the front of the classroom while the boys sat on the periphery or towards the back. Again, even where there were no chairs or desks, girls managed to get the teachers' full attention.

One possible explanation of the seating phenomenon might be that proximity to the teacher may be considered more suitable for girls as the 'weaker sex', while sitting at a distance from the teacher would be more masculine, as boys would then be far away from the watchful eye of the teacher. Another might be that boys do not need to be supervised, while girls need that 'motherly' protection of being close to the teacher. A third might be that boys do not think that they need the closeness of the teacher, as they were more *malolosi* (strong and independent). A final one is that the pattern could be a manifestation of the culture in the homes where boys as brothers are protective of their sisters, and would therefore defer to them in the classroom and allow them to sit closer to the teachers.

Whatever the explanation, girls sit in the front and by doing so could reap the benefits of teaching/ learning by being closer to the teacher and being able to see and learn from all the activities that go on as part of the teacher's own activities during a lesson. Teachers did not seem aware of the implications of seating arrangements on learning or if they were, appeared satisfied with the outcome of better achievement by the girls. If teachers were more conscious and deliberate in the way they arranged class seating, and balanced seating arrangements so that students are distributed equally (in terms of boys and girls) around the classroom, there might be different outcomes.

Teacher–student interactions

In language classrooms, girls were more active than boys, answering questions and carrying out demonstrations when asked. Girls also tended to volunteer more, for example, to read. Boys tended to be more reserved and quite reluctant to talk. When they did talk, boys struggled to find the words, especially in English. The girls were more fluent and more active in English. However, the differences in the Samoan classes were not as marked: the boys became more active and more relaxed in these classes and participated quite as actively as the girls.

Most observed science lessons were theoretical, based on teacher explanation: few practical classes were conducted. Again when questions were asked, the girls answered more readily. The science classes observed all had similar teacher–student interactions, wherein the teacher predominantly talked, explaining, showing and demonstrating, while the students looked on and listened. The reasons may have been that the teachers were overly teacher-directed in their approaches, while there was also a scarcity of resources to enable practical classes.

More active learning was observed in food textile and technology classes, where teachers and students were engaged in practical and hands-on work. The rapport between teacher and students was warm and there was a lot of interaction. Teachers used students' names more and generally there was much interaction between the teachers and students. It was also noticeable that there were resources available in these classes, and these were used by the teachers in all four schools. There were no boys in the FTT classes in three of the four schools.

Visual arts was an optional class offered in two of the four schools. All students in these classes were girls. Teacher–student interaction was characterised by on-task behaviour by all students and there was much enthusiasm to complete projects, which were then displayed. Tasks were accompanied by singing as the girls worked on *tapa* printing and tie-dyeing of fabric.

In the seating arrangements for whole-school singing, the girls were often seated in the front, while the boys were seated around the girls and tended to be towards the back of the classroom. It was noted that this was often the practice and the teachers did not direct the students on where to sit. It seems to be generally understood and is a practice.

School sports were often timetabled for one afternoon either on a Thursday or Friday. This was not the case for the all-girls school in the study, where no sports were organised. An issue of gender here is that the boys play rugby, while the girls play volley or netball. In one school, it was noted that in the principal's office, a number of trophies were lined up for rugby while there were not similar trophies for girls' sports.

Reflections

The observations illustrate that what goes on in the classroom with regards to teacher–student interactions or student–student interactions are mediated through the kinds of gendered notions held by teachers and students.

Seating arrangements were done by the students and showed that girls sat together, as did boys. This may be due to the fact that as young teenagers, affiliation among the sexes was stronger than between the sexes. Girls, however, sat at the front of the classroom while boys sat at the back. This implies that the girls are immediately in an important position of advantage, as the teacher tends to focus more on the group closest to the front of the class than at the back. This arrangement was also seen in other activities, such as whole school singing where the girls sat at the front of the choir while boys sat at the back. Teachers did not use seating arrangements as a tool to disburse teaching equitably around the classroom, and in this way may be contributing to supporting achievement by girls at the expense of boys. Seating arrangements, therefore, generally reinforce the more favoured status of girls.

Girls were more active and participated in more teacher–student interactions than boys in languages, science and in other subject areas such as food and textiles technology. Teacher–student interactions in the visual arts, where all students were girls, were more equal. In sports, girls played 'girls' sports' and boys played 'boys' sports'. Teachers tended to address all questions to the front of the class, which benefited the girls. Older teachers tended to use students' names more than younger teachers. In teacher–student interactions, girls were generally more active than boys in all subject areas. This was seen by teachers as just the way things are. They did not interrogate whether this was due to some 'self-fulfilling prophecy' effect. Teachers may be contributing to the lower achievement levels of the boys in the ways they handle classroom interaction.

Processes outside the classroom

This section discusses the processes and activities observed outside the classroom, both organised and informal, for both students and teachers. It also includes a discussion on the 'culture day' observed at one of the schools.

'Heavy' and 'light' work

In Samoan schools, students often carried out cleaning duties in the grounds, around the classrooms and in the toilets. Such activity can be given as an assignment or punishment for breaking school rules, such as lateness to school, not doing homework or for boys having long hair.

Boys were observed to be doing the 'heavy work', while the girls did the 'light work'. Heavy work meant cutting grass with a machete, lifting heavy objects and weeding in the banana plantation at the back of the school. Light work meant girls weeding the flower gardens at the front of the school, cleaning windows, sweeping the corridors, and picking up leaves and other rubbish. Toilet cleaning, however, was carried out by the girls of the girls' toilets and boys of the boys' toilets. Light and heavy work were also differentiated in tasks such as serving meals for the teachers, where it was noted that the girl prefects did this work while boy prefects marked the field for athletics day.

The gendered notion of boys doing heavy and more 'macho' work while girls should perform lighter tasks is common in many cultures. It is clear from these observations that schools reinforce gender-role specialisations in what goes on outside the classroom.

Culture day

A culture day is an annual event in most schools: it brings together all the teaching and learning that goes on in the school in the Samoan language and cultural studies. This special event was observed in one school, where traditional tasks of cooking by the boys and the girls were demonstrated as part of the learning outcomes in the Samoan language and culture. It was noted that cooking using the Samoan 'above ground' oven (*umu*) was prepared and carried out by boys, while meal preparation that uses boiling, frying or does not require cooking (for example, raw fish or *oka*) is carried out by girls. Craftwork also involves gender-specific roles. Boys weave rough baskets for collecting food, while girls weave the more refined baskets for women. Both men and women fish, but men go out on canoes and fish in the deep sea while women paddle in the lagoon for shellfish and sea slugs. The boys demonstrated the makings of the tools for deep-sea fishing, while the girls showed what they used in lagoon fishing.

For Samoan dancing, the students were divided into four groups and each group performed a final item where a girl (*taupou*) dances centre-stage while the boys providing the 'sidekicks' (*aiuli*) danced at the periphery. This is the Samoan 'last dance' (*taualuga*), which is more than just dancing. It reinforces the status of the people in a village community and it reminds people about their status in society. So the *taupou* is often the daughter of a chief, while the *aiuli* would be the sons of *tulafale* (orators). Hence proper etiquette is that the *aiuli* while 'whooping it up' with loud clapping and shouts should never be close to the *taupou*, who is always tantalisingly out of reach of the *aiuli*.

These types of teaching and learning epitomise cultural gendered notions and when taught in school, they reinforce societal notions of gender-specific roles and the reciprocal relationships that exist between male and female, especially that of a brother and sister in Samoan society. Students tend to regard all forms of traditional Samoan knowledge as inferior to '*palagi*' (Western, middle-class) knowledge, so culture days are often treated as a very brief digression from the main pursuit of Western knowledge.

Culture days are part and parcel of Samoan education. It is a means of reminding and reinforcing cultural norms and behaviour, and in this way they do reinforce cultural gendered notions of appropriate behaviour and observations of relationships.

Reflections

Boys carried out heavy work and the teachers expected them to do this while the girls did lighter work. Teachers explained this in terms of physical strength (boys are stronger than girls), expected role (boys should protect girls) and complementarity of roles (that tasks are done much faster and more efficiently if there is division of labour).

Boys worked at the back of the school while girls worked at the front. Teachers explained this in terms of the expected role of boys as protectors of girls. Boys work away from supervision by teachers, as there is an expectation that boys can look after themselves while girls need to be protected.

All culture day activities were demonstrated as work and tasks that were gender-specific to males and females. However, gender specificity is seen more as complementarity of roles rather than males and females doing the same tasks. Role complementarity does not preclude equity. Teachers' outside-classroom tasks were performed according to cultural gender-specific roles. However, these are also mediated by the concept of *va* – expected codes of behaviour that govern reciprocal relationships.

Conclusions and Policy Implications

Conclusions

The study found that the Samoan education system and schools do not challenge gendered roles as set by the *fa'aSamoa*: they tend to reinforce them, especially where they are concerned with 'appropriate' behaviour. The education system, in general, reinforces dominant gendered notions, stereotypes, identities and relationships. These notions are steeped in the values, beliefs, norms and expectations of Samoan culture, which have been moderated somewhat by the cultures of the Bible and Christian beliefs and values.

The study found that schools have the potential to facilitate the development of knowledge and skills and lay foundations for empowerment and transformation, but that the intentions and purposes of the co-educational schools and the single-sex school were different.

In the single-sex school, gender equality is considered to be a non-issue as there are only girls in the school. The principal and teachers interviewed are also unapologetic that they teach girls to be 'girls'. The purpose of the school, therefore, is to enhance the roles of females as generally perceived by Samoan society, which are to be good mothers and nurturers of family members and the community. The role of females as breadwinners is a secondary consideration in this school. Staff members hold strongly gendered, stereotypical beliefs about the roles of girls and women. The small total enrolment of students may reflect changing perceptions in the community and among parents in terms of their expectations of the education their daughters should get.

In the three co-educational schools, there is a general consensus that all students should have their individual potential developed through schooling processes. The general perception is that the opportunities, the provisions, the processes and management of school all contribute equally to the development of boys and girls.

However, the study found that boys may be placed in an unequal position relative to girls in the often unconscious processes of managing students in and outside the classroom, in classroom interactions and in the expectations of the teachers. All teachers expect that girls will do well and that boys will underachieve. Hence, there are strong elements of a self-fulfilling prophecy in the organisational decisions and activities carried out, especially by the teachers.

The study affirmed that girls and indeed females in Samoan traditional society have a high status within their own families, and in the rural areas in particular this translates into affirmative action that places girls in advantageous positions within the school. Schools in rural areas tend to reinforce the cultural norms of gender. The picture is not as clear for urban schools: there is some evidence that the cultural norms of gender are being challenged in these schools.

The study found that the experience of girls in the single-sex school was not the same as that of girls in the co-educational ones. In the single-sex school in the study, stereotypical roles of girls/females are strongly emphasised, which delimits opportunities for these girls when they leave school. The fact that stereotypical gender roles are actually encouraged in this school by the principal and teachers provides a real challenge. The study also found that the future of this school is uncertain, with falling rolls as parents opt to send their children to co-educational schools. It is possible that the ethos of this school has become outdated and less acceptable to parents.

There are school activities that encourage gendered notions held by the community, for example, the notion that boys should protect girls and defer to them in appropriate contexts. These notions affect people's behaviour towards one another. Yet they are being challenged as young people become more and more exposed to the outside world. If behaviour changes are observed whereby boys exhibit disrespectful behaviour towards girls, the school will challenge that behaviour by teaching the gender role of boys acting as protectors of girls.

Boys' underachievement is an issue in secondary schools and must be addressed by Samoa in order to adhere to its policies of equity, quality, relevance and efficiency. This study suggests that schools do reinforce the cultural gendered notions, identities and relationships of Samoan culture, with the resulting outcome of boys underachieving. The challenge is finding the best ways to enable gender equity and achieving equitable outcomes for both boys and girls. There is clearly a need for further research in this area.

Policy Implications

Participation in secondary education by all students in Samoa must be improved from its current level of about 48 per cent. This has implications for setting goals and action plans for improving gross and net enrolment at primary level. The latter is important, as this indicates the level of potential enrolments at secondary level.

Boys' participation and achievement in secondary schools must be addressed as a matter of urgency. Some of related issues that must be examined include the further development and sustainability of technical and vocational subjects in secondary schools. These issues have implications for both girls and boys.

There is a need to reform school pedagogy, management processes and teacher attitudes and approaches in order to address some of the gender issues of secondary schooling in Samoa. Some mission education systems might also need to address hard questions about educational equity. This is particularly so where single-sex girls schools still exist, propagating the traditional roles of women as mothers and family caregivers and nothing else, thus limiting opportunities for girls.

CHAPTER 6

A Gendered Analysis of Secondary Schooling Processes in India

Shobhita Rajagopal
Institute of Development Studies, Jaipur

Introduction

India is the seventh largest country in the world, with a population of more than one billion. The 35 States and Union Territories present a varied landscape as there is endless diversity of population, climate topography, religious beliefs, languages and social, economic and cultural settings. While India is recognised as one of the world's fastest growing economies, the problems of contemporary India in the key, interlinked areas of poverty, literacy, health and nutrition are extensive and continue to be influenced by caste, class and gender considerations.

Recent government reports indicate that the levels of both human and gender-related development indices went up between 1996 and 2006 in India, but gender-based disparities continue to exist. While the estimated Human Development Index (HDI) increased from 0.584 in 1996 to 0.648 in 2006, the Gender Development Index (GDI) score for India remained lower than the HDI score over that 10-year period. Nonetheless, GDI scores increased from 0.568 in 1996 to 0.633 in 2006, implying that progress has been made. The aggregate Gender Empowerment Measure (GEM) for India was 0.413 in 1996 and 0.451 in 2006. Although this is higher than the GEM scores for India estimated by the UNDP in 1998, the values attained still reflect the existence of sharp disparities in gender empowerment. The scores also reflect that women in India have particularly low power over economic resources (Government of India [GoI], 2009).

A critical issue in the Indian context is the marginalisation of women/girls that occurs based on gender – the social and cultural definitions of 'male' and 'female'. Gender-based inequalities/disparities are deep rooted in the realm of culture, and are found across social groups and communities. The material basis and unequal power that underlie social relations between men and women influence the allocation of resources, roles and entitlements at the level of individual households and thereby influence decision-making in relation to the education of children, especially girls (Nambissan, 2004).

Ensuring gender equality in education has been a key objective of educational policy in India for more than two decades. The National Policy on Education (NPE) formulated in 1986, articulated the commitment towards 'education for women's equality' as a vital component of the overall strategy of securing equity and social justice in education. The focus was not only on providing equality in educational opportunity, but on transforming the entire content and process of education, for achieving gender equality and a realignment of gender roles, to make them more equitable and harmonious. Notwithstanding policy vision and the improvements made over the years, educational statistics in India continue to reveal gender disparities in access and achievement that sharpen particularly at the higher stages of schooling.

In the context of the above, the present study focused on exploring whether classroom and schooling processes in secondary schools question or reinforce the dominant unequal gendered patterns and how they do that in an Indian context. The study attempts to unravel the 'hidden curriculum' of gender in schools and seeks to arrive at school-based strategies to overcome the gaps. It is based on case studies of four senior/higher secondary schools in urban areas[1] of Jaipur city, Rajasthan, wherein the interplay of gender in schooling processes was observed at the level of everyday school practice and experience.

The chapter is divided into five sections. The introductory section gives the background of the study, while the following section presents an overview of the status of secondary education in India and Rajasthan. The chapter goes on to provide an introduction to the surveyed schools where classroom processes were observed, and then presents the main findings of the study. The concluding section makes some suggestions for policy and action.

Setting the Scene

Education in India

The progress towards achieving Education for All in India presents a mixed picture given the vast dimensions and diversity prevailing in the country. The role of education in facilitating social and economic progress is well recognised within policy and the decade of the 1990s–2000 has seen noteworthy progress in the field of elementary education. The concentrated efforts made within the education system to include girls at all levels have also brought about significant gains.

The efforts towards universalising elementary education led to huge expansion in provision of educational facilities, as well as improved enrolments in schools. According to the Eleventh Five Year Plan (2007–2012) the total enrolment at the elementary level increased from 159 million in 2001–2002 to 182 million in 2005–2006 an increase of more than 23 million. The Gross Enrolment Ratio at the elementary stage increased from 82.4 per cent in 2001–2002 to 93 per cent in 2004–2005, an increase of 11 per cent. However, the dropout rate at the elementary stages continues to be as high at 50.8 per cent (50.5 for boys and 51.3 for girls), with dropout rates for children from socially disadvantaged groups[2] being higher. The social gap in dropout rates is acute with respect to girls. Two thirds of adivasi students do not progress beyond class 8. The Eleventh Plan acknowledges this challenge and the need to re-orient education programmes to meet challenges of equity, retention and high-quality education (GOI, 2008).

Secondary education is seen as a vital link between elementary and higher education. It is intended to equip students with education, knowledge and skills that will prepare them to be active citizens, as well as enable them to respond appropriately to emerging changes throughout their lives.

A review of secondary education reveals that during the decade ending 2004–2005, enrolment at the secondary level increased at an average rate of 5.32 per cent. According to the Eleventh Five Year Plan (2007–2012), there are 101,777 secondary schools and 50,272 higher secondary schools in India. There are 24.3 million students enrolled at the secondary stage and 12.7 million enrolled at the higher secondary stages. The Gross Enrolment Ratio (GER) at the secondary level is 51.65 per cent and for higher secondary 27.82 per cent. The combined GER for both levels is only 39.91 per cent. However, the gender gaps are clearly evident at these stages with the GER for boys being 44.26 per cent as against 35.05 per cent for girls – a difference of 9.2 percentage points. The GER for scheduled caste (SC) students at the secondary stage is 45.4 per cent and for scheduled tribe (ST) students is even lower at 37.2 per cent. The GER for girls from these disadvantaged groups is 37.6 per cent and 30.5 per cent respectively. The Plan acknowledges that secondary education suffers from poor access and participation as well as equity and quality issues, and proposes setting up of a Mission for Secondary Education at the level of the Government of India to meet these challenges.

Several other reports and documents have pointed out to the need for a renewed focus on secondary education. The report of the Central Advisory Board of Education Committee (CABE) on Universalisation of Secondary Education (2005) calls for a significant shift in conceptualising secondary education in its structural as well as curricular dimensions. Further taking cognisance of the prevailing gender gaps, the report notes that ' … *gender discrimination operates as a hidden curriculum at all times as an extension of patriarchy embedded in society. It is only when the school curriculum empowers the child adequately, initially to understand, then question and finally deal with inequality and justice would she be in a position to seek equality and social justice in her life after school'.* The report specifically emphasises that secondary education essentially has to be the education of adolescence and experiences in schooling have to be designed to be responsive to the needs of transition (GOI, 2005).

This renewed emphasis on universalising secondary education necessitates that gender equality concerns are brought centre-stage, to enable girls to move beyond the elementary stages and access secondary schooling.

Regional context

The State of Rajasthan, the largest state in India, is situated in the northwest of the country. It has been traditionally identified as a state ranking low on human development. Up until the early 1980s, the state exhibited slow progress on almost all economic and social indicators. Poverty levels were high, literacy levels were low, especially among women, and health and demographic indicators were indifferent (GoR and Institute of Development Studies [IDS], 2008). This situation was largely attributed to the vastly varied geographical and ecological dimensions of the state – i.e. large desert areas, scattered settlements and poor communication systems, which made it difficult to deliver basic services of health, education and water to people

The recent Rajasthan Human Development Report (GoR and IDS, 2008) points out that Rajasthan's ranking among Indian states improved from 12 in 1981 to 9 in the 1990s. The HDI has been calculated at 0.710. It also notes that Rajasthan might achieve some Millennium Development Goals (MDGs) like those in standards of living. The MDGs that address issues in human attainment might be more difficult to achieve. The persistence of gender-based inequalities in all spheres of life and society can be seen as influencing development outcomes – especially in areas of health, education and work. The issues faced by women in the state are wide-ranging and stem from patriarchal controls and gender discrimination, both within the private and in the public domains.

Rajasthan is also a state where several innovative programmes were implemented during the 1980s and 1990s with government and non-government partnerships. Educational programmes like the *Shikshakarmi* Programme and *Lok Jumbish* focused on new ways of addressing education challenges and forged links with civil society organisations/NGOs and communities. Both these programmes centrally addressed issues of gender inequality in education. Rajasthan in fact served as a laboratory for educational innovation during this period, producing concepts now adopted in many other Indian states including the use of para-teachers, micro-planning, school mapping and development of village education registers, and a focus on empowerment and equity (Clarke and Jha, 2006).

Education in Rajasthan

The status of education improved remarkably in Rajasthan in the 1990s. This advancement is particularly reflected in the significant increases in literacy and enrolment in education. The Census of India 2001 indicates that the overall literacy rate in the state rose from 38.5 per cent in 1991 to 60.41 per cent in 2001. The literacy rate among males improved from 54.99 per cent in 1991 to 75.70 per cent in 2001 and among females from 20.44 per cent to 43.85 per cent. There has also been a significant increase in the literacy rates for scheduled castes and scheduled tribes. However, the male–female gap in literacy in the state continues to be wide, as female literacy was still 31.8 per cent points lower than male literacy in 2001.

In Rajasthan, school education is provided by a network of government, government-aided and private schools. The state has witnessed considerable expansion in the number of schools in the past two decades, and it is claimed that all settlements have been provided with a primary school.

The annual progress report of the Department of Elementary Education states that there are a total of 12.89 million children enrolled at the elementary level in Rajasthan. Girls constitute 44.91 per cent of the total enrolment at the elementary stage (GoR, 2008a). Even though the state government has put in place various incentives to promote education of girls, the enrolment of girls has increased at a slow pace from 39.65 in 2000-2001 to 44.91 per cent in 2007-2008. While there is evidence that gender gaps are closing at the primary level, the gender gap at the upper-primary level continues to pose a challenge.

The Gross Enrolment Ratio (GER) is reported to be 115.03 at the primary level (115.81 for boys and 114.22 for girls) and 109.49 at the upper-primary level. The Net Enrolment Ratio (NER) at the primary level is 98.50 and 98.34 at the upper primary level (GoR, Data for Elementary Education [DISE] 2007-2008). However these official figures need to be read with caution, as they often do not reflect the 'real' picture.

One of the major problems confronting elementary education in the state is the low level of retention in schools. A large percentage of children who enter class 1 drop-out before completing class 5. The official data indicates that in 2007-2008, the retention rate at the primary level was 83.85. The dropout rate at the primary level was reported to be 12.44 per cent and for upper primary it was 5.85.per cent (GoR, AWPB Report, 2008-2009).

A major reason cited for poor retention in schools is the quality of education imparted in government schools. The Annual Status of Education Report (ASER) 2005 noted that students' learning levels, especially their writing and mathematical abilities, were extremely poor in Rajasthan. The report reveals 31.5 per cent of children (11-14 years) could not read a standard II level story and in basic arithmetic, 42.3 per cent of children (11-14 years) were unable to solve a division problem (3 digits by 1 digit) (Pratham, 2005).

The draft Eleventh Five Year Plan (2007-2012) document of the Government of Rajasthan points out that:

> '... though in the last five years issues related to access and infrastructure have been addressed to a large extent, still there are critical areas like quality of education, retention of students, gender disparity and upgradation of skills of teachers which have to be given focused treatment so as to ensure UEE [universal elementary education] and providing equal opportunities to disadvantaged groups' (GoR 2007:3.25).

While ensuring access to schooling is an important step towards UEE in the state, poor retention, high dropout rates and poor scholastic achievements have resulted in low enrolment ratios at the secondary level for both boys and girls.

Secondary education

The Department of Secondary Education manages secondary education in Rajasthan. Secondary schooling comprises classes 9–10 and senior/higher secondary includes classes 11–12 respectively. Public examinations are conducted by the Rajasthan State Board of Secondary Education for classes 10 and 12.

According to the Annual Report of the Department of Secondary Education (2007–08) there are a total of 8,288 secondary schools and 5,319 senior secondary schools functioning in the state. There are 301 secondary schools for girls and 504 senior secondary schools functioning exclusively for girls in the government sector (GoR, 2008b).

In the year 2007–2008 there were 2.17 million students (1.45 million boys and 710,000 girls) in the 14–18 years age group enrolled in secondary and senior/higher secondary schools. The percentage of girls to total enrolment was 32.9 per cent. While enrolment of girls has been increasing over the years, the trend over the last five years indicates that there has been only a marginal increase in the proportion of girls enrolled each year (see Table 6.1) (GoR, 2007).

The recent Gender Responsive Budgeting Report for Education published by the Government of Rajasthan (GoR, 2006) indicates that the low enrolment rate of girls in secondary schools is reflected in the lower state expenditure on girls for secondary education. In the year 2007–2008, 32.9 per cent of the total education budget was spent on girls. The expenditure per girl student works out to be 8000 Indian rupees (Rs) per annum.

Table 6.1. Increase in enrolment in secondary and senior secondary schools

Year	Boys (millions)	Girls (thousand)	Total	% of girls
2001–02	1.04	399	1.44	27.7
2002–03	1.11	435	1.55	28.2
2003–04	1.18	475	1.65	28.7
2004–05	1.24	513	1.75	29.3
2005–06	1.30	567	1.87	30.4
2006–07	1.35	656	2.00	32.7
2007–08	1.45	710	2.17	32.9

Source: GoR (2007–2008)

The near lack of focus on secondary schooling is clearly evident in the state. The high level of gender disparity at the secondary and senior secondary levels between boys and girls, indicates that girls tend to disappear from education over the age of 14 years, at a crucial age when aspirations can be channelled into opportunities.

Government initiatives to promote girls' education

Several initiatives have been put in place by the state government to encourage enrolment of girls in secondary education. These include:

- Girls enrolled in classes 1 to 12 are exempt from paying school fees.

- All girls studying in government schools are provided with free textbooks from class 1 to 12.

- To encourage enrolment of rural girls at the secondary and higher secondary stages, girls' hostels have been established in six divisional headquarters, each one catering for 50 girls.

- A *Balika Shiksha* (girls' education) foundation was established in 1994–95 to encourage education among girls. The foundation provides financial assistance for higher studies to deserving girls coming from poor families.

- Since 1997–98, the Board of Secondary Education, Rajasthan, has been providing cash awards to all girls who score more than 75 per cent aggregate marks in class 10. A scholarship of Rs1000/- per annum is provided to pursue education in classes 11 and 12.

- Several scholarships have also been provided for girls belonging to scheduled caste, scheduled tribe and nomadic families.

- The distribution of bicycles to girls who pass class 9 and are enrolled in class 10 has been initiated.

- Girls studying in classes 9 to 12 have also been provided with free transportation. The Rajasthan State Transport Corporation has been directed to issue free bus passes to girls studying in secondary and senior/higher secondary schools to ensure easy access to schools.

- An insurance scheme has also been introduced for girls enrolled in the secondary and senior secondary schools.

Despite the above-mentioned initiatives, gender-gaps continue to persist at all levels of education in Rajasthan and show that such gaps are bridging at a slow pace. It is evident that the socialisation of girls and gender-based division of labour continue to determine whether girls will be sent to school, for how long and why, thereby influencing educational access, participation and outcomes for girls.

The research

The schools and student enrolment

The four government schools identified for the research included two co-educational schools and two single-sex schools, one of girls and the other of boys respectively. Two schools were located in the urban periphery and two within the city limits. The four schools identified were:

- Government senior higher secondary school (GSHSS), HP (co-educational)
- Government senior higher secondary school, MW (co-educational)
- Government senior higher secondary school, MN (boys)
- Government senior higher secondary school, MN (girls)

All the four schools had classes from 6 to 12. The total enrolment in the surveyed schools was 1,288 (720 boys and 568 girls). There were a total of 69 teachers working in the schools (42 women and 27 men). In three of the schools, there were more women teachers than men teachers. According to government policy, no male teachers are appointed in schools that are exclusively for girls (see Table 6.2).

In all four schools, the language of instruction was Hindi. The schools offered only the humanities stream and the subjects offered in the senior classes included Hindi, economics, history, political science and geography. The lack of other streams like science and commerce were cited as being one of the reasons for students dropping out at the senior level in these schools.

A school fee is charged for all students in the schools, but varied according to the stage, sex of the child and caste affiliation. While policy pronouncements indicate that education is free for girls, girls enrolled in classes 6–12 have to contribute towards the development fund of the school. An annual sum of Rs75 (nearly US$1.5) is charged for girl students for upper primary, and Rs101 (nearly US$2) for secondary and senior secondary. Similarly, girls from the general category caste groups enrolled in classes 9–10 and classes 11–12 have to pay a sum of Rs200 and Rs300 respectively

Table 6.2. General information about the schools surveyed

School	Type of school	Level of school	Co-ed/ single-sex	Number of teachers		
				Male	Female	Total
GSHSS-HP	Govt.	VI to XII	Co-ed	7	13	20
GSHSS-MW	Govt.	VI to XII	Co-ed	11	4	15
GSHSS-MN boys	Govt.	VI to XII	Boys	9	15	24
GSHSS-MN girls	Govt.	VI to XII	Girls	–	10	10
			Total	27	42	69

towards the student fund. The girls from SC/ST and OBC category caste groups have to pay half the amount charged for general category caste groups.

School infrastructure and facilities

Physical infrastructure is an important aspect of the teaching/learning enterprise. While in recent years there has been a concentrated effort to improve infrastructure facilities in primary and upper-primary schools under various programmes, funds for improving infrastructure facilities at the secondary and senior secondary levels are usually raised at the school level, through the development fund or through individual donations.

All the schools surveyed functioned in government-owned '*pucca*' buildings and the school buildings were relatively in good condition and belied our expectations of poor infrastructure. The number of classrooms was sufficient given the present enrolment. In all the four schools, classroom furniture consisted of wooden or iron desks, benches and stools and a table and chair for the teacher. In most schools the furniture had been purchased out of the development fund.

Drinking water facilities were available in all the surveyed schools, but there were issues raised about availability of clean water. All the four schools had electricity, but in the schools located on the urban periphery the electricity supply was irregular. Separate toilet facilities were available for boys and girls, women and men teachers in all schools. In the HP co-educational school there was no tap connection in the toilets. This issue had been raised by the women teachers time and again. The girls in the MN girls' school complained that the toilets were unhygienic, as they were not cleaned every day (See Table 6.3).

A library facility with a separate room was available in only two of the schools (see Table 6.4). In MW co-educational school, the library was also the staff room and in the MN girls' school, the books were placed in the storeroom. The number of books in the libraries ranged from 450–2,700. The books included reference books, storybooks, life histories and inspirational material.

Table 6.3. Infrastructure facilities in the schools surveyed

School	No. of classrooms	Drinking water	Electricity	Toilet facilities			
				Common	Male	Female	Water facilities
GSHSS-HP	8	Tap	Yes	Yes	Yes	Yes	No
GSHSS-MW	9	Tank	Yes	–	Yes	Yes	Yes
GSHSS-MN boys	10	Tap	Yes	–	Yes	Yes	Yes
GSHSS-MN girls	8	Tap, water cooler	Yes	–	–	Yes	Yes

Table 6.4. Infrastructure facilities in the schools surveyed

School	Library facilities	Separate library room	Number of books	Play-ground	Games Girls	Boys	Computers (No.)
GSHSS-HP	Yes	Yes	2,700	No	Cricket, table tennis, *kho-kho*, *kabaddi*	*Kho-kho*, badminton	5
GSHSS-MW	Yes	With staff room	2,800	Yes	Cricket, *kho-kho*, *kabaddi*	Badminton, *kho-kho*, *kabaddi*	3
GSHSS-MN boys	Yes	Yes	490	Yes	Cricket, *kho-kho*, *kabaddi*	–	17
GSHSS-MN girls	Yes	With store room	450	Yes	–	Badminton, athletics, *kabaddi*	2

Computer science is a subject only in classes 9 and 10. All the schools had been provided with computers and had appointed computer instructors.

Out of the four schools, three had large playgrounds. The common games played by girls and boys included *kho-kho*, badminton, table tennis and *kabbadi*.

Position of teachers

There were a total of 69 teachers working in the four surveyed schools (27 men and 42 women). Their educational qualifications ranged from senior higher secondary to post graduation, with a required professional degree in education (BEd). In Rajasthan, the educational qualifications required for being selected as a government school-teacher are as follows:

- Primary teacher (grade 3 in Rajasthan): 12 years of general education and Before School Teaching Course (BSTC) training (2 years) qualified to teach classes 1 to 5.

- Senior teacher (grade 2 in Rajasthan): 12 years of schooling, bachelor's degree (BA, BCom or BSc) and one-year bachelor's in education (BEd) – qualified to teach classes 6 to 8.

- Lecturer (grade 1 in Rajasthan): 12 years of schooling, bachelor's degree and postgraduate qualification (MA, MCom, MSc) and three-year bachelor's in education (BEd) – qualified to teach classes 9 to 12.

In the surveyed schools there were 15 lecturers, 24 second grade teachers and 24 third grade teachers working (See Table 6.5). An analysis of the total number of sanctioned posts and vacant posts revealed some gaps. While teachers were in position, it was ironic that no teacher had been appointed to teach those very subjects that the school was offering as part of the choices open to students. In the MN boys' school, three second grade and three third grade teachers were on deputation to other schools, although their salaries were drawn/paid from this school. A physical training instructor (PTI) was appointed in all schools.

The poor quality of teaching/learning in the schools, inadequate numbers of teachers and teachers' lack of commitment are often seen as problems affecting the educational system across the state. Given that the schools covered in the present study were in urban areas, the problem of vacancy was not extensive. However, one of the major issues confronting the surveyed schools was that there were no teachers to teach some subjects, while there was a surplus in other subjects. Teachers' being on deputation to other schools was another problem area. It was pointed out that many of the teachers who were 'extra' or on deputation used political influence and always manipulated their postings.

Student enrolment in surveyed schools

The total enrolment in the surveyed schools in the year 2006–2007 was 1,288 (720 boys and 568 girls). The share of girls' enrolment was 44 per cent. The share of girls' enrolment in classes 6 to 8 was 46 per cent, while in classes 9–12 it was 43 per cent.

Table 6.5. Number of teacher posts sanctioned and teachers by grade

Type of Post	HP		MN		MN (Boys)		MN (Girls)		Total	
	PS	Working	PS	Working	PS	Working	PS	Working	PS	Working
Principal	1	1	1	1	1	1	1	1	4	4
Lecturer	5	5	5	4*	5	5	3	1	18	15
Grade 2 teacher	6	5	6	6	8	8 **	5	5	25	24
Grade 3 teacher	8	8	2	2	9	9 **	5	5	24	24
PTI	1	1	1	1	1	1	1	1	4	4
Librarian	1	1	1	1	1	1	1	Vacant	4	3
OA	–	–	–	–	1	1	–	–	1	1
UDC	1	1	1	1	1	1	1	1	4	4
LDC	1	1	1	1	1	1	1	1	4	4
Peon	5	1	4	3	5	4	1	1	15	9

PS=Posts sanctioned *Economics lecturer post is vacant ** Three teachers from each grade are on deputation

PTI=Physical training instructor OA=Office administrator UDC=Upper division clerk LDC=Lower division clerk

A comparison of the enrolment figures of the surveyed schools between the years 2001–2002 and 2006–2007, indicates that while the total share of girls' enrolment increased by 5 per cent, overall enrolment has fallen by 23 per cent over the five-year period (See Table 6.6 and 6.7). Reasons for the drop in enrolment can be attributed to the increase in the number of private schools in the vicinity, the poor quality of teaching and learning in the government schools and limited subject options.

Further, in the year 2001–2002 the ratio between boys and girls at the upper primary level was 53:47. This ratio dropped to 68:32 in classes 9 to 12, clearly indicating that there were fewer girls accessing the senior stages of schooling. In 2006–2007, while there was no significant difference in the ratio between boys and girls in the upper primary sections, the share of girls' enrolment in classes 9 to 12, increased by 11 per cent, an encouraging trend. This increase in girls' enrolment can be attributed to the various incentives introduced by the government to promote girls' education in the last five years.

Table 6.6 Enrolment in surveyed schools (2001–02)

School	Class 6 to 8			Class 9 to 12			Total		
	Boys	Girls	Total	Boys	Girls	Total	Boys	Girls	Total
GSHSS-HP	159	111	270	253	83	336	412	194	606
GSHSS-MW	68	68	136	43	66	109	111	134	245
GSHSS-MN boys	185	–	185	299	–	299	484	–	484
GSHSS-MN girls	–	190	190	–	136	136	–	326	326
Total	412	369	781	595	285	880	1007	654	1661
% share of enrolment	53	47	100	68	32	100	61	39	100

Table 6.7 Enrolment in surveyed schools (2006–2007)

School	Class 6 to 8			Class 9 to 12			Total		
	Boys	Girls	Total	Boys	Girls	Total	Boys	Girls	Total
GSHSS-HP	126	57	183	221	97	318	347	154	501
GSHSS-MW	72	69	141	61	73	134	133	142	275
GSHSS-MN Boys	77	–	77	163	–	163	240	–	240
GSHSS-MN Girls	–	109	109	–	163	163	–	272	272
Total	275	235	510	445	333	778	720	568	1288
% share of enrolment	54	46	100	57	43	100	56	44	100

Exploring the Bias: Gender & Stereotyping in Secondary Schools

The enrolment of students by caste indicates that a majority of boys enrolled in the schools are drawn from the SC (33 per cent), ST (5 per cent) and OBC (28 per cent) categories, while girls from the general category caste groups and SC/ST/OBC groups taken together are almost equal. The representation of students from the Muslim minority was negligible in the surveyed schools (See Table 6.8).

The enrolment data clearly indicates that government schools are increasingly catering to children from economically and socially disadvantaged groups, especially girls. Given the changing composition of the government schools, it is imperative that specific strategies are put in place to make schooling a meaningful experience for these students, particularly girls.

Main Findings

This section presents the main findings emerging from the case studies of the surveyed schools. These are based on observations, focus group discussions with students, teachers, and administrative staff and in-depth interviews with principals and education managers.

Classroom and outside-classroom processes

The relationship established between the students and the teacher within the classroom has a strong bearing on the quality of education, gender and social equity. The teachers are seen in their roles as 'knowledge providers' who will cater to the needs of both girls and boys equally. It is also critical to bear in mind that teachers do not enter the classroom as gender-neutral personalities, but are likely to have internalised a gender ideology through years of socialisation (Muoito, 2004). An effort was made therefore to understand whether these ideologies permeate into classroom practice.

Classroom observation was carried out in 22 classroom situations to gain some insight into current classroom processes and practices. The classes covered were classes 8, 9 and 10. The subjects covered included English, Hindi, science, mathematics and social science. Both male and female teachers were observed while

Table 6.8. Enrolment in surveyed schools by caste (2006–2007)

School	General caste		SC		ST		OBC		Minority		Total		
	Boys	Girls	Boys	Girls	Boys	Girls	Boys	Girls	Boys	Girls	Boys	Girls	Total
HP	83	44	122	51	13	4	129	55	–	–	347	154	501
MW	39	54	42	28	16	37	36	23	–	–	133	142	275
MN-B	92	–	87	–	9		48				236	–	236
MN-G	–	177	–	27	–	48	–	47	–	2	–	272	272
Total	214	275	251	106	38	89	213	125	–	2	720	568	1,288

teaching. The non-classroom activities observed included morning assembly, a computer class and games.

While some similar patterns were discernible in all four schools, each school also revealed some differences in the approach and process of teaching and learning.

The classroom setting

Box 6.1. A view of the classroom: extract from fieldwork

In a co-educational school

The classroom occupied by the students of class 8 in HP school was spacious with adequate light. There were 20 students present in the class, 10 boys and 10 girls. The teacher's table and chair was kept in front of the blackboard. There were three rows of iron desks with stools facing the teacher's table. Gender segregation was clearly visible. Girls were sitting on one side and the boys on the other. The primary teaching aids used by the teacher were a blackboard and chalk.

In a single-sex school

The classroom in the MN girls' school was airy and well lit, as there were several windows. A framed picture of Goddess Saraswati adorned the wall above the blackboard. The teacher's desk was placed in the middle of the room in front of the blackboard. There were several rows of wooden desks and benches facing the teacher's desk where the girls were seated. The classroom had fans, which were functional. All the girls had placed their schoolbags neatly on the back benches (Field Notes, 2007).

In the surveyed schools, the classrooms were airy, ventilated with adequate natural light, but they were poorly maintained. In the MN girls' school, the principal admitted that due to a shortage of support staff, girls had to clean their own classrooms. In the HP co-educational and MN boys' schools, the classrooms were not cleaned daily, but on a weekly basis by cleaning staff contracted to do this work.

The only teaching aids available in the classrooms were the blackboards and chalk. In two schools, some of the blackboards were in poor condition – the paint had chipped off making it difficult for students to read what was written. In some classrooms, there were no dusters to clean the blackboard and the teachers were seen using pieces of crumpled paper.

In all the classrooms, the teacher's desk and chair occupied a central place of authority. The general pattern was that the teacher's desk was placed in front of the blackboard and there were rows of desks and benches/stools (both wooden and iron) for the students facing the desk.

Sex segregation was ubiquitous in the seating arrangements in both the co-educational schools. Girls and boys sat separately in rows, an aisle acting both as a physical as well as a symbolic divide between them, a 'gender boundary' as it were. The teachers seemed happy with this arrangement and felt that mixed seating arrangements could lead to 'problems' and parents' displeasure. In the single-sex schools, the seating arrangement followed the same pattern – there were rows of desks and benches facing the teacher's desk where girls and boys sat with their friends.

According to government policy, textbooks are distributed to all students in government schools free of cost. In the surveyed schools, the prescribed textbooks had been distributed to students who had paid their fees and sought admission. Discussions with teachers revealed that a number of students had requested that they pay their fees in July, when the schools reopened after summer break. The inability of students to pay the fees was closely related to the fact that the majority students enrolled in these schools belonged to families with low earnings who could not pay the required amount on time. Some teachers also stated that they often paid the fees for students so that they could get the set of textbooks.

Teacher time and attention

As the academic session had only just begun at the time of the study, the teachers were in the process of teaching the initial lessons in all subjects. Most teachers seemed casual in their approach and were observed teaching without preparation. Only a few female teachers initiated the lesson by recalling what had been taught in previous classes.

The teacher time and attention in all four schools was contingent on the subject being taught as well as the sex of the teacher. For instance, those seen teaching social sciences were merely seen reading and dictating portions from the textbook. The transaction was mostly one way, the teacher dictating and students taking notes, with an occasional question thrown in. The science, mathematics and language teachers engaged more with the children and used the blackboard extensively.

There were nine girls present in class 10 in the MN girls' school. The topic being taught by Ms K, the English teacher, was the past indefinite tense and past continuous tense. The teacher wrote several sentences in Hindi on the blackboard and asked the girls to read out the sentences. The teacher wrote several other sentences on the blackboard and asked the girls to translate them into English, then wrote out a few 'fill in the blanks'. The girls copied the sentences from the blackboard into their notebooks. The girls discussed the possible answers among themselves. The teacher translated the Hindi sentences into English slowly so that the girls could comprehend.

It was observed that in both the co-educational and single-sex schools, teachers were familiar with the students and both women and male teachers made an effort to give positive reinforcement to both boys and girls. Most of the teachers used gender-neutral language. Some teachers addressed the students as *beta* (son), a generic term in Hindi which is used for both boys and girls.

It was also observed the overarching concern of the teachers was that the students should pass the annual examination rather than assessing if the students had actually understood a concept/lesson or not.

Student participation

Classrooms observation revealed that students passively received what was being taught and responded only when asked a question. No student made an effort to seek clarification or raise a question on his or her own.

There was a clear gender difference in the responses of girls and boys in the co-educational schools and the single-sex schools. In both the co-educational schools, boys studying in class 10 were more active compared to girls. The girls were shy and inhibited. When a teacher asked a question, they would stand up with their heads bowed. Even when they knew the answers to the questions posed they remained silent. In contrast, the boys were eager to respond. Discussions with teachers in these schools revealed that girls often chose to remain silent, as they feared ridicule by the boys, especially if they were not able to answer a question. It was also observed that when girls were in the majority in a class, they were more responsive and answered all questions.

Student–student interaction

The student–student interaction was limited to sharing a textbook or helping each other with answers to questions posed by the teacher. In the co-educational schools, there was no interaction between boys and girls within the classroom. The gender lines were clearly drawn. The space for healthy interaction between boys and girls was limited both within the classroom and outside.

Non-classroom activities

The non-classroom activities that the students were involved in included games, computer sessions and morning assembly.

A typical day in all the surveyed schools began with a morning assembly. The general pattern followed in all schools during assembly (across the state) is that the students recite a prayer and some *shlokas*, take a patriotic oath, read the newspaper and do some warm up exercises.

In the MW co-educational school, the morning assembly began at 7.15 am. Girls and boys stood in separate rows. The physical instructor (PTI), along with two girls who were leading the morning session, stood facing the students. Other male teachers stood behind the students. The assembly began with the girls reciting the prayers, which were followed by some *shlokas* and a patriotic oath. After the girls finished, a boy was asked to come forward and read out portions from the local newspaper. The PTI then made the students do some physical exercises. The entire assembly took 15 minutes. The assembly dispersed and the students went into their classrooms.

The games played by students in the schools included badminton, table tennis, *kho-kho*, *kabbadi*, racing, cricket and volleyball. Some students had also participated in school-level competitions and won prizes.

In one of the co-educational schools, it was observed that girls were playing badminton in the courtyard as there is no playground. Later discussions with girls revealed that they are not allowed to go out of the school gates during recess to play. In contrast, the boys are free to go out of the school premises and play. It was observed that even while playing the game, the girls were inhibited and shy. Their movement was restricted on the court. Discussions with the girls revealed that they also wanted to learn table tennis, but boys monopolised the table and girls never got a chance to play.

Computer education is part of the curriculum at secondary level in Rajasthan. All the surveyed schools had been provided with computers and instructors had also been appointed.

In the MW co-educational school, the computer class for class 10 was held in the computer room next to the principal's office. Three computers had been placed on computer tables along one side of the wall. There were no chairs, but benches to work on the computer. The young instructor started the lesson and informed the students he would be teaching them some basic operations related to Microsoft Word. He then proceeded to write the various steps in English on the blackboard. He asked the students to note down the steps in their notebooks. The instructor explained the various steps to the students in Hindi. He then asked four boys and two girls to sit at the computer table and demonstrated the steps to create a Folder. The instructor guided the boys and girls when they made mistakes. The teacher was friendly with the students and encouraged both boys and girls equally.

The observations clearly revealed that teaching and learning in the classroom is dry and didactic, with teachers reproducing textbook information while children listen passively. A few teachers were seen to engage more actively with the students, but this was not the norm. No effort was made by the teachers to link classroom knowledge to the everyday experiences of children. Nor was any effort made to use any teaching/learning material. Sex segregation is the accepted social norm, and is followed in most co-educational schools. The classrooms failed to provide an environment where gender differences are minimised and healthy interaction between boys and girls is promoted. The non-participation of the girls in the classroom and in games also reflected socialisation patterns wherein girls internalise a subordinate position vis-à-vis boys/men. While there was no overt gender differentiation in the attention teachers gave to students or in the use of language, the pervasive presence of gender and the constant legitimisation of gender distinctions were visible in classroom practices and environments.

Teachers' expectations, perceptions, language and behaviour

Focus group discussions with both female and male teachers clearly brought out their perceptions on gender and schooling processes. A total of 36 teachers participated in the discussions, representing both the younger and older age groups. There were teachers with experience spanning 30 years and others who had recently joined the profession. The majority had experience working in both co-educational and single-sex schools and in rural and urban areas.

Identity and self-image

Responses on self-image and perceptions regarding their own sexual identity as a male or female did not lead us far, although some of the responses were predictable and politically correct. The male teachers stated that they were proud of 'being men' and believed women and men to be equal. In their view, women and men had different sets of roles and responsibilities. Most men felt that their main role was to earn and provide for the family, and women were primarily seen in their role as 'homemakers' and 'caregivers'. Most women teachers forcefully stated that being a woman meant shouldering a whole range of responsibilities and maintaining a balance between the home and school, which was difficult due to absence of predictable support structures.

The women teachers in the MN girls' school felt that:

> '... even though we are educated, are working and contributing to the household income, the expectations within the household have not changed. If only the male members contributed to some work within the household we would feel less burdened.'

Equity issues and school policies

There was a clear divide in the perceptions of male and female teachers regarding equity issues in the schools. While most accepted that government policies did not discriminate/differentiate between women and men and the same rules were applicable to all, staff power dynamics were clearly discernable in task allocation, mobility and facilities.

Delegation of tasks

In all four schools, most teachers stated that the principal delegated various tasks to teachers on the basis of seniority, experience and interest. In each of the schools, teachers had been put in charge of various activities – admissions, cultural activities, the school development fund, shift in charge, health and sanitation, SUPW (socially useful and productive work), art education and so on. However, there were some

Exploring the Bias: Gender & Stereotyping in Secondary Schools

voices of dissent. Some teachers felt that personal preferences and whims of the principal influenced decisions related to tasks/responsibilities. Teachers generally felt that there was a 'coterie', which operated around the principal and decided 'who gets what'. This was also true of the single-sex girls' school, where there was a female principal and female teachers.

The women teachers in all the schools felt strongly that the entire education system was 'patriarchal', and gender inequality within school structures was a reflection of inequalities persisting in society. Male teachers were put in charge of important activities, while women were given responsibility for organising cultural activities. When a woman teacher was made responsible for an important task, male teachers did not like to work under her and did not co-operate.

The women teachers felt that they ended up having a greater workload than their male counterparts. For instance, they would often have to take more classes than the male teachers. A senior woman teacher in MW co-educational school stated:

'... there is a difference in the number of classes taken by women and male teachers. For example, according to government norms a lecturer is supposed to take 33 classes per week. The female teacher here takes 26 classes whereas the male teacher takes only about 11 classes. Similarly the second grade teachers are supposed to take a total of 36 classes. [Here] women take 30 classes, men only 22. When we discuss this issue in staff meetings it is not taken seriously.'

On the other hand, male teachers in the MN boys' school felt that they ended up doing all the work. They argued: '... there are too many problems with women teachers, they do not want to take responsibilities and always give an excuse and shirk work'.

Freedom and mobility

In all four schools, women teachers stated that male teachers had greater independence and mobility than women teachers. Men could come and go as they wished; they often went out of the school for their own personal work and no one questioned them. When a woman teacher left the school, it was always noticed and they had to give 'a thousand explanations'. The male teachers meanwhile complained that all 'outside' work had to be done by them, as women refused to do outside chores. The fact that most male teachers had their own vehicles, while women depended on public transport or a taxi service was also a reason cited for not delegating 'outside tasks' to women.

Facilities in school

One of the main issues raised by the women teachers with reference to gender equity policies was related to toilet facilities. The women teachers in the HP co-educational school complained that the toilets were located right in the courtyard and there was no privacy. There was no water connection in the toilets and the teachers said that they had made innumerable applications to the principal regarding a tap connection, but no action had been taken.

The non-availability of a separate staff room was also an issue raised by women teachers. In two of the schools, the teachers had to use the library as a staff room. In none of the schools was there any crèche facility for the young children of teachers.

Promotional avenues

Another point put forward by the women teachers related to the promotional avenues for women within the Department of Education. They pointed out that the chances of promotion and upward mobility for men were faster than for women. The women said that men had all the information, as they visited the offices of district education officers (DEOs) and other officials. Few women teachers had been promoted in the past 20 years (a point corroborated by the DEO for secondary schooling). The female teachers also resented the fact that there was no woman appointed as a DEO in the Department of Education, as there were several competent women who could do the job.

Attitudes towards gender equality

All the teachers were unanimous in stating that both boys and girls should receive equal educational opportunities. The women teachers in the MN boys schools were of the view that:

> 'In this modern world both boys and girls must receive education and must be encouraged to study. However, in the rural areas educating girls is still a problem and discriminatory practices are more visible there than in urban areas. Girls are groomed in a manner wherein they imbibe secondary roles and postures in school. Although we want the schools to provide an equal opportunity environment, society continues to treat women and girls as subordinate.'

Male teachers in the co-educational schools were of the opinion that:

> 'In recent years, women have joined various professions, which were traditionally male dominant. In this fast-changing world it was important that girls are educated and are encouraged to be economically independent'.

The majority of the teachers in the surveyed schools accepted that there were differences in the way boys and girls participated in the classroom. In the co-educational schools, the teachers felt that the girls were quieter in class and did not express themselves, but they worked harder and always finished their work on time. Boys were casual and had to be constantly pushed to work. All the teachers agreed that the boys always wanted to be 'one up', on the girls and were always competing with the girls. Some of the characteristics pointed out by the teachers for boys are girls are listed in Table 6.9 below.

Table 6.9. Gendered characteristics of students as seen by teachers

	Girls	Boys
	Responsible	Indifferent
	Quiet	Boisterous
	Serious	Laidback/casual
	Hardworking	Impatient
	Cautious	Competitive
	Disciplined	Aggressive
	Regular	Irregular

The teacher descriptions clearly point towards underlying social expectations, which cast girls as being responsible, quiet and hardworking. These notions highlight the continuities between socialisation into gender roles within the family and community and gender socialisation through schooling.

Teachers' expectations of students

There was a clear social bias in teachers' attitudes towards students from poorer and socially disadvantaged groups. The predominant notion held by the teachers (both women and men) was that the quality of students who enrol in government schools is 'weak'. Many of them are dropouts from private schools and their main aim is to pass the examinations. Some teachers felt that since the majority of the students belonged to socially marginalised groups and low-income families, their behaviour was not 'refined' – they used abusive language and the teachers had to control them. The teachers felt that they had to devote a lot of time and attention to see that 'these' children did well in schools. This middle-class bias was pervasive in all the schools.

Although teachers felt that all subjects were equally important for both girls and boys, in both the co-educational schools the teachers held the view that girls were better at languages, i.e Hindi and English. The teachers' views were divided on mathematics – some teachers felt that many girls feared mathematics and performed badly, while there were others who felt that both boys and girls feared maths. Many teachers were of the view that boys performed better in science than girls.

The women teachers in the both the co-educational schools as well as in the MN girls' school pointed out that due to the pressure of work in the household and lack of support, some girls were unable to devote time to home study. As a result, they found it difficult to complete their homework. They often carried these pressures to the school, and it was reflected in their academic performance.

Violence and harassment

All the teachers were of the view that they had to be extra cautious with girls, as they are more vulnerable to harassment and abuse. Under a special programme called *Operation Garima* (dignity), which aims to curb 'eve teasing' (harassment of girls) and is being implemented in the Jaipur district, a *Garima Prakosht* (a Dignity Cell) has been set up in the co-educational schools. In the MN girls' school, it was pointed out that some boys used to wait around the gate of the school and made lewd remarks at the girls. The school had to seek police intervention and plain-clothes officers were stationed in the area; they apprehended the boys who used to harass the girls.

In-service training

There is no institutionalised in-service training programme organised for secondary schoolteachers. Some teachers had attended training programmes on computer applications, life skills education, HIV/AIDS and the Scouts/Guides. None of the teachers had received training on gender issues. They felt that introducing gender issues in pre-service and in-service training would have only a partial impact. The teachers felt that attitudes needed to undergo a change at the household level. One of the teachers recollected how when she was posted in a rural school and had talked of equality between girls and boys, the community men had confronted her and asked, '*who was the teacher who was saying that boys and girls are equal*'. They were upset that she was giving the children 'wrong ideas'.

Guidance and counselling

The guidance provided by the teachers to students largely pertained to advising children on what subjects to pursue after schooling. The teachers also counselled children who wanted to discontinue their schooling, especially girls. Teachers cited several cases where girls wished to study further, but they had been withdrawn from school by their parents and 'married off'. However, no teacher had challenged or questioned the pressure to marry faced by girls.

The teachers we met spoke of gender equality at large and the importance of education for both boys and girls. They also agreed that there has been a discernable change in the past few years in terms of the enrolment of girls. Although most of the teachers accepted that there were marked gender differences in the behaviour of boys and girls within the classroom, few had made an effort to change the gendered environment or academic expectations. At the same time, however, it is also evident that workplace cultures and institutional habits are yet to become gender friendly. Issues related to status, conditions of employment and career development opportunities for women teachers point towards gender-differentiated patterns within the educational system and the limited spaces women have for voicing their concerns.

Gender analysis of textbooks and other learning materials

It has been argued for a long time that existing curricula in schools reinforce rather than question existing social norms and practices. A curriculum can be a gendered document in as much that it can express ideas about gender equality or it can reproduce ideas about divisions and inequalities stemming from caste, class, religion, ethnicity and national identities.

The textbooks of classes 8 and 10 were reviewed to understand how gender is represented in the textbooks with a focus on illustrations, content and pedagogy. The subjects reviewed included social science, Hindi, English and science. The textbooks prescribed up to elementary level (1–8) are published by the Rajasthan State Textbook Board, whereas textbooks for the secondary and higher secondary classes are produced by the Rajasthan State Board of Secondary Education.

An analysis by subject is presented below:

Social science

There is one textbook prescribed for social science in class 8 and two books for social science in class 10; they cover topics on history, geography, political science and sociology. All the textbooks are written by men. The lessons in the class 8 textbook cover a range of topics focusing both on India and Rajasthan. A review of 48 lessons reveals:

- The lessons are packed with too much information written in a brusque, monotonous style. There is an idealisation of Indian culture, traditions and society.

- All the illustrations presented in the class 8 book are poorly depicted, adding little value to the text. Representations of women are few and far between, with illustrations in just two lessons depicting women in non-traditional roles – as doctors, an engineer, a bus driver, a painter and a woman using an automatic teller machine (ATM). In the class 10 textbooks, there is not a single illustration depicting women. The chapter on 'Local Governance' shows two photographs of *gram sabha* and *gram panchayat* where there are only men sitting in the meeting. There is no mention of women as political subjects.

- There is a mechanical approach to the inclusion of gender in the textbooks. Women are only mentioned in six lessons. The opening chapter in the class 8 textbook entitled 'Social change' tries to present the changing role of women in India. It is stated that the social system is changing fast, and women are now seen as equal to men and are participating in all walks of life. The chapter goes on to describe the status of women in society. It also has a section on the various interventions/programmes being implemented for women.

- However, after this introductory chapter, in chapter 7 on 'Social and Economic Challenges' the section on sex discrimination reverts to clichéd statements like 'we need to bring harmony between men and women' and '*Yatra nariyastu pujyente, tatra ramante Devata'* – roughly translated as 'Where women are revered, there the Gods reside'– a common Sanskrit quote. In the class 10 textbook, the lesson titled 'Social Awareness' has a section on women's empowerment. Here again women are deified and the virtues of several women are eulogised. Names of a few contemporary women leaders are mentioned. The same section also talks about the various institutional mechanisms set up by government to combat social problems like child marriage, bigamy and the dowry system.

- The women protagonists who find a mention include Gargi, Maithreyi (women of intellect), Jhansi Ki Rani (the great fighter women), two women who were part of the tribal movement in Rajasthan and two local women saints – Gabri Bai and Amrita Devi.

- There is a clear absence of women's contributions in art and culture, science, mathematics and economics, the reform movement, the Indian freedom struggle etc. The contributions of male freedom fighters, leaders, local saints, scientists, mathematicians receive greater attention. Farmers are always depicted as male.

- Finally, the textbooks are full of stereotypical virtues of motherhood and clichéd concepts of femininity and women.

English

The English textbook for class 8 is authored by women, while the class 10 textbooks are written by men. There are two English textbooks prescribed for class 10 – a course reader and a rapid reader. The Preface in the class 10 textbook mentions that the textbooks have been prepared keeping in mind the background and standards of children in Rajasthan. There are a total of 57 lessons in the textbooks. The analysis shows that:

- Stories and passages by well-known male writers and authors – Rabindranath Tagore, Mahatma Gandhi, Ernest Hemmingway, Rudyard Kipling and J Krishnamurthy are included in the text. Only two stories written by women writers are included in the textbook.

- There are few women protagonists as compared to male protagonists. Out of 30 chapters in the class 8 textbook, women protagonists are present in just four lessons. Only two women are presented in non-traditional roles – as a scientist/doctor and a birdwatcher – while other women are seen in the roles of wife and daughter.

- Gendered titles indicating marital status are used in the text. There is considerable use of Anglo Saxon names in various lessons, presumably because it is an English textbook.

- The stories included in the textbook have titles like 'A Man's True Son', 'The Boy Who Tried', Jack and the Wolves', 'Man with a Magic Stick', as well as descriptions of men as merchants, kings, rich men, men as rescuers and as conquerors.

Hindi

Both women and men authored the Hindi textbooks. There are two textbooks prescribed for class 10 – one focuses on poetry and prose, while the other is a compilation of short stories and one-act plays. The review of a total of 62 lessons shows:

- There are 14 illustrations in the class 8 textbooks, of which six portrayed women.

- There is clear under representation of women writers/poets – in the class 8 textbook two stories are included by women writers and in the class 10 book only four stories were authored by women writers/poets out of 29 stories/plays/poems presented.

- Women protagonists are few and far between.

- The stereotype of a male provider and as a 'devta' (God) and marriage being central to a woman's identity is presented in a lesson called *Kartavya* (duty) in the class 8 textbook. Several stories depict men/boys as being strong, valorous, having high virtues of morality and character. Women are represented as mothers, as caregivers and as being emotional. In only two lessons are women represented as exercising a choice in marriage and as a fighter.

- Male writers dominate most of the literature presented. It is evident that the male-dominated literary discourse does not take into account women's lives, bodies or ways of being.

Science

The science textbooks are all written by male authors and cover biology, chemistry and physics. The class 8 textbook has 24 lessons, while there are two books prescribed for class 10. The review found:

- There are several illustrations in the class 8 textbook showing women in traditional roles – as mothers, woman serving food, women filling water at a handpump – while boys are shown riding a bicycle and going to school. The doctor is male, whereas a nurse is female. In the class 10 textbook, there is only one illustration of a woman – a photograph of Kalpana Chawla, the space scientist.

- The lesson on reproductive health talks about adolescence, the disadvantages of early marriage, especially for girls, and the need to make the right choices in a rather didactic manner.

- While a brief biographical sketch of Kalpana Chawla forms part of the lesson on 'Space and Information Technology' in the class 10 textbook, the following chapter on 'Life Sketch of Scientists and their Contributions' presents only male scientists.

- Women's contributions to science and technology are severely underrepresented.

The brief analysis presented above indicates that there is a trend among textbook writers to pack in as much of information or facts as possible, providing little space for self-exploration. The language used is also short and non-descriptive. Not surprisingly, the mode of communication in the classroom seemed determined by the text – dry and monotonous. In all the schools, teachers depended heavily on the textbook in the absence of any other teaching material.

Even though there have been some efforts to weave a gender perspective into the textbooks in Rajasthan, it is evident that these efforts have only led to 'token' shifts. Men continue to dominate the texts, both as writers and protagonists. Only the language textbooks in Hindi and English are authored by women, and under-representation of women is clearly evident in all the textbooks and across all subjects. There has been little effort to depict women in non-traditional roles or to portray them as capable of making choices. The textbooks are replete with traditional meanings of masculine and feminine.

It is clear that viewing gender in isolation from other hierarchies and asymmetries within society results in such tokenistic revisions. A gender perspective is not about adding a lesson on women's status or on women's empowerment, or making women visible in the text. It is important to recognise that unless a gender perspective is incorporated into textbooks, children will continue to absorb the biases of existing understandings of society and reproduce these ways of thinking in the future.

School management processes and practices

In the four schools covered during the study, the two co-educational schools had male principals, and the single-sex schools (girls and boys) had a female and a male principal respectively.

Awareness of gender

All the principals regarded gender issues as providing equal opportunities to boys and girls in schooling. They were of the view that since most of the students enrolled in their respective schools came from poor families, it was their responsibility as principals/teachers to guide the students and educate them so that they could improve their life situations.

The principals in the co-educational schools stated that their goal was to provide equal opportunities to both boys and girls and also to ensure that the teachers did not differentiate between girls and boys. They stated that in the school, girls were encouraged to speak their minds and be confident. The woman principal of the MN girls' school felt that in a co-educational or a boys' school, the principal had to maintain greater discipline and be strict. However, in a girls' school it was not difficult to maintain discipline: 'The atmosphere in this school is homely and the girls do not create problems'.

Delegation of tasks to teachers

All the principals were of the view that the teachers were given equal treatment in school and tasks were distributed on the basis of qualification and the teachers' interests rather than gender. The male principals pointed out that the women teachers were given extra consideration. Yet the male principals also had some reservations regarding their women colleagues. They felt that women refused to take on any extra responsibility and they also took too much leave of absence. They could not stay beyond school hours. One of the principals felt strongly that as head of the institution he had to keep a balance – '... male principals have to be very careful as women tend to allege harassment if action is taken against them. Women are vindictive and do not even spare other women'.

On the other hand, the female principal felt strongly that while official policies provided equal opportunities to both women and men within the Department of Education, there was a gap in implementation of these policies. Personal attitudes and preferences influenced many decisions. She also informed the research team that she was the one of the most senior principals in the district, but she had been sidelined and made a principal of an innocuous girls' school. The principal observed that:

> 'I have resigned myself to the situation. Women who are bold and articulate have no support within the system and women became easy targets for victimisation and character assassination. Women teachers are forced into silence, as they fear 'Badnami' (shame).

Her pessimism and cynicism perhaps echoed the state of women teachers within the larger system.

All the principals felt that apart from school-level responsibilities, the teachers were expected to participate in a number of government programmes: the pulse-polio campaign, census enumeration tasks, preparing and revising electoral lists etc. These tasks cut into teaching time. They felt that these added tasks disturbed the timetable, as substitute teachers had to be given teaching responsibilities.

Expectations of students

The principals were unanimous in stating that both boys and girls were intelligent and had unlimited potential. They felt that even though parents were not interested in educating girls, the girls were conscientious and hardworking, while boys were not interested in studies. They also felt that both boys and girl should be taught all subjects.

The female principal was of the opinion that socialisation patterns greatly influenced the behaviour of girls and boys in school. She felt that in a co-educational school there is a constant psychological pressure acting on the girls. Girls are scared that the boys will make disparaging remarks if they are active in class. As a result, only a few girls are able to speak up. Even if girls are knowledgeable, they are not articulate. She felt strongly that the parents were responsible for making girls 'weak'. She was of the view that since most of the girls in the school came from low-income families, they also witnessed violence around them. She stated that her aim was to provide a secure environment for girls in the school, as it was a space where they could be free from worries.

Curriculum and training

All the principals commented that there was scope for making the curriculum more gender sensitive. One male principal felt that gender issues could be taken into account in social science subjects, while in subjects like mathematics it was difficult to incorporate a gender perspective. They felt that regular teacher training and refresher courses should be organised for secondary and senior secondary teachers on various subjects, as well as on issues like gender. However, the male principals had clear reservations about introducing subjects like life skills education (LSE) and sex education in schools.

All the principals we met had years of experience behind them. Given the limited resources, the principals were all trying to make the best of their situations. They seemed committed to the idea of gender equality and improving the status of girls' education, but had done little to minimise gender differences in their respective schools. Their main preoccupation was limited to the day-to-day functioning of the school – managing school data, showing good results and steering clear of controversy. As one of the principals put it: '... the teacher can use any technique to teach the children – our concern is that the examination result should be good!'

Students aspirations, expectations, perceptions, language and behaviour

'My name is Pinky and I study in class 10 in the government secondary school. My father works in a shoe shop and my mother is a housewife. I have a brother who is three years younger [than] me. My parents want to educate me only up to standard 10, but I wish to study further. I wish to become a lawyer, but in our family girls are educated only up to secondary level.'

'My name is Rohit and I am a student of class 9. My father works in a steel factory and my mother is a housewife. I have a younger brother and a sister. I get up at 5.30 in the morning and get ready for school. After returning home from school, I have my lunch and do my homework. Thereafter I go out to play. I come back and eat with my brother and *sister. My brother and I rarely do any household work. My mother and sister perform all the domestic chores. I wish to study up to senior secondary level and then join the army.'*

Most students enrolled in the surveyed schools belonged to low-income families where the parents had varied occupations – drivers, tea vendors, electricians, tailors, laundry workers, painters and small traders, or they were involved in agriculture labour.

As the discussion method is rarely used in schools, a lot of interest emanated among boys and girls during the focus group discussions. While the gender divide was clearly maintained during the discussions, a noticeable difference observed was that the girls were equally articulate and forthright as the boys. The boys were eager to respond to all the issues, and it was difficult to ask them to wait for their chance to speak.

Self-image, aspirations and prevailing notions

The discussion in all the focus groups commenced by unravelling the notions of gender, self-image, perceptions and aspirations. The girls felt that they 'liked' being girls, as the government was supporting girls in many more ways than boys. The various incentives provided to the girls were making the girls more confident. However, the girls envied the freedom enjoyed by boys and wished that they could also have the same freedom and space as boys did. Some girls pointed out that, *'we cannot go alone to watch a movie. Our parents or someone older has to accompany us'*.

The girls clearly articulated that boys were given greater importance in families, as they are seen as 'heirs to the family name'. In most homes, the prevailing notion was that girls would study but get married and rear a family, while boys would study, get jobs and earn incomes. The girls felt that it was because of this image of a 'breadwinner' that boys were given more care and attention. The girls in the MN girls' schools articulated that though parents wanted to support the education of girls, if a girl failed to pass an annual examination, then invariably she was withdrawn from school. This was particularly true for the stages where public examinations are conducted, i.e. classes 8, 10 and 12. In contrast, if boys failed to pass an examination, they were given more chances to improve their performance. The girls were of the opinion that when parents are unable to pay school fees, it is invariably the girl who is withdrawn from school.

On the other hand, boys are proud to be born 'male' and did not want to exchange their sex and gender roles with girls. In the HP co-educational school, all the boys felt that they were better than the girls: '*... girls talk too much, fight a lot and have a habit of teasing'*, were the comments. Most boys accepted that few restrictions were imposed on them compared to girls.

The majority of girls wanted to continue their education, and their aspirations went beyond the household domain. They were confident that their families would support their pursuit of higher education. They aspired to be doctors, teachers, airhostesses, lawyers and government officers, while one of the girls wanted to do an MBA course. A few girls in the MN girls' school and the MW co-educational school were unsure whether they would be in a position to continue their education after schooling. The reasons cited included their family's poor financial situation, pressures to marry and the perceived low importance given to education of girls.

Most boys meanwhile aspired to be postgraduates and were confident that their parents would allow them to study as much as they desired. Choices of profession ranged from being teachers, doctors, cricket players, army and police officers, to chartered accountants and even property dealers. A few boys in the HP co-educational school had low-educational aspirations, as they knew they might not be able to continue their education beyond schooling. They stated that they would have to start work due to financial constraints. The expectations from boys within the household were that they would study and start earning. All the boys wanted to get married to girls who were educated.

Roles and responsibilities within households

The discussion on the nature of roles and responsibilities within households revealed that contributing to domestic chores was an intrinsic part of the daily routine for girls. The tasks included cleaning utensils, sweeping the house, cooking and serving food. Some girls said they liked to cook, other said that they did not like washing utensils and clothes, but there was little opportunity to refuse. Only a handful of girls said that they did not do any work, as there were others in the family who helped with housework. Some girls also said that they had to complete housework before coming to school.

'I get up at 5.00 in the morning. I sweep and mop all the rooms. I then get ready for school. I go back home and watch some television and do my homework. I then help to cook the dinner. My sister–in-law washes the [utensils]. Generally my father is served food first. My mother, sister-in-law and I eat after everyone has eaten.' **Parvati, class 10**

'My mother is a laundress and irons clothes from 8.00 in the morning to 8.00 in the evening. I have three brothers who are working. Since my mother is busy, I do all the household work and come to school. Sometimes I get no time to finish my homework.' **Geeta, class 9**

In contrast, the boys said that they get up early and get ready for school. A few boys performed outdoor tasks like going to the market, but none helped with other household chores. One boy said that, 'I have tried to make rotis, but I can never make them round'. Another commented that, 'I don't wash my clothes, my mother washes them for me'. All the boys accepted that girls have more responsibilities at home than boys.

Boys were not convinced that all the jobs could be done girls. They felt that since men/boys are physically stronger, they could accomplish several tasks that women/

Exploring the Bias: Gender & Stereotyping in Secondary Schools

girls could not do. Both boys and girls reported that there was no discrimination in distribution of food at the household level, and that all were treated equally by their parents.

Within the school

An effort was made to understand the roles and expectations of girls and boys within the school. The discussions on the distribution of classroom tasks revealed that in the co-educational schools both boys and girls were appointed as monitors. In the MN girls' school, the girls stated that a good student was chosen to be a monitor and it was her duty to clean the blackboard. The girls also revealed that they had to clean the classrooms, since there was no support staff in the school. In the HP co-educational school, the students stated that a member of the support staff carried out the task of cleaning the rooms. In both the co-educational schools the girls always led the morning assembly and recited the prayers. The girls were convinced that they could sing better than the boys. Table 6.10 outlines the gendered allocation of classroom tasks.

Both boys and girls were of the view that teachers did not discriminate in the classroom, and both boys and girls were made to work on the blackboard. It was evident that the students valued the teachers who were friendly and affectionate and disliked those who were strict and punished them. Most boys felt that female teachers were better than male teachers.

There was some difference in the subject preferences of boys and girls. The girls said they liked Hindi and English, which were followed by science and mathematics. Some girls indicated a dislike for social studies. The subjects preferred by boys included mathematics, English and science. All the boys wanted to be proficient in English as they felt it was a language that was widely used within and outside the country. The boys did not like Sanskrit, as they felt it was barely useful in everyday life.

Table 6.10. Gender allocation of classroom tasks

Tasks	Boys	Girls
Conducting morning assembly	–	✓(except in the boys school)
Fetching water	–	Girls serve water to visitors
Sweeping/cleaning classroom	–	✓(only in the girls school)
Monitoring class	✓	✓
Solving questions on blackboard	✓	✓
Running teacher errands	✓	✓
Serving tea for visitors	Carried out by	Carried out by
Teacher attention and behaviour	support staff	support staff

Extra curricular activities

In all the schools the students were unhappy with the limited games that they could play in school. The girls in the MN girls' school complained that there were very few games in the school, and some of the sport equipment was stored in trunks. The games girls played included *kho-kho*, *kabbadi* and athletics. Some girls had participated in tournaments in other districts. The boys in the MW co-educational school said that although they had a big playground, they played few games. The boys wanted to play volleyball and had requested that the principal get a net. A net had been put up the previous year, but it had been stolen. After that incident, a new net had not been purchased.

Under the aegis of socially useful productive work (SUPW), camps are organised in the schools in which both boys and girls participate. On national days like the Republic Day and Independence Day, girls actively participated in the cultural programmes that were organised in the school.

There is clear evidence that gender roles are sharply ingrained in the minds of girls and boys. Boys were seen as 'breadwinners' and girls as 'homemakers'. The educational aspirations of students were contingent on a variety of factors. Some students also realised that their aspirations might not be fulfilled. Subject preferences also indicate gender stereotyping – girls liked languages, while boys preferred maths and science. Individual teacher preferences were strongly linked to the affinity the teacher had with students. It is evident that schools are yet to become spaces where gender segregation is minimised and healthy interaction between boys and girls is promoted.

School system processes and practices

The secondary and senior/higher secondary schools are co-ordinated by the Department of Secondary Education. The administrative network is complex as well as large. Discussions were held with the DEO (elementary, who was holding charge of secondary schooling) and the Deputy Director (elementary) of the Jaipur district, to understand their views on gender in schooling and the problems faced by them as education managers. Both of them had long years of experience and had been closely associated with the innovative programmes implemented in Rajasthan, which had a special focus on expanding schooling opportunities for girls.

Gender equality and schooling

The DEO accepted at the outset that there were a lot of challenges in translating the goals of gender equality into reality at the school level. He felt that although the situation had improved in the last decade, gender gaps continued to exist at various levels and were particularly stark at the upper primary and secondary levels. He felt that socialisation processes and attitudes at the household level and within the schooling system were responsible for the gender gaps. He argued that schools were expected to play the role of a catalyst, but had failed to do so. He also reasoned that teachers had not worked towards minimising gender differences in schools. In his view, changes had to come about at all levels of education. The DEO strongly believed that motivational inputs were also needed for parents, so that girls could get equal educational opportunities.

Continuing problem areas

Several gaps were identified by the educational managers, which were seen to have an impact on enrolment, retention and performance of girls. These include:

- **Infrastructure:** The schools were lacking in gender-friendly infrastructure. A number of schools did not have clean toilets and common rooms for girls. In a recent meeting of all DEOs, a decision was taken that in schools that had common toilets, these would be converted into toilets exclusively for girls. This decision was taken because girls often hesitate to use common toilets.

- **Access:** While gender gaps were closing at the primary level, the situation at the upper-primary and secondary levels was disturbing. Even today girls are not sent to schools that are located far from home. A sense of insecurity continues to prevail among parents. In addition, in many secondary schools the numbers of women teachers are low.

- **Classroom interaction:** The two important issues at the classroom level are the curriculum and behaviour of male teachers. The curriculum needs to be improved and analysed from a gender perspective, so that the 'right message' is communicated to the students. In the co-education schools it is important that male teachers remain 'above board'. If at any point there is a sexual allegation against a male teacher, then the entire school environment is vitiated.

Assessment of male and female principals

The DEO felt that both female and male principals managed the schools efficiently. Women principals were appointed only in girls' schools, where they worked with women staff. In boys' schools, the male principals were usually considerate to women teachers. The deputy director opined that there was no difference in the working abilities of a male principal and a female principal – 'the person should have the right orientation and attitude'. He felt that women have similar capabilities to men and can make tough decisions. They are not 'weak' managers. However, he felt that some women principals were too dependent on male administrative staff.

Position of women teachers

The DEO pointed out that the number of women teachers had increased in the last few years due to special recruitment drives, but still their percentage was low. He also agreed that there were differences in promotional avenues and opportunities between male and female teachers. For example, women teachers who entered service in 1976 had been promoted to grade 2 only recently, while men who had joined the service in 1988 as grade 3 teachers had already been promoted.

Gender-specific issues

The education managers pointed out that the department had to be sensitive to the needs of women teachers. Women often came to them with various problems related to transfers/postings, and sometimes there were cases of harassment too. One of the common problems encountered by the DEO was related to training programmes. When women teachers were nominated to take part in training programmes, they came to cancel the nominations. He said that the department made efforts to adjust the training calendar in such a way that those women teachers could participate.

Training

Both the officers felt that it was crucial for the teachers to upgrade their skills, but no systematic trainings have been organised for teachers of secondary and senior secondary schools. The focus has largely been on training primary education teachers. More recently, with the introduction of the subject on life skills education (LSE), trainings have been organised at the regional level for both male and female teachers, including principals. Gender is an important component of LSE.

Gender-friendly schools

According to the education managers, some of the non-negotiables for a gender-friendly school are that the schools should be accessible to girls and the criteria for opening secondary and senior secondary schools should be reviewed. At present, the number of schools exclusively for girls at the secondary and senior secondary levels is just 10 per cent and 17 per cent. All primary schools should be upgraded as upper-primary and all secondary schools should be upgraded to senior secondary schools. This would help in curtailing the dropout rates for girls at the elementary and secondary stages as they would then be continuing in the same school where they had been studying.

The school infrastructure should fulfil needs pertaining to girls – toilets with water, common rooms, a playground, sports equipment and laboratory facilities. Women teachers should be appointed in all schools and should be treated on a par with men. The choice of subjects for girls should not be restricted to arts. Subject streams like science, commerce and home science should be available in all secondary and senior secondary schools.

It was also pointed out that various government initiatives and incentives provided to girls had led to an increase in girls' enrolment, but more effort was required. The continuing gender bias in textbooks also needs to be addressed. It was felt that the recent policy announcement and introduction of a transport voucher scheme to enable girls to access secondary schooling was a positive step.

Exploring the Bias: Gender & Stereotyping in Secondary Schools

The entire educational system is a network of complexities in which a range of issues is competing for priority consideration. While the educational managers we met were 'sensitive' and had the 'right' attitude, it was evident that they were surrounded by various other more pressing problems – like teacher transfers, litigation and fighting political pressures of various kinds. All these highlight the fact that 'gender concerns tend to get lost in the files' and are yet to become high-priority issues.

Conclusions and Recommendations

Conclusions

The present study reveals that despite a pronounced mandate for ensuring gender equality in education, the situation of secondary schools in the state largely remains unchanged and presents several challenges. It is clearly evident that gender is pervasive in the schooling experience of students, and there is a constant legitimisation of gender distinctions through everyday school practices. The hidden curriculum can be seen operating at all times – the seating arrangements, the task assignment and in gendered texts and play patterns.

While most teachers recognised and admitted to gender-based discrimination in society and spoke of providing equal opportunities to boys and girls, they have a limited role in transforming the gender patterns being played out in the classrooms. The relationships among women and men teachers also reveal gender discriminatory attitudes, where women teachers are not treated on a par with their male counterparts.

The teachers do not seem to be motivated to engage with the children outside the realm of the textbooks. Consequently, the teaching learning enterprise fails to promote critical thinking. The main concern of the teachers is to deliver satisfactory examination results.

While there have been some efforts towards curriculum reform in the state, the approach adopted has been 'add women and stir'. The curriculum continues to reinforce traditional gender roles, and does not offer learners the space to imagine a different future or set of gender relations.

Discussions with students reveal that gender stereotyping is strong at the level of the household, as gender roles and expectations for boys and girls within the household are clearly defined. The notions of restraint, obedience and sacrifice are so deeply ingrained that just as girls are supposed to be obedient at home, they are also expected to obey and conform in school. For the majority of girls, the burden of household responsibilities is 'real' and continues to hamper their legitimate participation in education. The boys, in turn, have the advantage of being born male. The girls expressed a wish for more freedom and have a strong desire to study further; however, many of them understand that their aspirations may not be realised, as the main purpose of girls' education is seen to be to enhance marriage prospects.

At the level of the state, the entire educational system is caught in a quagmire of politics, hostilities and litigations and changing the situation at the ground level requires huge efforts. The remark that 'the entire educational system is patriarchal' also holds true. The individuals who recognised the persistence of gender inequalities and injustice had little space to be critical and realised that their efforts may be undermined. However, they still endorsed the official policy viewpoint that the government is specifically concerned with the status of girls' education in Rajasthan.

Finally, the study clearly points out that concentrated efforts need to be made at different levels to shift the gender discourse from the margins to the centre of secondary education in the state.

Policy recommendations

Any approach for engendering development and education, in particular, must recognise the connections between universal education, social justice and equity.

At the policy level, the state needs to clearly plan the agenda for universalising secondary education. At present, the network of secondary schools is poor. A systematic mapping exercise should be initiated in the state, to assess availability of upper primary and secondary schools from the viewpoint of girls' access (and especially from the SC, ST and OBC groups).

There is a need institutionalise the concept of **gender-friendly schools**, which meets girls' requirements such as infrastructure, teacher positions, the curriculum, games and the quality of the educational experience. Several opportunities may open up with the new mission on secondary schooling.

The quality of education imparted in schools and other institutions depends essentially on the capacity of teachers. It is surprising to note that there are no teacher-training programmes for secondary and senior secondary teachers. More in depth, systematic and professional inputs need to be planned for teachers to upgrade their skills and improve teacher capacities. A gender perspective must be integrated in teacher education and training programmes, which will enable them to understand the pervasive presence of gender and initiate changes in school policy and classroom practices.

The curriculum is key to good-quality education and the textbooks are major instruments through which children learn about social values and norms. The task of reviewing textbooks has to be undertaken on a priority basis. Collaborations with women's studies centres, the National Council for Education, Research and Training (NCERT), the State Institute of Education, Research and Training (SIERT) and the District Institute of Education and Training (DIET) members could be sought to develop gender-sensitive curricula. The framework has already been provided by the National Curricular Framework (NCF) 2005.

An important aspect related to women teachers is the support provided to them within the mainstream educational system itself. There is a definite need to improve the status, conditions and career development opportunities for women. Creation of forums for women teachers seems essential, where they can collectively bargain and negotiate better working environments in schools.

Regular discussion forums should also be created at the school level, wherein students can be motivated to express and articulate their concerns vis-à-vis schooling and gender issues.

Finally, if education is the process of developing personhood and capacities such as independent thinking, autonomy and critical judgment, then schools must endeavour to provide gender-just institutional spaces.

Notes

1. The fieldwork was carried out in April and May 2007 after the new academic session had begun.
2. Contemporary government statistics differentiate four social groups: scheduled tribe (ST), scheduled caste (SC), other backward classes (OBC) and 'others'. Scheduled tribes, also referred to as adivasis, are indigenous peoples. Scheduled castes, also referred to as Dalits, used to be regarded as 'untouchables'. The ST, SC and OBC groups were 'scheduled' or recognised in the Indian Constitution for special development efforts.

CHAPTER 7

Gendered Education: A Case Study of Schools in Pakistan

Dilshad Ashraf
Aga Khan University Institute for Educational Development, Karachi

Introduction

Pakistan's position on the equal rights of its citizens is well articulated in the constitution of 1973, which ensures women's inclusion in all walks of life by denouncing any discrimination on the basis of sex alone. The constitutional position and emphasis on equal rights and opportunities for women was meant to address the traditionally low social status and minimal participation of women in most social sectors (Farah and Shera, 2007). In the years 1949–50, two years after Pakistan's independence in 1947, the overall gross participation rates at primary and secondary levels were low at 16 per cent and 9 per cent respectively. These figures were even lower for female participation i.e. 4 per cent at primary level and 3 per cent at secondary level (Jalil cited in Farah and Shera, 2007).

To improve female participation in education, all education policies formulated from the year 1970 to 1998 (the most recent policy being for the period of 1998–2010) have unanimously committed to ensuring provision of primary education. Each of these policies also committed to promoting girls' education. Pakistan is a signatory to international declarations and commitments made since the World Declaration on Education for All was adopted in 1990. Commitment to this declaration led Pakistan to pursue basic education as an integral part of the human development plan and as a means to eliminate all disparity, including those related to gender. Due to these efforts, overall participation in education has increased significantly since the 1950s, although the pace of change has been slow, particularly for women.

According to the Global Monitoring Report on Education for All (UNESCO, 2006), the female adult literacy rate in Pakistan in 2002-2004 was only 28.5 per cent, while the Gross Enrolment Ratio (GER) in primary education for girls was 69 per cent and the Net Enrolment Ratio (NER) was 56 per cent in 2004. Similarly, the female GER in secondary education was only 18.9 per cent. However, in the fiscal year 2004–2005, the female literacy rate had apparently increased from 28 per cent to 40 per cent (Government of Pakistan, 2005-2006).

In line with commitments to the international undertaking of the Millennium Development Goals (MDGs) and the Dakar Framework for Education for All, Pakistan has to accomplish a set of targets by 2015. The major commitment regarding universal primary education for all children rests in ensuring gender equality in education (Mukhtar, 2006; Khalid and Mukhtar, 2002). To meet these targets, the government of Pakistan developed a mid-term Education Sector Reform (ESRA, 2001–2005), and long-term National Plan of Action on EFA (NPA, 2001–2015) with an emphasis on overall education in the country and females' education in particular (Government of Pakistan, 2005–2006).

Improvement in the overall female literacy rate can be seen as a manifestation of Pakistan's international commitments. A review of the male and female literacy rates in both rural and urban centres, in Table 7.1 below, illustrates the nature of this improvement.

Pakistan's population is about 158.70 million (Federal Bureau of Statistics, 2007) of which more than 50 per cent live in rural areas. The table shows that only 29 per cent of the country's rural females are literate, while urban women's literacy is 62 per

Table 7.1. Literacy rates (10 years and above): Pakistan and provinces (%)

Province/area	1998–1999 *PIHS			2001–2002 PIHS			2004–2005 PSLM		
	Total	Male	Female	Total	Male	Female	Total	Male	Female
Pakistan	45	59	31	45	58	32	53	65	40
Rural	36	52	20	36	51	21	44	58	29
Urban	65	73	56	64	72	56	71	78	62
Baluchistan	36	54	16	36	53	15	37	52	19
Rural	33	51	12	32	49	11	32	47	13
Urban	56	72	39	54	71	36	60	74	42
NWFP**	37	56	20	38	57	20	45	64	26
Rural	34	54	16	35	55	16	41	61	23
Urban	53	66	40	56	70	41	61	75	47
Punjab	46	57	34	47	57	36	55	65	44
Rural	38	52	24	38	51	26	47	59	35
Urban	64	71	58	66	71	60	72	78	66
Sindh	51	65	35	46	60	31	56	68	41
Rural	35	53	15	33	51	14	38	56	18
Urban	69	79	58	64	74	54	72	80	62

Source: Pakistan Social and Living Measurement Survey (PSLM) 2004–2005, Economic Survey Pakistan 2006 (p.160) [*Pakistan Integrated Household Survey (PIHS)]
** NWFP=North West Frontier Province

cent – more than twice the rural literacy rate. Similarly, the table further indicates that in all provinces, the rural literacy rate is much lower than that of urban areas.

Furthermore, gender disparity is found at all levels of education. For example, at the middle level (gross middle-school enrolment) the gender disparity was 11 per cent in 2004-2005. The gender disparity is also found at matriculation level. However, if we examine the gender gap at the primary level of education in provincial, rural and urban levels in terms of GER and NER, we see great disparity. The disparity that is prevailing in rural and urban areas is alarming. A brief description of the gender gap in literacy and enrolment is shown in Table 7.2.

There may be various reasons for gender disparities – public expenditure could be one, for example. The government allocated 18.7 billion Pakistan rupees (PRs) to education in the budget for the year 2006-07, which is 2 per cent of the GDP and in some sources is 2.7 per cent (Ihtasham ul Haque, 2006). A lower financial allocation for education would mean less investment in initiatives to address such disparities. In the view of experts, this allocation should be not less than 4 per cent of GDP to achieve the MDGs (Ahmed, 2006). The Pakistan government has recently announced

Table 7.2. Gender gaps in literacy and enrolment at primary level (%) 2004-2005

Region/province	Gender gap in literacy %		NER gender gap at primary level		GER gender gap at primary level	
	2001–02	2004–05	2001–02	2004–05	2001–02	2004–05
Urban areas	16	16	3	3	7	7
Punjab	11	12	– 1	1	2	3
Sindh	20	18	6	5	13	9
NWFP*	29	28	8	6	14	16
Baluchistan	35	32	14	6	23	15
Rural areas	30	29	10	11	28	21
Punjab	25	24	6	7	19	14
Sindh	37	38	16	16	32	26
NWFP	39	38	16	15	44	30
Baluchistan	38	34	15	17	35	38
Total	26	25	8	8	22	17
Punjab	21	21	4	5	15	11
Sindh	29	27	12	11	25	19
NWFP	37	38	15	13	41	28
Baluchistan	38	33	15	15	33	34

Source: Pakistan Social and Living Measurement Survey (PSLM) 2004–05, Economic Survey Pakistan 2006: 166

*NWFP=North West Frontier Province

an increase to 4 per cent of GDP in principle; but putting aside 4 per cent GDP for education in theory only is not enough – the finance must be allocated in the annual budget by the government. So, it is important to increase GDP to achieve those targets and remove gender disparities in education. Other reasons for fewer enrolments of girls in schools may be poverty, social and cultural norms (Farah and Bacchus, 1999). One of the other constraints discussed in literature is parents' fear of girls' independent access to the outer world when they go to school. This access may have implications for girls' conduct, which is closely associated with a family's honour. Similarly, the gendered division of labour is widely stated as another factor that hinders girls' education. In conformity with societal norms, young girls start their caregiving role at an early age.

Sindh: The Study Context

Sindh is one of the four provinces of Pakistan and is located on the western corner of South Asia, with the Iranian plateau to the west. Geographically it is the third largest province of Pakistan, stretching about 579km from north to south and 442km (at the most) or 281km (average) from east to west, comprising a total area of 129,009 square kilometres of Pakistan's territory. Besides native Sindhis, different cultural and ethnic groups also reside here. The urban centres of Sindh accommodate migrants from all other regions of the country. Sindh is officially a bilingual province with large sections of the population speaking Sindhi and Urdu, while other languages spoken including Siraiki, Balochi, Brahvi, Punjabi, Pashto and Gujarati.

In accordance with the country's international pledges to promote Education For All, the Government of Sindh has taken a number of measures. Some of these include following:

- Free education for all children until they graduate with their Secondary School Certificate from government schools.

- Free textbooks for classes 1 to 5 and free textbooks for all girls studying in grades 6 to 10.

- Scholarships of 100 PRs per month are awarded for 10 months every year to all girls studying in grades 6 to 8 in government schools. In addition to this, girls who do well in classes 9 to 12 are also being paid scholarships.

- Twana Pakistan was launched in four districts i.e. Thatta, Badin, Tharparkar and Mirpurkhas to provide free lunch and other nutritional support to girl students in government schools.

Some of the above actions were launched under the auspices of the Compulsory Primary Education (CPE) ordinance, which was promulgated in December 2001. A study conducted by the Sindh Education Foundation (SEF) investigated the process of the implementation of the CPE ordinance and identified challenges and gaps in the implementation process (Kabani et al, 2003, quoted in Sindh Education

Foundation, 2007). The major findings of the study indicated that over-enrolment was one of the primary causes contributing to the deteriorating quality within schools. The study also highlighted teachers' incapacity to deal with the ever-growing number of students and the consequent inability to maintain a conducive learning environment within the classroom. Furthermore, the targets set out at the federal, provincial and district levels were primarily focused on raising numbers rather than launching educational reforms to attain qualitative revival and sustenance. At this point, however, quantitative targets also seemed elusive given the limitations of access and infrastructure (school preparedness) and affordability for parents to enrol at their children in formal schools (community readiness). In addition to the CPE study and participation in various EFA forums, it has been learned that so far the emphasis of government and donor agencies has been towards achieving quantitative targets (i.e. increases in enrolment) rather than seriously considering the issue of quality. Moreover, there is a dearth of research work focusing on the impact of EFA on the quality of education by critically evaluating at the 'pre' and 'post' stages for EFA initiatives.

Another critically important study has recently been conducted by the Sindh Education Foundation (Sindh Education Foundation, 2007), which examined the impact of EFA on the quality education in Sindh. Quality was defined as: i) whether or not the initiatives taken under EFA are relevant to the educational context of Pakistan and particularly to the province of Sindh; ii) whether quality enhancement is the priority of various stakeholders involved in the implementation of EFA at different levels; and iii) what processes have been employed for the implementation of EFA at the grassroots, district, provincial and federal levels and how they are linked to the quality of education. The Sindh data discussed in the study report provides the quantitative side to the qualitative outcomes of the present study, which aims at developing insights into secondary school processes from a gender point of view. While two of the four schools in the study come under the government Department of Education's jurisdiction, a discussion on the overall situation of achieving the EFA goal of ensuring access and eliminating gender disparities in education would allow deeper insights into the findings of the present study. Eliminating gender disparities in primary and secondary education to date remains a distant reality. The challenge is well articulated in the figures in Table 7.3.

Table 7.3. Number and distribution of schools in Sindh

	Primary schools	Middle schools	Secondary schools	Total
Boys' schools	17,813	1,202	902	19,917
Co-educational schools	16,232	485	270	16,987
Girls' schools	6,514	713	516	7,743
Total number of schools	40,559	2,400	1,688	44,647

Source: SEMIS quoted in Sindh Education Foundation (2007)

Exploring the Bias: Gender & Stereotyping in Secondary Schools

The above table clearly illustrates the discrepancy between primary and secondary schools, for boys as well as girls. For females, however, this discrepancy is all the more problematic for reasons such as lack of money, migration, the distance to school from home, poor facilities, involvement in economic activities, homework, and parents not valuing education for girls and lacking interest. More alarming still is the vast gulf between the number of girls' schools and boys/co-educational schools, a trend that remains consistent at all levels of schooling in terms of simple ratios: at the primary level, girls' schools account for a mere 16 per cent of the total number of schools. The significant number of co-educational primary schools allows better access to education for girls. However, their enrolment from grades 5 and above can nevertheless be hindered by varying and often conservative cultural attitudes, especially in the rural areas.

Table 7.4 clearly indicates the net effect of this discrepancy. There is a 15 per cent difference between the participation rates (the ratio of enrolment figures to the total population) of girls and boys at the primary level. Furthermore, the dramatic fall in participation rates, for both girls and boys, at the middle and secondary levels is reflective of the gap between the numbers of primary and secondary schools. Overall however, gender disparity in participation rates stands at 10 per cent – a figure that clearly reflects the divergence from EFA commitments, under which Pakistan had committed itself to end gender disparity at the primary and secondary levels by 2005.

Table 7.5 presents the figures for out-of-school children in Sindh, which at the primary level stands at 50 per cent for boys and 65 per cent for girls, while the figures

Table 7.4. Enrolment and participation rates in Sindh

School level	Population		Enrolment		Participation rates	
	Boys	Girls	Boys	Girls	Boys	Girls
Primary	3,445,499	3,105,939	1,715,629	1,074,532	50%	35%
Middle	1,568,086	1,301,055	283,107	197,603	18%	15%
Secondary	746,679	632,410	146,215	100,350	20%	16%
Total	5,760,264	5,039,404	2,144,951	1,372,485	37%	27%

Source: SEMIS quoted in Sindh Education Foundation (2007)

Table 7.5. Out-of-school children in Sindh

School level	Boys	Girls
Primary	50%	65%
Middle	82%	85%
Secondary	80%	84%
Total	63%	73%

Source: SEMIS quoted in Sindh Education Foundation (2007)

for the middle and secondary levels are significantly worse. Overall, 63 per cent of boys and 73 per cent of girls remain out of school.

However, efforts to increase enrolment at all levels have often been impeded by several factors including lack of access, poor infrastructure, the presence of 'ghost schools' (schools that exist only on paper as teachers never go and open the school) and the low quality of education. Incentives to increase enrolment have been provided by state and donor agencies with mixed results. In this regard, a case study on enrolment of girls in secondary schools will aptly indicate the difficulties faced in increasing enrolment and participation on schools.

According to the statistics given Table 7.6, the enrolment of girls increased by an absolute number of 775 (0.38 per cent) from 2001–02 to 2002–03, while the enrolment jumped by 62,695 from 2002–03 to 2003–04 (31.14 per cent). The reasons for the jump in enrolment include the following:

- The direct impact of the financial subsidy on the enrolment of girls in secondary schools, which would point to poverty as one causal reason for out-of-school girls.

- The direct impact of the enrolment drive conducted in the province of Sindh by UNICEF. The drive registered more than 300,000 children for school in six weeks, of which 42 per cent were girls and 58 per cent were boys.

There are no statistics available separately on the enrolment of girls in secondary school in Sindh in 2004–05 to gauge the effect on enrolment in the long run. However, the SEMIS data reports that the number of girls of school-going age who are out-of-school in 2003–04 stood at 84 per cent of the entire secondary school-going female population in the province. To that end, the increase in absolute numbers is comparatively small if total enrolment is to be achieved for girls by the year 2015.

Studies conducted in Pakistan (e.g. Jan, 2007; Hafeez, 2004; Zafar and Malik, 2004; Pasha, Ismail and Iqbal, 1996) have largely dealt with both supply and demand factors that hinder girls' education in Pakistan. For instance, the arrival of an unwanted sibling in the family, parents' perceptions about investing in a girl's education, and the sense of security due to the distance between school and home are all recognised factors that influence the parents' decision about sending a female child to school. The absence of a school within the neighbourhood, the non-existence of boundary walls, lack of toilets and non-availability of adequate numbers of female teachers are all reported supply-side factors that impede female access to school. The respondents

Table 7.6. Total number of girls enrolled in public secondary schools in Sindh

Period	2001–2002	2002–2003	2003–2004
Girls	200,516	201,291	263,986

Source: SEMIS quoted in Sindh Education Foundation (2007)

of the studies mentioned above in particular viewed the poor quality of education and teachers' attitudes, including corporal punishment, as major reasons for girls' dropping out of school. These findings warrant researching school-based conditions to identify factors that are likely to contribute to gender disparities in education. A quick review of research carried out around gender issues in education identifies a dearth of such research in Pakistan. For instance, studies need to increase understanding of how school policies, structures and teaching and learning processes can influence male and female students' participation in education. Very few studies (e.g. Zainulabdin, 2007; Ali, 2006; Rarieya et al., 2006) have actually examined teachers' instructional practices and their beliefs about female and male students' academic performance. The findings of these three studies shoe the strong influence of teachers' gender-related beliefs on their practices. The participants of these studies (primary and secondary schoolteachers) considered girls hardworking and serious while boys were seen as intelligent beings, assertive and full of energy, which makes them hard to control. The present study takes a more comprehensive approach to understand school structures and processes from a gender perspective.

The Study Schools

Overview

The research methods are outlined in the introductory chapter of this book. The research was conducted in the following four schools situated in the province of Sindh:

- Government girls' higher secondary school, Karachi

- Government boys' secondary school, Karachi

- Muslim Community School (MCS), Karachi

- Quaid Secondary School (QSS), Karachi (a community-based school)

Two of the four schools are run by the provincial government's Department of Education and the two are community-organised schools. Both public schools are officially single-sex and are situated in rural Sindh. However, the single-sex boys' school has a long history of admitting female students. Their admission to the boys' school is recognised, as they are allowed to study alongside the boys from grades 6 to grade 10, when they graduate after completing their public exam. The private schools of the study are situated in urban areas; nevertheless they are away from the centre and the hustle bustle of the city.

The government girls' higher secondary school caters for the rural community settled around it. It is a public-run school with 207 students currently enrolled in grades 6 to 12. Courses of study in humanities and physical sciences are offered to the students of higher grades (from grade 9 onwards). Around 16 teachers are teaching in the school, the majority of whom are qualified to teach in secondary school. The school has some teaching positions that remain vacant, as qualified female teachers are not willing to work in a rural setting.

The government boys' secondary school is a Sindhi-medium school and is situated in the rural catchment areas of Karachi city. The school was constructed in 1905, first as a single-sex boys' primary school. However, at the request of community, girls were admitted later to study with boys. As a response to the ever-increasing number of students, the school was upgraded to secondary level in 1979.

The MCS community school is an urban, co-education secondary school with a total of 509 students enrolled (244 girls and 265 boys). Although the school is an urban school, it is situated in an area that is away from main city. Historically the school was established as primary school and it has been upgraded gradually. The 2007 grade 10 students were the first group to sit for the Secondary School Certificate exam. The school started as a co-educational institution, but recently switched to single-sex classrooms for grades 6 to 9 (this is discussed further below).

The QSS is a faith-based school run by a trust. The school was established in 1990 to cater for the educational needs of those sections of the community from a lower socio-economic background. The vision of the school states its aim is to: *'uplift the community economically, academically, spiritually, morally, physically, socially, aesthetically and mentally.'* The school further aims at providing quality education to its clientele with affordable fees. Furthermore, it has a policy of awarding fee remissions and waiving fees altogether for the needy students. The school places special emphasis on providing an environment and culture conducive for learning.

School management

All four study schools have different layers of administration for school management. QSS and MCS (the private community-based schools) have well-structured external bodies – the Board of Governors and School Management Committee – that oversee overall school functioning. The membership of these two structures is taken from the schools and respective communities. The majority of the members are male. The principal heads the school-based administration in MCS, supervising management of the school's academic affairs and the smooth functioning of school administration. The school-based administration in QSS School has two distinct offshoots: one headed by the principal, who leads academic matters, and one headed by administrators, who look after finance and other administrative matters. The school-based management teams in both private schools comprise of males and females. QSS has a predominantly women-led academic team, with the finance department run by male accountants. MCS has predominantly male-led academic team, with finance and administration again handled by men.

Parent–Teacher Associations (PTAs) form external bodies in both government schools to oversee school management, with community and parent representation, the school principal and a teacher forming the membership. The government boys' secondary

Table 7.7. Demographics of the study schools

		Government girls' higher secondary school, Karachi	Government boys' secondary school, Karachi	Muslim Community School (MCS), Karachi	QSS secondary school, Karachi (community-based school)
Status of the school		Single-sex girls' school	Officially single-sex boys' school, but co-ed in practice	Co-ed, with primary and secondary sections	Co-ed, Montessori, primary and secondary sections
Status of school building		Purpose-built building with basic amenities	Purpose-built building with basic amenities	School housed in a community hall and number of adjacent small residential apartments	Grand multi-storey building with fully equipped classrooms, staffrooms, principal's office and administration blocks
Gender equity measures		Free books for girls, stipend PRs1,000/year, School Management Committee, girl prefects	Free books for students, stipend PRs1000/year, School Management Committee, leadership opportunities for girls and boys as class prefects	Leadership opportunities for girls and boys as prefects, fee concession for deserving students, School Management Committee, health club, students' council	Parent Advisory Committee, leadership opportunities for girls and boys as class prefects, Early Childhood Centre, special counselling sessions for girls and boys
Provision of facilities and amenities		5 toilets, drinking water tank, playground, library, computer lab with no computers, canteen, 3 science laboratories	Drinking water cooler for girls, one toilet for girls, playground, library, computer laboratory equipped with computers, 3 science laboratories	Separate toilets for girls and boys, drinking water for girls and boys, computer laboratory with 14 computers	Library, computer laboratory, 3 science laboratories, separate toilets for girls and boys, separate play grounds for girls and boys, toilets, water cooler for girls and boys (on each floor)
No. of students	Girls	207	207	244	1,173
	Boys	–	289	265	1,201
No. of teachers	Female	16	18	28	127[1]
	Male	1	6		71
Extra-curricular Activities		Occasional quiz programmes, recitation of Holy Qur'an and religious poems	Poster competition, quiz programmes, recitation of Holy Qur'an and religious poems	Discussion forum, poster competitions, quiz programmes, annual school picnic, recitation of Holy Qur'an and religious poems	Annual school picnic, separate discussion forum for girls and boys, poster competition, quiz programmes, recitation of Holy Qur'an and religious poems

school has an all-male PTA membership, while the government girls' secondary school has a mixed-gender PTA, although the female principal is the only woman on the committee. School-based management in these two schools is headed by the principals, who besides looking after academic affairs also supervise finance and administration. Male staff members make up the teams that handle financial and administrative matters in both schools.

Secondary School Certificate examination results

The Secondary School Certificate public examination is viewed as an important milestone in schooling processes and students' learning outcomes. A school's performance is generally measured by its students' grades in the Secondary School Certificate examination.

Curriculum and textbooks

All four schools follow the national curriculum prepared by the Federal Ministry of Education's curriculum section. Teachers use textbooks published by the Sindh Textbook Board Jamshoro, Sindh. These textbooks are developed with approval from the Federal Ministry of Education's curriculum section, and they are reviewed by the National Textbook Review Committee. These textbooks are available in Urdu, English and Sindhi to cater for the different mediums of instruction in the province.

Table 7.8. Secondary School Certificate (SSC) examination results, 2006

Name of the school	Total no. of students		Passed		Failed	
	Girls	Boys	Girls	Boys	Girls	Boys
Government girls' higher secondary school, Karachi	52	–	47*	–	5	–
Government boys' secondary school, Karachi	39	70	36	69	3	1
MCS community school, Karachi	17	22	The first group of students reached grade 10 in 2007	n/a	n/a	n/a
QSS secondary school, Karachi	35	37	35	37	Nil	Nil

* The single-sex girls' school showed poor result in the grade 10 public examination, with only two girls securing a B grade while others secured C (31) and D (14) grades. Five girls failed. The majority of the students (both girls and boys) from the government boys' secondary school and the QSS secondary school secured A and B grades, with rare exceptions of grades C and D.

Education options

The data analysis reveals that the education options in the two private schools are determined by the availability of both financial and human resources. Information technology, biology and commerce are three options offered by the QSS secondary school, while the MCS community school offers science subjects to its students.

The government girls' higher secondary school offers two options: science (physics, chemistry and biology) and humanities (civics, home economics). The latter is a legacy of past practices by the government's Department of Education that, through teaching girls home economics, prepared them for their caregiving familial roles. Boys' schools, in line with socially constructed gender roles, always offered subjects related to science and technology. The girls, by the virtue of being enrolled at the government boys' secondary school, studied science subjects.

Teachers' qualifications and professional development

In line with government's defined criteria, the teachers of both government-run schools are professionally qualified. The majority have a bachelor's in education (BEd) or a master's in education (MEd). Due to the schools' status as higher secondary schools, many teachers have a master's degree in a particular school subject and are called 'subject specialists'. Both the private schools assign secondary classes to the teachers with a bachelor's or a master's degree. Experience of teaching is another criteria used to assign teachers at secondary level. In-service or continuous professional development of teachers is a priority in these private schools. Through their capacity-building initiatives, these schools have developed their senior teachers as teacher educators who are then able to plan school-based professional development for colleagues. Collaboration with other teacher-training institutions was also reported by these schools. The government schools' teachers joined the schools with a teaching qualification, but have had no in-service professional development opportunities. None of the principals or teachers from the study schools has attended a course on gender.

Three schools (the MCS, QSS and government boys' secondary school) have both male and female teachers; the latter, however, has only one woman teacher. The allocation of teaching subjects at times seemed guided by the widely dominant gender ideology. For instance, the whole of the primary section at the MCS school is assigned to the female teachers, while the secondary section is taught by male teachers with the exceptions of female teachers teaching Urdu and biology. The male teachers and the single woman teacher in the government boys' secondary school are given equal numbers of teaching periods. Teachers are also delegated responsibilities other than teaching assignments in this school. For instance, the male teachers are given tasks such as collecting fees from students, and filling in examination, discipline, and maintenance forms etc. The only female teacher has been given

Exploring the Bias: Gender & Stereotyping in Secondary Schools

responsibility for listening any girls' problems that they cannot share with the male teachers.

The possibility of hiring more female teachers in the government boys' secondary school was rejected due to the principal's particular reservations:

> 'There is no need to have more female teachers in the school as female teachers, particularly married ones, come with lots of their domestic [problems]. The home problems affect their work, so it's better to have only male teachers, even in co-education.' **Interview, 6 April 2007**

Frequent unplanned leaves by the female teachers, due to their health and domestic issues, and a preoccupation with domestic issues were seen to be important reasons by the principals for women teachers' inefficiency. This reveals the gendered positioning of both male and female teachers in three co-educational schools. This situation in secondary schools poses a critical question about the messages that are being passed on to students through teachers' gendered attitudes. A later section of this chapter explains further the implication of this in terms of students' views on gender.

The dress code observed by male and female teachers varied in all four schools. Male teachers from the MCS and QSS schools wore pants and shirts, while the majority of male teachers in the government boys' secondary school were seen in *shalwar qameez* (baggy pants and a long shirt with slits on both sides). Female teachers in all four schools wore *shalwar qameez* with *dupatta* (a long, wide scarf or shawl). Some used their *duppattas* to cover their heads and upper parts of the body. Others used a *hijab* (a separate scarf to cover their heads).

Interestingly, despite the *hijab* being part of the official dress code for girls, many women teachers at the QSS school did not conform to the practice of wearing the *hijab*. The attitude of the female principal in this school regarding the freedom of teachers to choose whether or not to wear the *hijab* was reflected in teachers' dress code. Some covered their heads with 'proper' headgear, while others wore the *dupatta* (shawl) covering their shoulders. The principal reported the reaction of a donor who was on a visit to the school. He saw a female physical education teacher teaching children outside in the playground without her head covered. He immediately turned back and expressed his disapproval and anger over the female teacher's dress. In response, the principal remained persistent on her view of not jeopardising female teachers' autonomy and freedom.

Findings and Analysis

Views on gender

The principals and the teachers at the study schools interpreted the concept of gender generally as segregating males and females on the basis of their sex. The majority of teachers, principals and the management staff shared this fundamental premise, with minor differences. The female principal of QSS secondary school, for instance, viewed gender both in terms of biology and male and female characteristics approved by society. One such characteristic of females is obedience and non-assertive behaviour. This, according to her observations, was reflected in girls' behaviour during the initial days of the school. The principal reported that the initial passiveness was due to their first experience of co-education, but was gradually replaced by more active participation in the teaching and learning processes.

For the principal of government boys' secondary school, the word 'gender' means segregating males and females on the basis of their sex. He saw segregation of this kind as a cultural norm. Since the school is a village school and all teachers and students come from villages, they (referring to himself, teachers and male students) have to adhere to cultural norms, in which they respect women. For example, they cannot penalise female students, even if they make a mistake. On the other hand, 'We can beat male students, but sometimes we use [a] warning to girls as well'. The gender-related views of the female principal and her teachers from the government girls' higher secondary school were quite in line with the views of the male principal. They perceived gender as 'men' and 'women' with the given tasks of 'providing' and 'caregiving' respectively. Female teachers in this school in particular identified men's job to be the provider and family head. Despite earning a significant income through teaching, these teachers did not consider themselves to be providers. Rather they termed their work as 'giving financial support to their families'. Women teachers viewed educated women's role to be disciplining the family, fulfilling home-related responsibilities and maintaining better relationships with their immediate and extended family members. One of them stated 'She [a woman] helps her husband with children's education for a better future'. These women teachers were convinced that exchanging their caregiving role with men's role of provider and decision-maker was not an option for them due to the innate challenges of the latter role.

With the exception of female students' future aspirations (which were somewhat similar to boys') all participants of the study viewed gender within the dominant parameters of productive and reproductive roles. Some male students from one school considered the gender division of space as 'public' and 'private' to be a culturally acceptable phenomenon. In general, male students were quite cognisant of their future role as providers:

> 'We boys are like chlorophyll for the family.' [meaning the family is dependent on boys for survival, just like a plant depends on chlorophyll]

> 'We boys are the backbones of our families.' **Boys in focus group discussion, MCS community school**

Boys believed in the dominant gender ideology. They considered themselves future providers for the family, which warrants their hard work as students to become qualified for good professional colleges. This, they believed, would enhance their ability to secure a well-paid job. Caring for elderly parents, supporting their siblings' education and getting their sisters 'married off' were some of the responsibilities boys believed that they would have to assume as adults. The value of education for them is seen as different from girls due to boys' future productive roles. The same line of argument is also noticeable in the value these boys accorded to the support extended to them by their mothers and fathers. Analysis of the data reveals that the boys were only concerned about support from their fathers, who would ensure financial assistance for their education. Their mothers' support was not viewed as important, as one of the said:

'Ammi ki support nabhi ho tao koi perwa nahi hai. Aaboo ka support hona zaroori hai. Iss liyee ke woo kamatee hain' [it does not make any difference if there is no support from mother, but father's support is necessary as he earns money] **Focus group discussion, 13 April 2007**

This quote reflects boys' understanding of the gendered relationship as two distinct spheres of work and responsibilities for women and men to undertake.

Girls' perceptions of gender can also be viewed under the auspices of the wider gender ideology. All of them had a pride in their ability to perform multiple tasks ranging from household chores, school studies and religious rituals 'We are proud of being girls, as it allows us to perform variety of roles'. They believe their female identity provides them with a broad sphere of activity in comparison with their male counterparts. All of them were cognisant of their reproductive roles and believed 'no one else except a mother can perform the children's upbringing well'. One said:

'Men always need women's support to get their work done, because women are good advisers and they respond to situations accordingly – being more rational and cool-minded as compared to men.'

Also expressed was the vulnerability related to being female, particularly by one student from the rural government school:

'We females are like a white handkerchief; any small mark of ink on it will be very visible.'

This was an explanation of how family honour is associated with its female members' conduct. Even the slightest move away from the set norm of female conduct can cause a huge furore in close-knit communities and can also risk the continuity of a girl's schooling. Girls' actions, according to them, face scrutiny for potential threats of defaming the family's name and honour. Girls consider themselves intelligent and brave and that despite all the difficulties (e.g. restricted mobility, pressure to perform the familial role), they do not get discouraged.

Women's lower status as compare to men's concerned girls from all four schools. Their particular reservations were about girls' restricted mobility. In the context of their province, girls from the government girls' higher secondary school strongly denounced the oppression by men that confines women to within the four walls of the house. These girls seemed quite conscious and concerned about the injustice meted out to them at home – whereby a male child is given more importance, as males are the family 'breadwinners'. The birth of a boy calls for jubilation and celebration, while the birth of female child fills the environment with sorrow and sadness. They mentioned girls' powerlessness:

> 'First, as a daughter, we have to listen to our parents, then after marriage we are expected to be obedient wives of husbands, then we have to sacrifice our lives for their children. So when will we live our own lives?' **Focus group discussion, 13 April 2007**

Lack of opportunities for education and early marriages are some of the challenges these women face in Pakistani culture. Discrimination against them, they believe, is rooted in the patriarchal structure of the society that leads to a strong preference for the male child. While girls expressed their persistence in the face of multifarious challenges, the lack of future vision was yet another manifestation of their deprivation in a patriarchal context.

An interesting analysis of students' classroom participation was offered by the female students from the co-education schools. These girls thought that teachers generally treated both male and female students equally. While there was a general consensus among the girl participants of the focus group discussion on teachers' attempts to give all students equal attention, an explanation of teachers' different views of boys and girls was also presented by one of the girls:

> 'I think that boys are confident enough and they can ask questions in the class. This gives teachers the idea that they are understanding the topic and boys are intelligent. We girls also want to ask questions, but we are shy and cannot ask questions. Thus, we become only listeners in the class.' **Focus group discussion, 13 April 2007**

Unquestioned conformity to parents and other elders in extended families is an expected norm, and is one that women/girls are required to follow in particular. Socialisation in such an environment apparently instils in them a tendency not to ask questions which is, according to the above explanation, interpreted by teachers in a different manner.

Students' career aspirations

The career aspirations of the boys were clearly shaped by expectations of parents and society. They saw the value of education to be different for them compared to girls, who will assume caregiving responsibilities in future. Boys reported that due to societal perceptions (the gendered division of roles), girls – despite being professionally qualified – could not continue their careers, while they (boys) have the freedom to seek the best available careers and are expected to have a bright future. Most of the boys in the group discussions aspired (and were guided by their parents) to take up professional careers in the fields of engineering, information technology, the armed forces, banking and professional sport. One boy expressed his desire of becoming an education minister to improve the system, while some wanted to carry on to doctoral studies. In terms of professional aspirations, they feel the 'sky is the limit' as they are confident of support from their parents and other family members. With strong determination, perseverance and hard work, they are confident of achieving their goals in life. The focus group participants from the government boys' secondary school and the MCS school envisaged poverty and their family's limited financial resources to be constraints on the achievement of their future goals. Freedom of mobility was perceived to be a privilege by the boys, as the girls, they admitted, were socially constrained in this respect.

Girls from all four study schools expressed various fields of interest for their future careers, which included flying, chartered accountancy, commerce, medicine and the armed forces. One girl wanted to go on to study for a PhD. They believed that their passion, hard work, encouragement from parents, teachers' and parents' blessings would help them achieve their future goals. As a supporting factor, the presence of qualified family members (male relatives) provided most of them with optimism. The majority of the girls believed that their parents would support their studies financially. Some, nevertheless, had not thought clearly about their future, as they believed family attitudes might hinder them in realising their dreams. Girls, particularly those from rural schools, envisaged early marriages, parents' disagreeing with their ambitions, and opposition from the extended family and the family patriarch as possible constraints.

Lack of thought over a career also surfaced during the students' description of their future aspirations. Two of the focus group participants from the rural schools hoped that medicine would be their future field of study; however, this did not fit in with their present studies in humanities. Some realism also surfaced, as these girls continued discussions on the likelihood of achieving their future goal. More optimism was shown about joining traditionally female areas such as nursing and teaching than becoming a pilot, for example. Despite parents' consent to their education, girls also envisaged that lack of resources would hinder their dreams of further education. Girls from the rural schools reported that as an indigenous cultural practice, the family patriarch or the patriarch of the community generally makes decisions related to family and community matters. At the behest of the family patriarch, female education is generally discontinued after grade 10 public examinations. One of the girls referred to her grandfather's opposition to girls' education: he had earlier prevented an older granddaughter from accessing education. Their brothers' influence over decisions about whether or not to send girls to school also surfaced as a hindering factor.

Students' daily routines

The gendered differences between how girls and boys spend their day were reflected in all accounts given by the participants. Female participants from all schools begin their day with prayers before dawn. After school activities varied due to their positions in sibling order, and also the presence of other active and older females in the family influenced their afternoon routines. Some of the girls took care of domestic needs after school (e.g. cooking, washing). Some also reported going to private coaching in the afternoon. Staying at home watching TV and visiting relatives living close by were some other engagements reported by students. Generally, girls' after school routines took place inside the home, except for a few who went for private coaching.

The gender divide between public and private was obvious in these young girls' lives, as compare to their brothers' activities outside. Girls identified differences between theirs and their brothers' routines, who regardless of their age and status were more mobile in public sphere. Some of them were employed while some studied. The girls' brothers also spent their time outside the home playing or studying at private coaching centres. In comparison with male siblings, girls had limited option in terms of studying at home. Many of them spend their time after school performing caregiving roles. Many, unlike their brothers, lacked opportunities for private coaching, as such centres catered for boys only. Girls indicated a gender divide in families in relation to available resources: the male members of the family (including siblings) get preference in terms of the best food, clothing and education.

Generally, according to the female participants, parents liked their daughters to demonstrate utmost obedience. Girls from rural schools reported their parents' approval for their conforming to the traditional dress code and fulfilment of religious rituals as part of their daily routines. They invoked their parents' disapproval for not wearing their headgear properly. Frequent or independent mobility beyond the four walls of their homes was seen as prohibited by the parents (fathers) of all female students. While girls took pride in their ability of performing multiple tasks, they also showed their dislike for household chores such as cooking, washing dishes and laundry, which they reported interfered with their studies.

Male students' daily routines were very different from their female counterparts. Parents' expectations of the boys to prepare themselves for their future role as a provider put these youngsters under a lot of duress and pressure. Boys found it difficult to put prolonged time and energy into their studies, because other distracting factors around them. The majority of them managed to remain focused, as poor academic performance could upset their parents; their understanding of their future role also contributed to them staying focused.

School experiences

School experiences are enhanced by frequent extra-curricular activities (e.g. speech and debate competitions, recitation of the Holy Qur'an and religious poetry) and sports events. Boys from the QSS school reported their better performance compared to girls in these events (particularly in debates and speech) due to their confidence, which, they feel derives from their experience and exposure to the outside world. Nevertheless, they also noted that sometimes girls perform better and sometimes they remain equal. In this school, the games are gendered as girls play badminton and handball while boys prefer to play cricket and soccer. The boys termed these games as 'girls'' and 'boys'' games. They felt that the girls could not play 'boys' games' as they need more energy and power.

Conformity to a certain dress code was observed in all four schools. Male students, except in the government-run boys' school, wore pants and shirts with ties. Besides the uniform (knee-length shirt and *shalwar*), girls in all four schools covered themselves with a dupatta in line with the dominant code of dress for women in general society. However, the practice varied from school to school. In all three co-education schools, girls were more conscious of maintaining their conformity to this practice. In MCS school, girls loosely covered their head and upper part of their body with a *dupatta*. Strict conformity to this practice was specifically demonstrated in the QSS school and the government boys' secondary school. Girls from the government girls' higher secondary school were observed wearing the complete *hijab* - a long, loose gown with head gear and a veil - while commuting between home and school. This dress code was an unwritten rule and was followed by all female students, who took pride in conforming to the 'religiously defined code of dress'.

While all four schools clearly marked gendered spaces inside and outside the classrooms, the girls' single-sex school posed restrictions on girls' movement inside the school. For instance, girls were not allowed play in the school courtyard due to the presence of male guard at the gate. This school has two cemented courtyards. According to the principal, due to absence of the physical education teacher, the school sports equipment could not be used. During their recess hour, girls spend time in the courtyard that is not manned by the male guard inner. Younger girls were running around and chasing each other, while the older ones sat or walked in groups. One explanation for not playing given by the girls was 'we are too big to play around'. There is a staircase present in the courtyard, but the girls are not allowed to go upstairs because that would expose them to the neighbourhood.

The government boys' secondary school also stands out for its strongly gendered outlook. Separate lines of girls and boys are made during the morning assembly. It is always the boys' duty to recite in the morning assembly. The boys have a five-minute recess before the girls. In addition, they are supposed to go outside the school premises, while girls are supposed to stay on the premises during recess. There are two hawkers allowed to bring food for the girls to buy on the premises of the school, but they come with the school's permission and sell under the observation of male teachers. Every class, as reported by the principal, has two prefects: a boy and a girl. However, the boy prefect is overall responsible for discipline and dealing with class issues. The principal said:

> 'We don't give such responsibility to girls. Boy prefects can deal with both girls and boys, but girls prefects cannot.' **Interview, 6 April 2007**

Each girl prefect is expected to deal with the girls only - for example, she can only collect fees from girls. Moreover, it is not considered culturally appropriate for a boy to collect fees etc. from the girls. That is why the school has to have girl prefects. The girls and boys are assigned different tasks, for example, the girls are responsible for cleaning their classrooms, and boys clean the areas outside the classroom, such as the playground during the 'Hafta-E-Safai' (Week of Cleanliness).

Gendered spaces beyond school buildings also provided a reference to the extent students felt or experienced mobility. Commuting to school was especially taken care of by parents: girls were either escorted by a male member of their families or they commuted in groups. Many of them reported being stared at and teased by males on their way to school. Their response to the situation is to walk away with their eyes on the ground. Some girls are chaperoned by their father or a brother to ensure their safety during the commute, while the majority walk in groups and wear the full *hijab* for security.

Examples of considering girls' developmental were also present. In three schools, girls said that advice on their monthly menstrual cycle was available. Students from one school had arrangements to meet their menstrual needs. Girls reported teachers' flexible attitude towards their needs – for example, to leave class if necessary. In one school, students reported being able to meet with a particular female teacher who would help them.

Teachers' perceptions

Teachers' views about male and female students across the four study schools reflected the gendered image of their students.

Gender and space

Gender differences were observed in terms of how male and female students occupied physical space. Observations of classroom teaching and learning, games lessons and recess hours revealed a gendered pattern. For instance, girls were found huddled together both inside and outside the classroom, while boys occupied space more comfortably by spreading around. This was also explicit in one teacher's description of how boys and girls occupy the space available in the science laboratory. According to the science teacher, girls generally hover around one table while doing experiments. Boys, on the other hand, spread out and occupy all the tables. The science teacher interpreted this as girls' attempts to seek security and help from their peers. The patterns in which students occupy space, in other words, can be associated with hierarchical social structures in which women are considered weak and dependent. Furthermore, the socialisation of females into femininity and feminine ways to conduct themselves could be yet another explanation of this behaviour.

Learning styles and needs

Male teacher/s reported that boys are visual learners while girls are auditory learners and require teachers to repeat concepts often; boys in contrast do not seek repeated explanations. Teachers also reported gender differences between girls' and boys' responses in written work. Girls reproduce the given text, while boys have the ability to articulate the same concept in their own words. A set pattern for a question paper was considered to be helpful for female students' written responses, as they 'regurgitate' text following the expected pattern of examination. According to a male teacher, changes in the pattern of questions, content and the context of an assessment affect girls' performance in other institutions where they go after graduating from this school.

Disruptive behaviour by boys was observed in two schools, and an explanation was given. Male teachers believe that due to boys' certain developmental needs, they must take part in physically engaging activities. This also hinders boys' concentration on their studies. All the teachers were conscious of boys' responses to their teachers, which can sometimes be disruptive. Girls take teachers and teaching relatively seriously. Male teachers reported that girls relate emotionally to their teachers, while boys relate to teachers through content.

Boys are 'intellectual' and girls are 'hardworking'

The data reveals teachers' unanimous agreement on boys being more intelligent than the girls. This notion is reflected in the fact that teachers believe boys are good at physics, chemistry and computer studies, while girls do better in Urdu and Pakistan studies. These two groups of subjects are perceived to demand different levels of intellectual engagement by students. In curricular activities, however, all the study participants observed girls' better performance. One explanation of this phenomenon was given by the teachers to be girls' serious attitude towards their academic performance through preparation for all tests and examinations. Boys, on the other hand, choose to work hard only for the final examination. All the teachers unanimously agreed that girls outperformed boys in tests and exams, but said this was because of previously established patterns in the exam papers. According to a male teacher's analysis, boys do better in assessment that requires application of their learning, while girls generally reproduce answers. Teaching boys was perceived to be more challenging than girls. Engaging girls in a relatively plain and boring lesson was easier, but a monotonous lesson could easily put boys off – which then leads to disruptive behaviour. To avoid such situations, teachers are constantly required to update their lessons with more challenging tasks.

The data from the co-educational schools reveals that having girls and boys studying in the same classroom is considered to provide a competitive edge for both, as they want to perform better. This helps students build their confidence, interpersonal skills and improves their academic performance – a prerequisite for their entry into colleges. However, according to some boys, sitting with girls may damage boys' confidence as they hesitate to participate in the class for fear of the teacher telling them off for giving a wrong answer. Such a response from a teacher would be damage their self-image in front of girls – an unacceptable situation.

Studying together

The case study schools offer an interesting picture of schools' and the community's efforts to ensure gender equity in accessing education at the secondary level. Apart from the single-sex government girls' school, all three schools offered co-education. To address disciplinary issues arising from boys' conduct towards girls in the MCS school, the school administration and the board of governors decided to shift to single-sex classrooms for boys and girls. Presently, girls and boys from grade 6 on-wards study in their own sex groups. The chair of School Management Committee regarded this a timely measure to avoid the likelihood of girls discontinuing their education. The single-sex policy has posed a huge challenge to the teachers. The boys' disruptive attitudes have been reported as a constant hindering factor in the boys-only classrooms. Boys admitted creating havoc in the classrooms, and believed that girls' presence there would have made them more focused on their studies, as their underperformance in front of girls would be unacceptable to them. Girls, how-ever, felt more comfortable in single-sex classrooms and did not see any reason to return to co-educational classes. Having minimum interaction with boys, they be-lieve, makes the classroom an enabling environment and more acceptable to their parents.

Girls and boys from the MCS school seemed to follow the same 'minimum interac-tion' approach during recess, forming their own single-sex groups. However, the building compound's limited space made the groups stay closer to one another. Many men and boys were observed watching the students' recess time while standing on their apartment balconies at various floors. Some women were also seen, but they were busy putting clothes on washing lines.

The QSS school started off as a secondary school, with single-sex instruction for girls and boys. The school management, particularly the principal, found boys underperforming due to their disruptive behaviour in the classroom and decided to switch to co-education as a measure to address this issue. Both female and male students find co-education boosts their confidence, and that it keeps the boys fo-cused on their studies. Male students do not like to be seen to be unable to respond to teachers' questions or participating poorly in classroom processes in their female classmates' presence. Studying together with boys in the same classroom boosts girls' confidence and morale. Besides, girls reported the liveliness of the classroom envi-ronment due to boys' constant jokes.

Observations and focus group discussion data reveal boys' visibility in the class-rooms through their jokes and disruptive attitudes. Teachers were observed spending significant amounts of time having to discipline boys. In one instance, an extra teacher was present to monitor boys' engagement in the assigned tasks. While there was unanimous agreement on bringing challenging tasks to the teaching and learn-ing environment to engage boys, female teachers disagreed with a male teacher that boys posed more challenges to female teachers than to the male teachers. QSS offers an opportunity for boys and girls to study together throughout their school years in the same classrooms. However, the gender divide is clearly visible outside the class-room. The playgrounds and courtyards where students spend their recess and sports periods are separate for boys and girls. Both courtyards have a separate tuck shop with exclusively male and female staff.

The government boys' secondary school offers instruction in the provincial lan-guage Sindhi. The school started officially as a single-sex boys' school, but opened its gates to girls later on. Now, the school has girls enrolled throughout grades 6 to 10. Yet the increase in female students in this school has not warranted the entry of more female teachers. At the time of writing, the school had only one female teacher teaching the lower grades. The teachers as well as the students belong to the local village community, and they developed a shared sense of urgency for female educa-tion at community level. The community, according to the teachers, was greatly concerned about girls' inability to find a high-quality Sindhi-medium school and negotiated with the provincial Department of Education to allow girls' enrolment in the school. Now girls can officially sit for their grade 10 public examinations.

The school provides a 'protective' environment to girls, as reported by the students and teachers. Certain policies and practices are enforced to avoid any interactions between female and male students. Seating arrangements in the classrooms portray gender segregation. Girls are sent home earlier than boys as the school day ends. At the same time, the water facility placed near the principal's office is apparently only for girls: boys are not allowed to come to the tap in the presence of girls during class. During recess, boys leave the school premises while girls must remain there.

Observation data reveals no evidence of interaction between female and male stu-dents. Any interaction with male students, according to the girls, may invite teachers' scrutiny and doubts. This data also reveals that boys are the focus of teachers' atten-tion, who directed their explanations and questions towards them.

Teachers' disciplinary measures further explained the gendered nature of teachers' interaction with their students. Teachers reported that they might beat boys when they misbehaved in class; however, they could only reprimand girls, but not punish them physically. According to the teachers, the sight of boys being beaten was warn-ing enough for girls to make them realise that they could also be penalised for not listening to the teacher. This attitude on the part of teachers was apparently directed and guided by culturally approved seclusion of both genders, 'We cannot touch (physi-cally punish) girls as they are mature and grown up', said the teacher in a focus group discussion (6 April 2007).

Teaching and learning processes

Teaching/learning processes in all four schools were clearly influenced by the domi-nant gender relationships of the society. Gender segregation worked as a basic principle to guide these processes in all the schools. The single-sex girls' school was established on the basis gender segregation, while the other three schools dem-

onstrated their belief in gender segregation through their practices and arrangements that discouraged interaction among girls and boys inside and outside
the classroom.

Gendered teaching and learning

Textbook reading and 'chalk-and-talk' were the widely used teaching strategies in
all four schools. Within this conventional teaching approach, the gendered nature
of teaching was obvious. More visible gender messages surfaced specifically in
co-educational instruction.

In the government boys' secondary school, the teacher-centred lecture method was
used in biology and chemistry classes. Male students were the main focus of the
teachers' attention; they maintained eye contact with the boys and most questions
were directed at them. Furthermore, the distance between the teacher and the boys
was always less compared to the distance between the teacher and the girls.
For example, in the chemistry class when the teacher showed a diagram in the
textbook, it was kept in front of the boys' row; the girls were unable to see the
diagram clearly.

Assigning tasks to boys and girls was seemingly determined by the level of challenge
it may pose to students. For instance, in one English lesson, the teacher asked girls to
read the given passage from the text while boys were asked to summarise the lesson
– the task required an advanced level of comprehension and language skills. In
another lesson, while explaining the digestive system, the teacher directed all the
teaching towards the boys, hastily passing through content that pertained to particular parts of the body. Teachers also reported their difficulty in teaching such
'sensitive' topics in the presence of girls. Interactions between strangers are not
approved of, while discussions on sex and related topics are taboo in the context of
these schools.

Gender-segregated classrooms

The seating arrangements inside the classroom, as shown in Figure 7.1, depicted
visible gender segregation at different levels. Boys and girls sat in pairs at separate
desks in the co-educational schools. In QSS, students did not follow a set pattern in
terms of seating arrangement, but same-sex pairs were always the basic organising
principal. Here, males and females were sometimes observed sitting in the same
rows. They were also seen exchanging jokes, accessories and books. Nonetheless,
even with this rather flexible seating arrangement, teacher-directed interaction among
male and female students was not observed.

The seating arrangement in the government boys' school enforced a rather stringent
divide between the two genders. While girls and boys sat in different rows, the space
between the two rows was maintained at certain level in all the observed classrooms,
which required students to walk up to the other row if they needed to exchange any

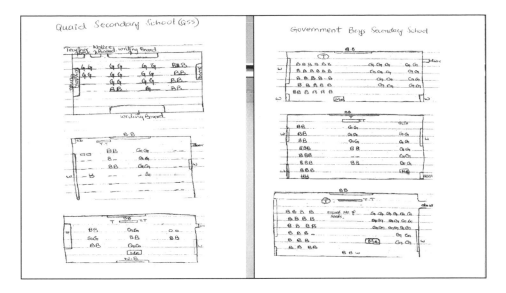

Figure 7.1. Seating arrangements inside the classroom for the QSS school and the government boys' secondary school

item. The classroom here had big windows on one wall and the smaller, sometimes only one, window on the other wall. It was also observed that girls always sat by the wall that had fewer, smaller windows. Student interactions with fellow students proved to be non-existent in this school.

The seating arrangements in the schools were apparently meant to discourage any possibility of male and female students' interaction. Nonetheless, the flexible seating arrangements in the QSS secondary school did allow students to talk frequently and exchange accessories. The female students from QSS reported frequent interactions with boys, who they thought made the classroom lively with their jokes. Yet despite this apparent flexibility, a sense of (gendered) interaction is present when boys and girls divide tasks according to the nature of those tasks. For example, the boys made the stage for a particular function and carried out tasks to be done outside the school premises; the girls, meanwhile, performed tasks inside the school.

Student–teacher relationships

Two of the four schools (QSS and MCS) had both male and female teachers working at the secondary level. The study revealed the students' views on how they related to their teachers. Interestingly, boys and girls shared their liking for male teachers. These feelings were based on how these teachers related to the students during the lessons. The students reported use of different pedagogical skills by the male teachers. Female teachers, on the other hand, were categorised as 'not favourite' by some of the students. In one school, the boys reported liking female teachers' presence in the class when they were in the mood for playing pranks. A female teacher was also named as the most disliked teacher for her blunt behaviour towards students.

A sense of comfort with male teachers surfaced in girls' views. For instance, although girls from the government boys' school wished for more female teachers to be present in the school, teaching by male teachers was reported to be equally acceptable to them. While effective teaching strategies in a 'lighter' mood of teaching were the general criteria used by the students to judge their teachers, male teachers' physical behaviour in class was yet another criteria used by female students. A group of girls denounced a particular male teacher who, while teaching, would casually move around and pat girls on their backs just as he would do to the boys.

An analysis of the observations quoted above demonstrates students' increasing recognition of their gendered selves in the manner in which they relate to their teachers. Boys made their male identity obvious by disrupting female teachers' lessons, while girls observed their interactions with male teachers in accordance to their (male teachers') culturally appropriate or inappropriate behaviours.

Equity of access by schools

The focus group discussions with teachers and the principals from the QSS secondary school, MCS school and the government boys' school articulated a realisation about female education being a matter of urgency. Various steps have been taken in these schools to ensure girls' as well as boys' access to education. For instance, girls were admitted to an officially single-sex boys' school as a gender equity measure. A shift from co-educational instruction to single-sex instruction was made in the MCS school to ensure continuity of girls' education. This contrasts with the QSS secondary school, which moved to co-educational instruction from single-sex classrooms to improve boys' underachievement. The community's role in managing school administration and finances, through an active board of governors or a school management committee, ensures students' access to a physically enabling environment. Although the government boys' school has an active Parent–Teacher Association (PTA), the interests of students are well taken care of by the teachers, who have their own children studying in the school. Girls' introduction to what was 'officially a boys school' was possible because of these teachers, who needed proper schooling for their own daughters. Therefore, a sense of community presence and monitoring female students' participation in the school prevails. In contrast, the government girls' higher secondary school did not report community involvement in female education, except the presence of a rather inactive PTA.

The data revealed parents' indifference towards their daughters' schooling. The majority were concerned with the girls passing the grade 10 public examination to obtain their Secondary School Certificate, but were less interested in whether they had quality learning opportunities in the school. Girls' absenteeism was a grave issue facing the schools, which teachers and principals saw to be rooted in the low value given to girls' education by their parents. A family affair (a wedding, birth or a death), the sickness of a family member or the pressure of studying were frequently observed excuses for sometimes a week-long absence from school. The teachers also reported pressure from parents in response to teachers' attempts to take disciplinary action. The prevailing low value that is put on education for girls has a visible impact on students' outcomes, particularly in the grade 10 public examination (see Table 7.8). Issues such as vacant teaching positions and disparities in the language used for instruction are worthy of serious attention to improve learning opportunities for girls in the single-sex girls' school.

Female education in a single-sex school

The study data reveals the challenges facing girls to secure equal learning opportunities in the co-educational schools. The same struggle, however, also surfaced in the single-sex girls' school. This school seems comfortable in the dominant gender ideology, which has implications in terms of the overall quality education offered to girls. The principal believes the manner in which boys and girls are nurtured ought to be different because of their fundamental differences: '... boys can be out and can go out, but we have to control girls. We need to treat girls as girls'. School, in her view, teaches girls the etiquette of behaving within the specified norms and culture of society. In other words, school is engaged in nurturing (female) students' femininity with constant reminders. 'Be like girls' (teacher's emphasis to the girls in a physics class). A talk about an academic task by the teacher could also be accompanied by a piece of advice or a reprimand about the students' femininity. One teacher explained to the girls the rationale behind her reprimanding them during the academic year:

> 'My objective of reprimanding you was just to ensure that you have [a] proper upbringing ... because not the certificate but your behaviour will reflect your education. For instance, how you behave when there is a guest at home.' **Grade 9, physics lesson**

This view, along with parents' low expectations for their daughters' education, seems to be determining the low-quality learning opportunities in the school. Parents' attitudes towards girls' education are constrained by cultural norms of early marriage and girls' and women's status in the patriarchal society. The incongruity of using multiple languages for teaching, homework and examination apparently also has serious implications for students' motivation and performance in physics (as well as in all other subjects taught in a language other than the language of instruction). The complexity of this issue hinders the quality of teaching/learning processes, which leads to the below-average academic performance of these female students. Their poor performance in public exams diminishes their chances of further education in a context already burdened by poor resources and negative attitudes towards female education.

Beyond the prescribed curriculum

The study schools all functioned within Pakistan's prescribed curriculum examination system, and teaching and learning were geared towards preparation for public examinations. The frequency of extra-curricular activities followed a similar routine, with most schools organising such events in the middle or at the beginning of an academic year. The QSS secondary school, in collaboration with an NGO, initiated a programme to contribute to the social, moral and physical health of its students. This was the only school that offered some 'out of the box' options to students such as interior decoration and woodwork. Initially, there was a gender division in these subjects (e.g. interior design for girls and woodwork for boys). However, this division was later abolished. Some girls in particular performed very well in woodwork. Teachers, nevertheless, were not sure if any boy has crossed the gender divide. The data did not reveal any evidence of teachers' attempting help students move across the socially constructed gender boundaries.

Teaching aids and displays

Observations of lessons taught in all four schools revealed exclusive use of textbooks and the blackboard. No other teaching aids were used. Fast approaching secondary school examinations were one explanation for this phenomenon. Displays inside and outside the classroom were also a rarity, although the QSS secondary school had some displays in and around the classroom. Quotes, drawings of science experiments and concepts, and inspirational religious lessons were also on display. Both male and female students made those displays there were. The MCS school had a few displays that portrayed the demonstration of 'action' words (e.g. cook, run, play) and some male saints. The few displays also portrayed gender in a traditional manner: a number were made by girls who, for example, drew boys kicking a football and running; girls meanwhile were shown watching television and reading inside the home. Government schools had a very small number of displays containing scientific concepts and verses from the Holy Qur'an.

Textbook analysis

To achieve curriculum objectives, Pakistani schools rely heavily on textbooks as the legitimate and only source of knowledge. Therefore, textbooks were analysed to understand what gender-related messages were being passed on to the students. While all textbooks were scanned to identify gender messages, Urdu and English books were analysed most closely, because all secondary school students study these books, regardless of their subject stream. The analysis revealed the following:

- Deeply rooted traditional beliefs and perceptions of women's position in society were portrayed in the text and illustrations. Women are shown in their reproductive roles. Men, on the other hand, are portrayed in productive and decision-making roles.

- The visibility of women is low as compared to the appearance and visibility of men in the textbooks.

- Women and men are identified with certain stereotypical attributes. Men, for instance, are portrayed as being brave, heroic, honest and strong, while notions of caring, self-sacrifice, love and kindness are associated with women.

- Members of textbook review committees and textbook authors are almost all men, with an insignificant number of female writers. However, in one instance, a team of female authors and reviewers were able to produce a comparatively gender-inclusive textbook (class 9).

The analysis confirms that textbooks used in secondary schools perpetuate the dominant gender ideology. Through highlighting gender-related attributes, textbooks are found to be reinforcing the stereotypes that students carry with them to schools. Such presentation of gender ideology through textbooks not only limits girls' chances of having equal opportunities, it also prevents young secondary school students more generally from being prepared for more gender-aware roles in their future lives.

Conclusions and Recommendations

Conclusions

The study draws the following conclusions on the basis of the findings discussed above:

- The concept of co-education surfaced more in the context of the three secondary schools that offer schooling to boys and girls in the same premises and during the same hours. Boys and girls (in two instances) perceived the presence of the opposite gender as boosting their confidence and preparing them for adult life. However, no visible attempts by the teachers or schools were seen to use the presence of both genders as an opportunity to create a conducive learning opportunity. Conversely, every attempt was made to discourage any interaction between boys and girls to promote their academic strengths. Gender segregation remained the underlying principle in all schools, both inside and outside the classrooms. As a result, boys more than the girls appeared to be trapped in dominant gender relationships – by having to exhibit a 'macho' image, for example.

- The single-sex school for girls is engaged in socialising girls into a passive role within existing gender relationships, with little or no concern for encouraging their future potential.

- Despite the equity measures taken by the schools and government Department of Education, boys and girls have different learning opportunities inside the classroom. Girls remain invisible by being task-oriented and demonstrating obedience to teachers. Boys get more than their fair share of the teachers' attention.

- The equity measures (e.g. yearly scholarships, provision of textbooks and free education) taken by the Department of Education attempt to address poverty (which is recognised as being a major hindrance in retaining girls in schools, particularly at secondary school). However, school management processes – including teaching and learning processes – have not been explored to develop insights into how such processes facilitate or impede gender equity as the school level. Thus, schools as a whole continue communicating to young people the dominant gender ideology that views men and women within the strict boundaries of productive and reproductive roles.

- The teachers and principals from all four schools hold preconceived notions of their students' capabilities and attitudes towards learning on the basis of gender. This is reflected in teachers' pedagogical practices and has implications for teaching/learning at the classroom level.

- Expectations of boys and girls are significantly gendered. Male students live the dominant image of masculinity with attributes such as being assertive, moody, adventurous, intellectually demanding and uncontrollable. This has implications for the quality of teaching and learning processes – both in single-sex boys' classrooms and in co-educational settings.

- Teaching and learning processes, particularly through displays, textbooks and teacher–student interactions, perpetuate dominant gender ideologies. This dilutes any concerted efforts carried out by schools to ensure equity of access to all students.

Recommendations for policy and practice

Federal Ministry of Education

- Integration of a gender perspective into school processes needs a clear articulation in education policy. This will help generate resources and develop mechanisms for the successful implementation of such policy.

- An analysis of the situation is fundamental for the Federal Ministry of Education to understand the gravity of the existing situation in schools and beyond. A situation analysis will help develop a comprehensive gender strategy.

- The Federal Ministry of Education needs to develop a gender focus group, with specialists in gender in education and a portfolio to plan and implement gender strategies at the provincial level. Some of these strategies should include advocacy campaigns, curriculum and textbook guidelines, capacity building for teacher educators, curriculum developers and textbook writers, and developing a mechanism for the implementation of a gender strategy.

- Public–private partnerships – the government needs to develop partnerships with private organisations to build its strength for effective gender-based interventions at the macro and micro levels.

Exploring the Bias: Gender & Stereotyping in Secondary Schools

Capacity building for teachers and management teams

- Teacher empowerment through equipping them with appropriate skills, knowledge and attitudes is fundamental for promoting gender equalities at the school and classroom levels.

- Teacher training curricula (both pre- and in-service) need to be revised to eliminate concepts and contexts that are gender insensitive. Furthermore, a component of gender in education needs to be offered in all teacher-training programmes to help teachers develop relevant skills, knowledge and attitudes to ensure gender equity at the classroom and school levels.

- A leadership and management-training programme can be offered to the principals of secondary schools, with a focus on how a gender perspective can be integrated into school management policies and practices to ensure gender equity.

Curriculum and textbooks

- The composition of textbook author teams needs to be revised to ensure equal participation by women. Gender training should be a prerequisite for inclusion in textbook author teams.

- Textbooks need to be reviewed to identify what gender messages are conveyed through the text lessons and illustrations.

School based interventions

- Developing and establishing school (and district level) forums (e.g. students' debate and literary groups, councils) can help male and female students express their beliefs; this is fundamental if these young people are to act as more gender-fair adults – men and women.

- Schools with a co-educational setup need to appoint a gender focal person who can ensure gender equity across school policies, structures, the distribution of resources and processes.

Exploring and disseminating good practices of how teachers and schools have been able to promote gender equality at the school and classroom levels will help practitioners develop their ideal of gender-informed teaching.

Note

1. This number includes teaching and other academic staff (e.g. floor supervisors, lab attendants, librarians, computer instructors).

CHAPTER 8

The Reproduction of Gendered Inequalities in Nigerian Secondary Schools

Dr Salihu Girei Bakari
State Universal Basic Education Board, Adamawa State

Introduction

Nigeria's development and gender profile

Nigeria, on the west coast of Africa, has an area of 923,769 square kilometres. In 2006, its population of 140,003,542 spoke more than 400 languages and belonged to more than 250 ethnic groups (Federal Republic of Nigeria, 2007). It has a low Human Development Index – ranked 158 out of 177 countries (UNDP, 2003) and high ethno-religious and regional tensions. The struggle for economic and political dominance leads to high-profile assassinations, religious intolerance and ethnic clashes at the slightest provocation. This situation, coupled with the political influence of kinship, lack of transparency in government and other factors creates space for corrupt practices and disregard for the rule of law. This in turn paves the way for marginalisation of less powerful groups and individuals.

Women face discrimination in the economic, political and social spheres and in educational opportunities. Nigeria's Gender-related Development Index (GDI) was 0.551 in 2006, ranking 139 out of 157 countries and only 18 positions away from the worst performer. Fafunwa observed that:

> '... for too long, woman has lived in the shadow of her male counterpart and this has, over the centuries, created a psychological complex in the female gender as she is made to play a second fiddle.' (1990:7)

Generally, socialisation patterns in Nigeria place enormous restrictions on women, while demanding a higher input to domestic labour. Girls are in many cases, reportedly denied the same quantity and quality of food as their brothers. Moreover, parents generally prefer to have boys because of the higher prestige society accords males. Indeed, Anyawu (1995) observed that nursing mothers are better cared for if the baby is a boy. A UNICEF and National Planning Commission (NPC) report further states that:

'In Nigeria's patriarchal society, women suffer marginalisation even at the family level. Just as girls in some parts of the country are excluded from decision-making concerning their choice of spouse, women are often not allowed to take part in decisions on how many children to have or when to have them. The right to make such decisions, especially among the Yoruba, is seen to be exclusively that of the man.' (UNICEF/NPC, 2001: 256).

The same source noted that women were often excluded from family decisions on matters that are deemed important. It noted further that at the community level, women 'have traditionally been excluded from direct participation in decision-making' even though some women's forums provided avenues for females' expression of their aspirations. This is because decision-making is 'considered the man's exclusive domain' and because 'they were considered too weak and emotional to exercise responsible leadership' (ibid.). While such attitudes are prevalent throughout Nigerian society, they are likely to be more deeply rooted in the North, where it was only in 1976 that a decree allowed women to vote in, or to contest, elections. UNICEF/NPC gave an account of how a female political activist was expelled from Kano,[1] flogged in Zaria[2] and imprisoned 17 times during Nigeria's First Republic (1960–66) for participating in politics (Bakari, 2005).

Despite Nigeria signing up to the Convention on the Elimination of All Forms of Discrimination against Women (CEDAW) in 1985, there is still institutionalised discrimination against females, as the instances below illustrate:

- The Penal Code (applicable in the North) excludes forced 'sexual intercourse by a man with his own wife' from the definition of rape as long as she has attained puberty.

- Sections 350 and 363 of the Criminal Code cover the same offence (unlawful and indecent assault), but provide for a lesser punishment when the victim is female (two years' imprisonment) compared to when the victim is male (three years).

- Wife beating is seen as a legitimate practice under many traditional Nigerian customs. The Penal Code [Section 55 (1) (d)] does not recognise as an offence those acts that do not occasion grievous harm and are done by 'a husband for the purpose of correcting his wife, such husband and wife being subject to any natural law or custom in which such correction is recognised as lawful'.

- A husband is generally regarded as having the legal power to decide on family property, even without consulting the wife. Irrespective of the wife's contribution, assets are usually acquired in the husband's name.

- Under customary law, the wife is often treated as property in the event of her husband's death. Especially in the South East, 'she is one of the properties to be inherited' (UNICEF/NPC, 2001: 238–239).

　　　　　　Exploring the Bias: Gender & Stereotyping in Secondary Schools

Such discriminatory practices as sanctioned by the state no doubt have a telling effect on education institutions as well. This research will contribute towards exploring how such discriminatory practices impact on education institutions.

Nigeria's education system

Overview

Nigeria's formal educational system has been considerably transformed since independence. The overall philosophy of education in Nigeria, as outlined by the National Policy on Education, is to live in unity and harmony as one indivisible, indissoluble, democratic and sovereign nation founded on the principles of freedom, equality and justice, and to promote inter-African solidarity and world peace through understanding. The National Policy on Education gave the basis for the nation's philosophy of education as:

• The development of the individual into a sound and effective citizen,

• The full integration of the individual into the community,

• The provision of equal access to educational opportunities for all citizens of the country at the primary, secondary and tertiary levels both inside and outside the formal school system.

Formal education in Nigeria is highly rated in the nation's development plans, as education is viewed as the instrument for change and the attainment of national development goals.

Nigeria currently operates a three-tier formal educational system, known as the '6-3-3-4' system of education. This comprises basic education (comprising six years' primary and three years' junior secondary education), three years' senior secondary education and four years' tertiary education. As at 2006, there were more than 54,000 primary and more than 18,000 secondary schools across the country (Federal Republic of Nigeria, 2007). There are also some 200 universities, monotechnics, polytechnics and colleges of education, which enrol hundreds of thousands of students. These institutions have been set up and are run by a variety of proprietors including the federal, state and local governments as well as corporate bodies, NGOs and individuals.

Gender and education

In its national education policy, the Federal Government of Nigeria (FGN) recognises that education is 'an instrument par excellence for effecting national development ... and a dynamic instrument of change'. The national education policy is based closely on Nigeria's national goals and identifies the following as the core beliefs underlying the country's philosophy on education:

- Education is an instrument for national development; to this end, the formulation of ideas, their integration for national development, and the interaction of people and ideas are all aspects of education,

- Education fosters the worth and development of the individual, for each individual's sake, and for the general development of the society,

- There is need for equality of educational opportunities to [sic] all Nigerian children, irrespective of any real or imagined disabilities, each according to his or her own ability,

- There is need for functional education for the promotion of a progressive, united Nigeria; to this end, school programmes need to be relevant, practical and comprehensive, while interest and ability should determine individuals' direction in education (FGN, 1998: 7).

Nigeria is also a signatory to international commitments that guarantee human rights, especially those to do with the right to education. It has signed up to the Dakar Framework for Education for All (the EFA goals), which includes eliminating gender disparities in primary and secondary education by 2005 and achieving gender equality in education by 2015, with a particular focus on ensuring girls' full and equal access to and achievement in basic education of high quality. Nigeria has also expressed its commitment to the Millennium Development Goals and targets to be achieved by all UN member states by 2015. Member states are expected to reflect the MDGs in Programmes of Action as part of their development plans. All MDGs are gender responsive, but specific to education and gender equality are Goals 2 and 3, which aim to achieve primary and secondary education for all children and to eliminate gender disparity in education.

The Nigerian education philosophy is therefore based on: (i) the development of the individual into a sound and effective citizen, (ii) the full integration of the individual into the community, and (iii) the provision of equal access to educational opportunities for all. The application of this philosophy is, however, complicated by ethno-religious and geopolitical differences in the country, which result in perceptions of marginalisation and mutual mistrust.

In 2005, the Universal Basic Education databank released projected figures for primary school enrolment up until 2016. The expected number of students enrolling for junior secondary school in 2005, for example, was 20,688,772 (11,458,355 boys and 9,230,417 girls). The growth rate for enrolment is assumed to be 2.5 per cent; therefore, a total of 32,326,206 (17,903,680 boys and 14,422,527 girls) may be registered for junior secondary school in 2007.

Most secondary schools in Nigeria are government owned, but there are few private schools owned by individuals and private or religious institutions. The government controls all matters related to policies and programmes through the Ministry of

Education at the federal level and State Ministries of Education at the state level, while management processes fall within the purview of individual schools.

In Nigeria, 35 per cent of youth aged 12-17 years attend secondary school. Young people in urban areas in the south and those in more economically advantaged households are most likely to attend.[3] There is concern that education largely reproduces and reinforces the wider social discrimination and economic and political disparities experienced by girls and women.

Significant gains in terms of gender equality can be made at the secondary school level. Through education, girls can become more empowered and self confident, as they acquire the knowledge, skills, and attitudes and values that are critical for negotiating their place in society. In this regard, many of the benefits normally attributable to education issue from the secondary rather than primary level, which underlines the importance of building on any gains at the primary level with high secondary participation rates.

Literature suggests that multidimensional factors account for students' selection of subjects. Parental influence, students' interests and aspirations, as well as certain factors within the schools, all play a complementary role in determining what students study. Leach (2003a: 102-104) observed that females are encouraged to study traditionally 'feminine' subjects to maintain the public versus private domestic spheres and because science and mathematics are seen as high status, difficult and objective, while 'feminine' subjects 'are seen as less important and suitable for the less intelligent'. Women sometimes feel unable to study sciences, and both male and female students believe some subjects, particularly home economics, are more appropriate for females and the core sciences for males (Harding, 1992; UNESCO, 1997; Dunne, Leach et al., 2004). In these cases, gender, rather than ability or capacity, plays a role in determining what subjects students choose to study.

The Research and the Sample

The research

The study was carried out in Kogi, one of 36 states in Nigeria, situated in the north-central part of the country. Kogi is a historic state also referred to as the 'Confluence State' because two major rivers that run through Nigeria (the River Niger and River Benue) converge in its capital city of Lokoja. Kogi State is not only a confluence of rivers, but also of cultures, religion, ethnic groups and languages: the state therefore provides a rich source of data for the survey.

Fieldwork was carried out from 4-24 May 2007 by a team of eight researchers: four men and four women. In common with all the countries in the study, the Nigerian exploration used classroom observation, focus group discussions with students, administrative staff, school inspectors and support officials, as well as interviews with teachers and principals and senior education managers.

The field researchers made several field trips to the schools in groups of three to five. For every visit, the team would spend the whole day in school, making observations and conducting interviews and discussions.

Different instruments were applied in addressing the main task of the research, but the chief instrument used was in-depth interviews. A semi-structured interview schedule was developed by the research team in collaboration with the central facilitator at the Commonwealth Secretariat. Other instruments used were documentary evidence, observation and focus group discussions with students (males and females), teachers and principals and education ministry officials. The interviews were guided by the research task, as well as by the insights gained through documentary evidence and classroom and other related observation.

Five schools were involved in the study, each unique in its type, nature and location, to enable the researchers to capture a wide range of responses as regards gender practices across cultures, language, religious and ethnic groups. The selected schools covered all the three senatorial districts in the state. They were:

- A boys' government secondary school located at a suburban town about 60 kilometres from the state capital

- A co-educational community secondary school located at a rural settlement about 200 kilometres from the state capital

- A girls' government secondary school located in a rural settlement about 300 kilometres from the state capital

- A co-educational government secondary school in an urban setting within the state capital

- A co-educational private school located in a suburban area on the outskirts of the state capital

The schools

All the schools had the same pattern and levels of classes stipulated by the government as enunciated in the National Policy on Education, although not all had complied with the recent prescribed format for separating grades 7 to 9 from grades 10 to 12. The different levels or grades are shown in Table 8.1.

Table 8.1. Grades by junior or senior secondary level

Level	Grade	Level	Grade
Junior secondary 1	7	Senior secondary 1	10
Junior secondary 2	8	Senior secondary 2	11
Junior secondary 3	9	Senior secondary 3	12

Exploring the Bias: Gender & Stereotyping in Secondary Schools

The term 'grade' is equivalent to that found in the British school system. Students transiting from the junior to the senior levels must sit a nationwide promotion exam to qualify. Differences in student enrolment at senior secondary level (as will be seen in the analysis) are often connected with this process.

Three out of the five case study schools are government owned; one is a community initiative supported by government, the other is a private school. Three schools are co-education secondary schools, while the other two are single-sex schools: one boys' school and the other girls'. Although there are certain basic features that cut across the structure of all school types, management processes and practices are based on the individual school's discretion. All were established between 1923 and 2001. The older schools have witnessed various administrations and management styles. In three of the schools, the principal is assisted by two vice-principals: one is in charge of personnel/student administrative matters, while the second handles academic matters.

All schools have teachers employed by the government, Parent-Teacher Associations (PTA), the National Youth Service Corps (NYSC), or by private institutions and there are more men than women. In addition to their teaching roles, teachers also sit on various committees. There was a high rate of teacher attrition in almost all the schools and students are sometimes left alone without subject teachers. In some of the schools, the PTA is actively involved in the management processes and takes decisions[4] on such issues as employment of part-time teachers or repair of toilet facilities etc.

Enrolment in all five schools reveals 34.96 per cent girls compared to 65.04 per cent boys with a 15–30 per cent drop-out rate for girls and a 7–18 per cent drop-out rate for boys. The most common reasons for boys' dropping out of school are monetary (where parents cannot afford the financial demands of their schooling) and male truancy. The reasons for girls dropping out of school are financial (where parents are gender-biased in choosing whose education is funded by available household resources) or associated with early pregnancies. Reasons for dropout by both sexes include household chores, especially for girls, child labour or the death of a parent, family member or benefactor.

The Findings

Education system and processes and practices

Education managers and inspectors, predominantly men, revealed their thoughts and practices as regards gender. They believe that efficiency in performance of principals and teachers is gender-related and its impact can sometimes be negative or positive. When female principals or teachers are absent for pre-natal or post-natal reasons, they are interpreted to mean incompetence occasioned by 'natural deficiencies', which impacts negatively on their jobs. According to them, in the course of their supervision and inspection of schools they come across problems with female teachers and managers much more often than they do with males. For example, they frequently referred to female teachers as being always on maternity leave, leaving early to breastfeed their babies or nursing their sick children in the hospital etc. In essence, they identified what Connell (2001:34) calls the 'reproductive arena' as a 'deficiency'. Connell explains:

'In gender processes, the everyday conduct of life is organised in relation to a reproductive arena, defined by the bodily structures and processes of human reproduction. This arena includes sexual arousal and intercourse, childbirth and infant care, bodily sex difference and similarity'.

This finding is in agreement with Connell's (2002) observation that some males accept women's rights in principle, but engage in habitual practices that perpetuate male domination of the public sphere. With this strong belief and thought-pattern, female heads and teachers tend to exert themselves twice as hard (compared with their male counterparts) to please education managers and school inspectors.

This position corroborates the affirmation by the top management officers that schools and offices in the education ministry headed by females do better. Their performance is, however, ascribed to females' weaknesses and paradoxically, to their 'natural tendencies' to be thorough as a result of '(extreme) fear of intimidation'. In this regard, the good performances of females in managing educational institutions and departments are seen not as a result of their competence, but out of fear of failure, which make them work harder and spend extra time to 'measure up'. This is a clear case of deliberately misrepresenting merit and ridiculing women's success, which is occasioned by the gendered notion that the female sex is weaker and not supposed to lead males. Feminine 'deficiencies' were exploited to naturalise male authority through the institutionalisation of a firm male-dominated management hierarchy, both at the student and staff levels. Both male and female staff and students interviewed appeared fully aware of this discourse.

Male respondents displayed prejudice against female leadership in various ways and strongly opined that male-dominated school management has nothing to do with gender inequity. Rather, it is seen as an appropriate action taken in order to ensure effective management of schools. Dismissing gender considerations in appointments, a top senior officer in the Ministry of Education declared that gender was not an issue in the ministry, because 'as you can see, some of our departments are being headed by women'. He used this as an excuse to downplay the need for gender sensitivity in appointment of staff to positions of higher responsibility.

Most of the male respondents agreed that the management of schools is male dominated, but they believe that the status quo will not harm female teachers or students. Ironically too, even though some school inspectors claim that gender is not an issue in terms of school headship/leadership, they still believe that it is more convenient or even necessary for a female to head a girls' school and a male to head a boys' school, on the basis of each 'understanding their own gender better'.

While it was claimed that gender is not a factor in the provision of equipment and instructional materials in schools (since the same policies, type of education and opportunities applied to all), students were however given access on the basis of preconceived notions of the types of subjects suitable for the different sexes.

It does appear that the education managers interviewed are gender-unaware. This is because they feel strongly that gender issues should not be considered or infused in the preparation of curricula themes, schemes of work or lesson delivery, because there is no glaring gender disparity in the current uniform practices. It is also understandable for them to think the way that they do, as none of them has ever attended training to enhance their knowledge and skills in gender-related issues, let alone gender-related interventions. In such situations, school, rather than being life enhancing, might be life impairing.

School and class environments

Classrooms, like any other structure around the school compounds observed, were built with block and cement. Only two out of the five schools had an adequate number of classrooms that were also in good condition, perhaps owing to their recent establishment. The other schools not only had insufficient classroom numbers, but these rooms were old, dilapidated, poorly furnished (seats and desks were often provided by individual parents, with students having to carry them to and from school), some with dusty non-cemented floors, others with no doors or window shutters and roofs partially blown off (exposing students to the elements). Not having enough classrooms means that rooms are over-crowded: a normal class scenario witnessed 64 students seated in one classroom. This situation seems to disadvantage girls, in particular, who are expected by society, school officials and male students to be shy, quiet and timid.

Three out of five schools observed had school compounds that had no fencing or clearly defined boundaries. One particular school compound was a thoroughfare, as vehicles and people pass freely, even when classes and exams are going on. The school environment therefore did not seem to be conducive for effective teaching and learning for both sexes.

Although the schools are visibly connected to an electric power supply, electricity was not constant and this interrupted the schools' daily activities. The standard of hygiene and sanitation is very poor in four of the five schools observed. Inadequate water supply was another challenge that students faced, as they had to trek long distances to fetch or buy water. The lack of water in the schools also affected the state of toilets (where available); for example, in one of the schools, teachers bluntly refused to teach as a result of the stench from the toilets. Absence of water and hygiene facilities, and poor hygiene practices are important reasons for children, especially girls, not to go to school or to drop out. It is difficult for girls to remain in school in such harsh school environments as the ones reported on here.

Even more serious than these grave issues, was the fact that the trek to collect water exposed girls to the threat, and sometimes reality, of rape en route – purportedly by a gang/or gangs of male students. Such a situation potentially undermines any of the benefits of school; this is even more the case given the high HIV/AIDS prevalence in many areas of Nigeria.

School management

The spillover effect of the influence of education administrators is the gender spread of principals and their deputies across the schools surveyed. Among the five principals, four were men and one was a woman; of the 10 vice-principals, nine were men and one was a woman (she was also the principal of the affiliated junior secondary school).

The female principal was head of the all-girls school. Her deputies, however, were men: they are expected to guide her in the running of the school, since women are thought to lack the requisite leadership qualities and skills. The principal narrated the experience of her former employment as the head of a co-educational school where upon resumption of duty, several male teachers resigned their appointments because they could not tolerate a female principal. The ministry reasoned with the 'protesters' and posted her to the girls' school. She also reported on having been intimidated to be hyper-aware of her actions, so that she would not be labelled as a 'non-performer' as a result of her being female. This finding is important in the sense that it explains one of the reasons why schools reproduce and transmit gendered beliefs and practices from one set of students to another. Provided that gendered micro-politics persists among teachers and are actively supported by the policy-makers as shown in this case, there is little hope for redressing and structurally eliminating harmful gendered traditional practices.

The school management on its part plays a strong role in gender stereotyping by delegating assignments and headship of various departments and committees based on gender. For example, committees such as those managing finance, exams, continuous assessment and the timetable are headed by males, while the social and food committees are headed by females; this was the pattern throughout the survey. Invariably, the students see the same trend in larger society replicated in their schools, and form attitudes reminiscent of societal gender expectations. Specific facilities for female teachers such as maternity leave, being able to leave early for nursing mothers and separate toilets (for males and females) were allowed. However, there is no recognised government policy to allow paternity leave (for males) in Nigeria.

Consciously or unconsciously, gender determines teacher/student interactions and responses. For example, most male students are said to be rude and disobedient to female teachers, but respectful and obedient to male teachers. This is because students believe that it is only male teachers who have the authority, as well as the physical power, to control them. In matters of health, however, female students prefer to approach women teachers and male students prefer men teachers. In class, both male and female students prefer female teachers because they were perceived to be kind, gentle and responsive: 'just like mothers'.

Students were involved in classroom management as monitors and prefects. Their assignments include keeping order and discipline in class and assisting teachers in many different tasks. These assignments differ in some cases for boy and girl prefects/monitors. For example, matters concerning discipline and supervision of boys and girls were exclusively for boys. This is because, according to the school ethos, girls are not expected to exercise control over boys, who consider it degrading to receive directions from or obey their female colleagues.

Most schools (especially the co-educational and girls' ones) had special rules for girls in addition to the common rules and regulations for boys and girls. These rules have to do with dressing, movement and association. They are justified as being in girls' own interests, to reduce their risk of suffering harassment. Girls must be seen to dress decently and should not mingle with boys or men, visit boys' hostels or receive male visitors in their hostels. None of these rules applied to boys' conduct, thereby entrenching the biased nature of responsibility. The schools support division of labour based on sex/gender roles. Both boys and girls performed chores such as sweeping, fetching water, dusting the blackboard and picking up refuse, but girls were held more accountable. Boys were assigned physically strenuous tasks and any considered to be dangerous for girls.

Teachers

In theory, teachers attach great importance to educating both girls and boys. However, they believe that there are some differences in capacity and performance in certain subjects for girls and boys, and also that there are differences in their expressed choice of subjects. They think that girls tend to like and do better in arts subjects, while boys aim for science subjects. There were exceptions, however, where some girls do better in the sciences and some boys do better in the arts.

Teachers used the same strategy in teaching boys and girls and believed that if there was any difference in the way girls and boys learn, it must be attitudinal. For example, it is generally believed that girls tend to be more attentive and more disciplined than boys with lessons. Table 8.2 gives an example of the characteristics of girl and boy

Table 8.2. Perceptions of the characteristics of male and female learners

Girls	Boys
Love/preference for art subjects	Love/preference for sciences
Like maths	Like maths
Timid and shy in class	Confident, domineering in class
Look up to boys in class	Look down on girls in class
More serious, disciplined	Less serious, less disciplined

learners from the co-educational schools' perspective, as seen by teachers and school managers.

However, teachers' role is seen to be paramount in students' choice of subjects. In one school, for example, both boys and girls performed well in mathematics because they liked the two teachers of that subject. In the sciences (biology, chemistry and physics) teachers think that boys do better than girls (??? physics), while in the arts (languages and social sciences), girls do better than boys.

Teachers were of the general opinion that male and female students should be allowed to assume their natural roles in future, depending on their choice, even if that choice is influenced. This means if a girl chooses to play a 'feminine' role or 'masculine' role, she should not only be allowed, but also encouraged in that direction. However, they strongly objected to the idea of allowing boys to study 'feminine' subjects such as home economics. Teachers exhibited preconceived notions and strong prejudices as to the roles of females and males. The schools, undoubtedly, seemed to be preparing students to conform to the society's gender stereotyping of girls and boys.

In terms of behaviour, teachers believed that students generally misbehave and are very difficult to control. Students commit offences such as stealing, loitering, truancy or absence from school, violence against male teachers who try to correct them, bullying, rape and many other types of violence (for example, a girl could instigate her boyfriend to attack and beat up other students or even male teachers who disapprove of their promiscuity). To maintain discipline, teachers use corporal punishment on both male and female students, but in different ways. Male students are considered stronger and worse behaved and tend to receive harsher punishments than girls. Gender also determines the type and method corporal punishment. For instance, boys would be flogged on the buttocks, while girls would be caned on their palms. One of the teachers explained that they could not flog girls on their buttocks without evoking sexual connotations.

Most of the teachers are concerned about the numerous cases of sexual harassment by male students and teachers to female students and teachers, and by female students to male teachers.[5] Such cases often result in teenage pregnancies, which may lead to abortion and other reproductive health challenges. The issue of violence, particularly against female students, appears to be serious. Reports indicated various forms of violence such as 'senior' boys sexually harassing girls, including junior girls (12–15 year olds); groups of boys collectively raping girls; harassment of teachers (male and female) by boys and even girls (through their boyfriends); male students physically assaulting male and female teachers; bullying etc. Even as the researchers were leaving a particular school, they witnessed a male student slapping a male non-teaching staff member when he tried to stop the boy from beating a girl. Yet laws / policies fail to mention or address harassment in schools. Such cases were left for the school authorities to deal with. The only form of reprimand or punishment for such behaviour is a transfer or withdrawal from school[6] of the students involved.

The situation in the single-sex schools was different. Female teachers were said to be punishing girls, often accusing them of enticing male teachers to befriend them. Girls disagreed with this assertion, but rather claimed that male teachers harassed them sexually and they were too afraid to report such cases. They claimed further that female teachers harassed them verbally and assaulted them physically for allegedly having male teachers as boyfriends. In the boys-only school, meanwhile, there are reported cases of bullying of younger students by older ones. Coined as 'seniority', the school ethos permits some students to send others on errands. Refusal to obey such directives attracts physical assault and other forms of 'punishment' from the older students. Within this context, too, some older students snatch food items and money from junior students. Victims hardly ever report such cases for fear of reprisal attacks by the older students.

Teachers believe that laws/policies are neither definitive nor practicable on harassment, because most such cases are not considered to be harassment or violence, even by the school management and/or the Ministry of Education. For instance, it is not unusual for a senior boy (student) or a teacher to 'befriend' an adolescent girl and have sexual relations with her. If she becomes pregnant, the penalty only applies to the girl. She would be withdrawn from school and becomes the victim who loses the chance to continue schooling, while the boy (or male teacher) go unpunished.

Students

The students appeared aware of the different social expectations of boys and girls. The boys were happy and indeed proud to be boys: thankful to God for their ascribed roles as males, and liked the qualities attached to boyhood. A boy said he liked being a boy and gave the following reasons:

> 'When I exercise authority in the house, my parents are happy. They both like me for doing manly jobs like washing their cars, playing football, protecting my sisters from any danger or fighting bad boys. Also to make sure that they don't go out especially at night. I pity my sisters, but that's how God made them'.

Boys liked the authority and physical power associated with being male and some said they would prefer to die than to be born female.

Girls also projected themselves as proud and happy to be girls, but there were certain qualities attached to being girls that they did not like. These include their vulnerability and lack of security, weakness, lack of freedom and feminine roles assigned them by society. Girls want to study to become nurses, accountants and teachers. When asked why the preference for being a nurse instead of being a doctor, the response was: 'I prefer to be doctor, but I am not good in the subjects (sciences). I know I can be a teacher or nurse. Then I can marry a doctor'. Others feel that society, particularly family institutions and negative values attached to educated females, could serve as a hindrance to their education. Boys and girls live in mutual suspicion, in a kind of love/hate/fear relationship. Some of the boys claimed girls were 'seductive' and that this distracts boys from being serious about their studies.

Boys were confident and ambitious to take any of the courses or subjects perceived to be difficult and 'no go areas' for girls. The girls were ambitious and confident to study as far as possible and become doctors, engineers, journalists, politicians, actresses, pharmacists etc, but societal/parents' expectations (desires and demands) keep them from actualising their dreams.

The schools' ethos and practices, as translated in teachers' attitudes and behaviour, did more to direct students to take courses based on gender, as well as reinforcing gendered beliefs, than any other factor. One girl was afraid of any mathematics-related course and suggested that this was because she was female. A boy wanted to study home economics, but could not do so as a result of prejudice against a boy taking the course by teachers and students alike. In another instance, the male-only secondary school didn't teach home economics, because it was taken for granted that boys do not need such a subject. Boys in the school claimed that, even if they were interested in registering for the subject, they would not be able to do so.

Girls also complained of little or no time to study to get good grades. According to them, their average day begins at 5 or 6 am and ends at 8 or 9 pm, with hardly any time for rest or recreation. Table 8.3 provides an overview of girls' and boys' routines during an average day: during term-time and the holidays.

Further concerns expressed by both boys and girls related to school welfare and security. Different factors affect their studies such as lack of teachers in some subjects, the distance to school, lack of water supply, lack of toilets (poor hygiene and sanitation), lack of furniture in the class (students having to carry desks to and from school every day), lack of security (the school compound is open and unprotected), exposure to snakes and scorpions while trekking long distances in search of water and the seemingly incessant cases of sexual harassment, especially rape.

Textbooks and learning materials

Teaching and learning materials in classrooms range from the blackboard to illustrative maps and charts. All the schools have libraries, but most lack books. Where science laboratories exist, equipment was in short supply or not available at all. Male students were favoured in science subjects over females, and formed the majority in science classes.

Although textbooks and learning materials were in short supply, a gender analysis was conducted on samples of those available. Two textbooks were analysed, one each for English and chemistry. The textbook on English language was chosen because it is a core subject and all students in all the schools use it; the chemistry textbook was chosen because chemistry is a core subject for all science students.

Table 8.3. Gender differentiated daily schedules: term-time and holidays

Time	An average school day	
	Girls	Boys
5–7 am	Wake up, help mothers sweep compound, prepare breakfast for family. Attend to young ones	Sleep, wake up, listen to radio, wait for breakfast
7–7.30 am	Eat breakfast, bathe and go to school	Eat breakfast, bathe and go to school
2–3 pm	Return from school, eat lunch, wash dishes	Return from school, eat lunch, rest
3–6 pm	Prepare supper	Sleep/rest/go out to visit friends, play football
6–8 pm	Eat supper, wash dishes	Read, watch TV or go out
8–10 pm	Watch TV, video, read	Watch TV, video, read, go out
10–11 pm	Go to bed	Go to bed
Time	An average holiday day	
	Girls	Boys
5–7 am	Wake up, help mothers sweep compound, prepare breakfast for family. Attend to young ones	Sleep, wake up, listen to radio, wait for breakfast
7–8 am	Eat breakfast, wash dishes and bathe	Eat breakfast, bathe
8 am–1 pm	Wash clothes (for juniors, parents), run household errands, prepare lunch	Help father in market, farm etc./ sometimes free
1–3 pm	Eat lunch, wash dishes	Eat lunch, rest
3–6 pm	Prepare supper	Go out (visit friends, play football etc).
6–8 pm	Eat supper, wash dishes	Eat supper, watch TV, go out
8–10 pm	Read, watch TV etc.	Go out, read, watch TV etc.
10–11 pm	Go to bed	Go to bed

The cover page of the English textbook (Titled: *Senior English Project for Secondary Schools Students Book One* authored by NJH Grant, S Nnamonu and D Jowitt) shows a picture of six males and a female. The illustrations in the textbook do not depict males and females in equal or close to equal numbers. Pictures of boys/men outnumbered those of girls/women by 11, i.e. 22 male compared to 11 female pictures. Nor are the images similar in size, position or aesthetics: the pictures of girls are smaller than those of boys, as if viewed from a distance. The illustrations also depict males and females in a variety of roles, traditional and non-traditional. Images of males include the following:

• A man standing with a long hoe in a discussion with another male farmer

- A hardworking farmer ploughing with an ox

- A farmer resting under a tree with a hoe beside him (implying rest after hard work)

- A man tilling a piece of land

- An old man telling other males the history of their locality

- Men playing musical instruments, with some dancing and others fishing

- A male poultry farmer

- Two men walking through a forest

Females, on the other hand, are shown carrying baskets of fruit, carrying a baby and dancing. Table 8.4 lists the gender roles as depicted in the book.

On the whole, this book depicts a great deal of gender bias and stereotyping, showing men as hardworking, landowning, controlling finances, making decisions for the family and as managers. Roles or positions such as priests, warriors, rulers/leaders etc. were exclusively for males. Boys were regarded as heirs to the men. The females, on the other hand, were depicted as mere helpers to men or domestic servants. However, non-stereotypical and non-prejudicial terms such as 'passenger', 'people', 'being', 'individual', 'veterinary doctor', 'secretary', 'parent', 'humanity' etc were also used.

The chemistry textbook was written by ST Bajah, BO Teibo, G Onwu and A Obikwere. It made use of tables, graphs, circles, test tubes, drawings and so on. The drawings were clear and of different shapes and sizes. The front page depicted a male and a female: the male is shown dying a material, while squatting, while the female is depicted carrying out an experiment in a laboratory; she is wearing a white apron. Gendered pronouns 'he' and 'his' were used, especially when pointing at contributions made by different authors. No female scientist was acknowledged throughout the text, whereas male scientists dating back to 1787 were acknowledged for their contributions.

Table 8.4. Gender analysis of textbook imagery

Male	Female
Hardworking, own land, controls finances	Good housewives
Protectors	Helpers
Marry women and protect them in a house	Involved in petty trading
Men as heirs	Potters and weavers
Name newborn babies	Perform domestic chores
Adventurers	Wash men's clothes
Conquerors	Cook meals for the household
Holy priests	

Processes within and outside classrooms

One key feature in all the co-educational schools studied was the gendered nature of student interactions both in and outside the classroom. In the classroom, gendered interactions were noticeable through the creation of gendered space. All sitting arrangements were structured in such a way that boys and girls grouped themselves differently. The boys tended to sit separately and tended to occupy the front seats, while the girls occupied the rear seats. It is also striking that students reveal that they choose to sit along gender lines without influence from the school authority. However, school authorities approved of this arrangement and said it's a logical thing to do.

The same practice was observed outside the classrooms. Observation in the playgrounds, morning assembly and dining areas all showed a segregated cluster of boys and girls working, playing and standing separately. Only occasionally, did we see boys and girls interacting.

The major reasons advanced for this segregation ranged from religious to cultural and biological explanations. It was explained that boys and girls were encouraged to observe strict seclusion, especially during adolescence. Both boys and girls also cited religious factors and physiological factors (especially for girls during menstruation), as reasons for segregated seating arrangements along gender.

Classroom Processes

Most classrooms observed recorded high student numbers (for example 48–64) to one subject teacher. This questions teacher productivity and students' receptivity in terms of learning. The teaching method used by a majority of the teachers is the lecture method, with occasional questions to students to get feedback. As a result of large number of students in one class, the teachers could hardly spend two minutes with any one individual student.

Tasks on classroom upkeep were shared out among students. An example of a daily schedule in a co-education school is presented in Table 8.5.

Table 8.5. Gender analysis of a typical school's daily classroom schedule

Tasks	People responsible	
Conducting morning session	Boys	–
Fetching water	Boys	Girls
Sweeping/cleaning classroom	Boys	Girls
Monitoring class	Boys	–
Solving questions on blackboard	Boys	Girls
Running errands for teacher(s)	Boys	Girls
Serving tea to visitors	–	Girls

When some students were asked if they were comfortable with this arrangement, both boys and girls said they did not want to change the way things were because it fits with their gender roles. However, some male and female students argued that boys should be spared fetching water, as this is perceived to be the responsibility of women. This is unsurprising because students are blinded by gender-stereotyped socialisation and engage in gender inequity and discrimination without the slightest notion of the harm that can be done to their development processes as a result. Although there were fragments of empathy for the different gender roles, especially by the boys, students are generally oblivious of the interventions that could be made through policy. This finding shows that the schooling process is already preparing students to accept and appreciate their assigned gender roles in preparation for adulthood.

Sport and recreation activities

In all the co-educational schools studied, different sports and recreation activities exist for both boys and girls. In the single-sex schools, too, sports that are deemed inappropriate for a particular sex were not available. For example, football and badminton facilities were not provided in the girls' school. Perhaps more disturbingly, the teachers in charge of sporting facilities in the co-educational schools have preconceived notions about the types of sports male and female students should engage in, which in all cases is reflective of the opinions of school management/authority. Table 8.6 lists recreation and sporting activities and students' participation by sex.

Girls play all the balls games played by the boys, except football, although some girls expressed their desire to play the game had it not been for discouragement by society as translated in the school ethos. There is little or no form of encouragement from teachers in charge of these sports for students to engage in sports across 'gender lines', as girls are rarely considered or groomed to become captains of teams. For example, sports kits are provided through the sports captains, who are often boys (except in the female-only school). In addition, it was observed that girls were hampered by their skirts (which is the approved mode of dress) during sports: they could not run or jump as easily as their male counterparts.

Table 8.6. Gender analysis of sporting and recreation activities

Sport	Boys	Girls	Recreation	Boys	Girls
Football	X		Debate	X	X
Volleyball	X	X	Dancing		X
Basketball	X	X	Music		X
Handball	X		Snooker	X	
Athletics	X		Picnics	X	X
Badminton	X		Field trips	X	X
Table tennis	X		Knitting		X

Conclusion and Policy Suggestions

This study concludes that the lack of a policy that specifically addresses gender discrimination is one of the major causes of the institutionalisation of discriminatory practices in schools. This policy gap is itself a product of patriarchy, which strenuously attempts to institutionalise male norms as the standard. Neither national nor local policies consider gender as an essential issue to be addressed, hence the lack of policies or affirmative action that take into account the strategic needs and circumstances of girls.

The study found that both institutional (school-related) and societal factors have a strong influence on the preservation, refining and transmitting of gendered belies and practices in the schools surveyed. The schools appear to be erecting powerful barriers to females' entry into the world of work. This is being done through the inculcation of the belief that boys should be prepared to dominate their physical environment, while girls should be prepared for marriage, child rearing and 'playing second fiddle' in society. Indeed, the study established that apart from deliberate discrimination against girls in the types, forms and processes of education provided for them, their personal integrity is also at times attacked in schools. Issues such as physical assault and sexual violence against women and girls appeared to be an unfortunate reality in some of the schools studied.

This study reveals first of all that parents prefer to educate their sons rather than their daughters, even if they can afford the education of both sexes. Therefore, under conditions of extreme poverty, girls are easily withdrawn from school. Regrettably, some of the girls tend to agree with their parents' positions, believing that if they acquire higher qualifications, they would be less likely to get married. Teachers, therefore, being part of society and many being parents themselves, they are influenced by such beliefs. Thus, teachers' attitudes and behaviours tend to favour male students over their female colleagues. Many teachers (both male and female) hold the belief that male students are more competent and able than female students. Teachers see girls to be the 'weaker sex' and more fragile physically, intellectually and socially than boys.

The study further reveals that boys and girls are encouraged by the school ethos and practices to choose subjects along gender lines. More males than females choose science subjects, while teachers and the general school environment encourage male students to chose and perform better in these subjects. A subject such as home economics, which is largely seen as feminine, is not even taught in the boys-only school. What is more disturbing is the fact that none of the teachers or officials interviewed supported the idea of infusing gender issues into the curriculum, and no one liked the idea of students being encouraged to take subjects across gender lines.

The management of the schools studied also reveals strong male bias. Perhaps, the major problem is the way in which schools reinforce the perpetuation of this maleness in leadership. Boys were found to play a more predominant role than the female students. The head boy was generally more active and has authority over both boys and girls, while the head girl has authority only over girls.

There is a strong interrelationship between existing patriarchal policies and formal and informal practices in the schools. This study has concluded that patriarchy is the main covert principle that determines policy formulation and/or its lack of implementation. The schools' ethos tends to ignore or suppress females' gender identity. In other words, discrimination based on gender is legitimated and often 'encouraged'. This legitimisation cuts across the hierarchy. The schools' staff members and students are ideologically stratified into binary opposition camps: feminine and masculine, with the major focus of discourse by both sexes centring on feminine 'inferiority'.

The main finding of this study is that institutional life in the schools studied is gendered and that gendered relations affect retention, participation and performance of boys and girls. To borrow Connell's words, the schools studied are 'substantively, not just metaphorically, gendered' in that 'organisational practices are structured in relation to the reproductive arena' (Connell, 2001:35). Since school is a 'masculine' institution, whose 'cultures appeal to highly masculine values of individualism, aggression, competition' (Collinson and Hearn, 2001:146), gender 'neutral' equitable policies on the ground become largely ineffective in addressing gender-discriminatory practices. Indeed, such policies tacitly reinforce gendered perceptions, beliefs and practices with negative consequences for gender-fair practices. The practices in these schools are themselves a reflection of the patriarchal values dominant in the wider society, as respondents consistently referred to practices and beliefs in society to explain or justify what went on in the schools.

The following actions need to take place:

- The development of a gender-sensitive policy framework for schools in Nigeria. Without a legal framework, victims of gender discrimination stand unprotected and this viciously sustains and promotes the discrimination against them. Such a policy needs to be formulated so that it can redress the existing gender imbalance as a short-term strategy, as well as ensure gender-fair and gender-sensitive education institutions in the long term.

- A concerted effort to infuse gender issues in the formal school curriculum at all levels.

- The development of school-level gender equity policies to guide recruitment, admissions, course placement, promotion etc. of teachers and other staff.

- The development of a comprehensive policy on sexual harassment, with clearly defined procedures for complaints and investigations, which do not result in further risk or threat to the complainant. Such a policy requires the active involvement of all stakeholders, i.e. male and female members of staff and students.

- The development of less hierarchical in-school relationships, especially between members of staff and students. There is the need to reduce the unequal power relations existing between students and teachers.

- Teacher training and awareness raising on gender issues as they affect enrolment, retention and achievement and the consequences of teacher action and inaction.

- The infusion of gender issues into teacher education curricula, with a view to re-orienting teachers and helping them unlearn the gendered perceptions of their worldview.

Notes

1. This is an ancient Islamic city/state and now one of the northern states that practises the Sharia legal system.
2. An ancient Islamic city and now part of Kaduna state.
3. Nigeria DHS EdData Survey 2004: Key Findings.
4. Community ownership of schools is vital to a conducive learning environment.
5. It is considered to be 'sexual harassment' against male teachers by girls if the girls dress in an 'attractive' manner.
6. Withdrawal hardly ever takes place because the (female) victims are seen to be attracting boys through their behaviour and style of dress in such cases.

Glossary of Gender Terms

Sex	Sex describes biological characteristics and differences (such as physical features related to the capacity for childbearing and breast-feeding for women and voice-breaking for men) between girls and boys, and women and men.
Gender	The socially constructed differences between women and men. These differ from one culture and society to another, change over time and define who has power and influence over what.
Gender analysis	The systematic study of the differences between men's and women's, girls' and boys' roles, positions, privileges and access to resources. Gender analysis involves collecting sex-disaggregated data; in other words, data that present information separately for women and men, girls and boys.
Gender-aware (and gender-sensitive)	Able to highlight gender differences and issues and incorporate them into strategies and actions.
Gender balance	Equal or fair distribution of women and men within an institution or group. It gives equal representation.
Gender equality	Means women and men have equal rights. They should have the same entitlements and opportunities. Equality is rights-based.
Gender equity	Means justice so that resources are fairly distributed, taking into account different needs. Note: 'gender equality' and 'gender equity' are sometimes used interchangeably; there is no agreement about the exact difference between them.
Gender-inclusive	Language or behaviour that minimises assumptions regarding gender.
Gender mainstreaming	The process of integrating gender into all policies, programmes and activities.
Gender parity	Equal numbers. In schools, an equal number of boys and girls.
Gender policy, types of:	
Gender-blind	Ignores different gender roles and capabilities. Assumes everyone has the same needs and interests.
Gender-neutral	Not aimed at either men or women and assumed to affect both sexes equally. However, it may be gender-blind.
Gender-specific	Recognises gender difference and targets for either women or men within existing roles.
Gender-redistributive	Seeks to change the distribution of power and resources in the interest of gender equality.

Gender relations	Social relationships between people (women and men, women and women, men and men). They reflect gender difference as constructed in a particular context or society. Gender relations intersect with other social relations based on age, class, ethnicity, race, sexuality and disability.
Gender-responsive	Able to respond to and deal with the gender issues that are revealed by gender analysis.
Gender roles	Learned behaviours in a society/community. They condition which activities are seen as male and female. Gender roles are affected by age, class, race, ethnicity and religion and by geography, economics and politics. Gender roles often respond to changing circumstances, e.g., development efforts.
	Both women and men play multiple roles, such as productive, reproductive or community roles. Women often play all three roles at once, hence the terms 'triple role' or 'multiple burden'.
Gender system	The socially constructed expectations for male and female behaviour. Prescribes the division of labour and responsibilities between women and men and gives them different rights and obligations. The gender system defines males and females as different and justifies inequality on that basis.

Exploring the Bias: Gender & Stereotyping in Secondary Schools

Glossary of Non-English Words and Phrases

Malaysian

Word or phrase	English translation
Bahasa Malaysia	Malay language
dia	she/he
Itu biasa	That is normal
Itu kerja wanita	It's girls' work
lelaki	boy
Sekolah Kebangsaan	National School
Sekolah Jenis Kebangsaan	National Type School

Samoan

Word or phrase	English translation
aiga	family, normally meaning the extended family
aiuli	one who dances in support of
alofa	love or compassion
a'oga faife'au	pastor's school
aualuma	social aggregate of all the daughters of the village
aumaga	social aggregate of all the sons of the village, also untitled men
faaaloalo	respect
Fa'aSamoa	the Samoan way of doing things
fai ava	a married man living in his wife's family or village
feagaiga	relationship between a brother and sister, governed by protocol
fono a matai	the council of chiefs in a village
Fono Tele	General Assembly
ie toga	a very fine mat that is used in special rituals
Koneferenisi	Conference
le mafaufau	one who does not use his/her brain
malolosi	very strong and powerful
mana	spiritual gift of wisdom
matai	a man who holds a title of the family
nofo tane	a married woman living in her husband's family or village

nuu	village
palagi	a European person
siapo	cloth that is made from the bark of the mulberry tree
tamaiti	children
taualuga	last dance in a Samoan recreational programme
taupou	daughter of the highest village chief
upu taufaifai	word of ridicule
va	relationships between people that is articulated in mutual respect
va fealoaloai	respectful and reciprocal protocols in a relationship
va tapuia	sacred protocol in a relationship

Hindi

Word or phrase	**English translation**
Adhyapika Manch	Women Teachers' Forum
badnami	shame
beta	son
dari	cotton carpet
Devta	God
kartavya	duty
kho-kho, kabbadi	local games
Garima Prakosht	Cell constituted in co-educational schools to handle cases of harassment
gram sabha/panchayat	village-level councils of local governance
Operation Garima	A programme to curb 'eve teasing' (harassment of girls/women) implemented in Jaipur district
rangoli	floor patterns drawn with rice powder or coloured powder
salwar kameze	a two-piece dress with a long shirt and loose trousers
shabash	very good
shlokas	hymns/chants
rotis	bread made out of wheat flour
Sarva Shiksha Abhiyan	Government of India's umbrella programme for universalising elementary education

References and Bibliography

Abdullah, Maria Chin (2006) Addressing Gender-based Violence in Malaysia. A survey conducted for United Nations Population Fund (UNFPA), 17 April 2006. Petaling Jaya, Malaysia: UNFPA.

Aikman, S and E Unterhalter (2005) Beyond Access: Transforming Policy and Practice for Gender Equality in Education. Oxford: Oxfam.

Albert, MC (2005) Underperformance of Boys in Secondary Schools: Extent, Reasons and Strategies. Unpublished MA thesis.

Ali, S (2006) Exploring perceptions and practices of science teachers about how boys and girls learn science. Unpublished master's dissertation. Karachi, Pakistan: Aga Khan University, Institute for Educational Development.

Anyawu, SO (1995) 'The Girl-child: Problems and Survival in the Nigerian Context'. Scandinavian Journal of Development and Alternatives, 14 (1–2):85–105.

Arifin, Jamilah (2004) Gender Critiques of the Millennium Development Goals: An Overview and an Assessment. Paper presented at the International Council on Social Welfare (ICSW) 31st International Conference on Social Progress and Social Justice, 16–20 August 2004, Kuala Lumpur, Malaysia.

Ashraf, D (2004) Experiences of women teachers in the Northern Areas of Pakistan. University of Toronto, Canada.

Bakari (2005) Gender and Equity in Teacher Education: A Case Study from Nigeria. D. Phil. thesis submitted to the University of Sussex.

Brown, L (2005) 'Gender and academic achievement in math: an examination of the math performance data on seven to nine-year-olds in Trinidad and Tobago'. Caribbean Curriculum, Vol.12, No.1:37–58.

Brown, M (2006) Gender differentials at the secondary and tertiary levels of the education system in the Anglophone Caribbean: Specialist study: Dropout from educational institutions in three CARICOM countries. Mona, Jamaica: Regional Co-ordinating Unit, Center for Gender and Development Studies, University of the West Indies (UWI).

Central Intelligence Agency (2007) The World Factbook: Trinidad and Tobago. Retrieved from: https://www.cia.gov/library/publications/the-world-factbook/print/td.html [accessed 15 May 2009]

Central Statistical Office, Trinidad and Tobago (2005) Report on education statistics, 2001–2002. Port of Spain, Trinidad: Central Statistical Office.

Chevannes, B (2001) Learning to be a Man: Culture, Socialization and Gender Identity in Five Caribbean Communities. Kingston, Jamaica, Barbados: University of the West Indies Press.

Clarke, P and J Jha (2006) 'Rajasthan's Experience in Improving Service Delivery in Education'. In Vikram K Chand (ed.) Reinventing Public Service Delivery in India. New Delhi: Sage Publications.

Cohen, L, L Manion, and K Morrison (2000) Research Methods in Education (5th ed.). London: RoutledgeFalmer.

Colclough, C, S Al-Samarrai, P Rose and M Tembon (2003) *Achieving Schooling for All in Africa: Costs, Commitment and Gender.* Aldershot: Ashgate.

Collinson, D, and J Hearn (2001) 'Naming Men as Men: Implications for Work, Organisation and Management'. In S Whitehead, and FJ Barrett (eds.) *The Masculinities Reader:* 144-169. Cambridge: Polity Press.

Connell, RW (2001) 'The Social Organisation of Masculinity'. In S Whitehead and FJ Barrett (eds.) *The Masculinities Reader:* 30-50. Cambridge: Polity Press.

Connell, RW (2002) *Gender.* Cambridge: Polity Press.

Convention on the Elimination of All Forms of Discrimination Against Women (CEDAW) website: www.un.org/womenwatch/daw/cedaw [accessed 15 May 2009]

De Lisle, J (2006) 'Dragging eleven-plus measurement practice into the fourth quadrant: the Trinidad and Tobago secondary education assessment (SEA) as a gendered sieve'. *Caribbean Curriculum,* Vol.13:91-129.

De Lisle, J, and P Smith (2004) 'Reconsidering the consequences: gender differentials in performance and placement in the 2001 SEA'. *Caribbean Curriculum,* Vol.11, No.1:23-56.

De Lisle, J, P Smith and V Jules (2005) 'Which males or females are most at risk and on what? An analysis of gender differentials within the primary school system of Trinidad and Tobago'. *Educational Studies,* Vol.31, No.4:393-418.

Dunne, M (1996) 'The Power of Numbers: Quantitative Data and Equal Opportunities Research'. In L Morley and V Walsh (eds.) *Breaking the Boundaries: Women in Higher Education:* 236-256. London: Taylor and Francis.

Dunne, M, and F Leach, with B Chilisa, T Maundeni, R Tabulawa, N Kufor, D Forde and A Assamoah (2004) *Gendered School Experiences: The Impact on Retention and Achievement.* London: DFID.

Fafunwa, AB (1990) Women: Able Partners in the Development Process. Women and Leadership: Proceedings of the Conference on Women and Leadership, NAUW (Lagos Chapter) 21-23 February 1990, National Endowment for Democracy, African American Institute.

Fairbairn-Dunlop, P (1991) Women, education and development in Western Samoa. Unpublished PhD thesis. Melbourne: Macquarie University.

Farah, I, and K Bacchus (1999) 'Educating girls in Pakistan: Tension between economics and culture'. In Fiona Leach and Angela Little (eds.) *Education cultures, and economics:* 225-237. New York: RoutledgeFalmer.

Farah, I, and S Shera (2007) Female education in Pakistan: A review. In R Qureshi and Jane Rarieya (eds.) *Gender and education in Pakistan:* 3-40. Karachi: Oxford University Press.

Federal Bureau of Statistics (2007) Pakistan Statistical Year Book 2007. Ministry of Economic Affairs and Statistics, Government of Pakistan. Retrieved 24 August 2008: http://www.statpak.gov.pk/dept/index.html

Federal Republic of Nigeria (1988) National Policy on Education. Lagos: NERDC Press.

Federal Republic of Nigeria (2007) Annual Abstract of Statistics, 2007. Abuja: National Bureau of Statistics.

Female Education in Mathematics and Science in Africa (FEMSA) (1997) Parents' and community attitudes towards girls' participation in and access to education and science, mathematics and technology (SMT) subjects. Forum for African Women Educationalists (FAWE). Retrieved 15 January 2007: www.nicef.org/education/educprog/ste/projects/girls%20arica/femsa/femsa/femsa6.html-45k

Figueroa, M (1996) Male Privileging and Male Academic Performance in Jamaica. Paper presented at the Symposium on the Construction of Caribbean Masculinity. St Augustine: Centre for Gender and Development Studies, University of the West Indies.

Gan Wan Yeat et al. (2005) *Biologi*. Bakaprep Sdn. Bhd., Malaysia.

Government of India (1986) National Policy of Education, Department of Education. New Delhi: Government of India.

Government of India (2003) Select Educational Survey. New Delhi: Government of India.

Government of India (2005) Report of the CABE Committee on Universalisation of Secondary Education, Ministry of Human Resource Development, New Delhi.

Government of India (2007) Draft Report of the Sub-group on Secondary and Vocational Education for Eleventh Five Year Plan, Planning Commission. New Delhi: Government of India.

Government of India (2008) Eleventh Five Year Plan 2007–2012, Volume II, Planning Commission. New Delhi: Government of India.

Government of India (2009) Gendering Human Development Indices: Recasting the Gender Development Index and Gender Empowerment Measure for India, Department of Ministry of Women and Child Development, New Delhi.

Government of Malaysia (not dated) Education Development Plan (2001–2010). Kuala Lumpur: National Government Printers, Malaysia.

Government of Malaysia (not dated) Eighth Malaysia Plan (2001–2005). Putrajaya: National Government Printers, Malaysia.

Government of Malaysia (2006) Ministry of Women, Family and Community Development, Implementation of the Convention of the Rights of the Child. Malaysia's First Report 14 December 2006. Available from: http://www.kpwkm.gov.my/portal/BM/Upload/20080618_124906_26531_Pelaksanaan%20Konvensyen%20Mengenai%20Hak%20Kanak-Kanak%20 (CRC).pdf

Government of Malaysia (2005) National Education Policy. Putrajaya: National Government Printers, Malaysia.

Government of Malaysia (not dated) Ninth Malaysia Plan (2006–2010) Putrajaya: National Government Printers, Malaysia.

Government of Malaysia (not dated) Seventh Malaysia Plan (1994–2000) Putrajaya: National Government Printers, Malaysia.

Government of Pakistan (2006) Economic Survey, 2005–2006, by Ministry of Finance. Retrieved 18 December 2006 from: http://www.finance.gov.pk/survey/home.htm

Government of Rajasthan (2006) Gender Responsive Budgeting of the Department of Education, Department of Planning. Jaipur: Government of Rajasthan.

Government of Rajasthan (2007) Draft Eleventh Five Year Plan (2007–2012). Jaipur: Planning Department, Government of Rajasthan.

Government of Rajasthan (2007–2008) Data for Elementary Education (DISE, 2007–08). Jaipur: Department of School Education, Government of Rajasthan.

Government of Rajasthan (2008a) Annual Report, Department of Elementary Education. Jaipur: Government of Rajasthan.

Government of Rajasthan (2008b) Annual Report, Department of Secondary Education. Jaipur: Government of Rajasthan.

Government of Rajasthan (2008c) Appraisal Report of Annual Workplan and Budget 2008-2009. Rajasthan: Sarva Shiksha Abhiyan.

Government of Rajasthan (2009) Annual Workplan and Budget 2008-2009. Jaipur: Government of Rajasthan.

Government of Rajasthan and Institute of Development Studies (2008) Rajasthan Human Development Report, An Update. Jaipur: Directorate of Economics and Statistics, Government of Rajasthan and IDS.

Government of Samoa–Asian Development Bank (2004) Survey of the Education Sector 2004.

Hafeez, M (2004) Communities' perceptions on girls' education: A study of six UPE-project districts in Punjab. UNICEF/NORAD.

Haque, Ihtasham ul (2006) We are doing all within our means to achieve MDGs. Retrieved 23 January 2006 from: http://www.dawn.com/2006/10/15/ebr14.htm.

Haralambos, M, and M Holborn (2000) *Sociology: Themes and Perspectives*. London: Harper Collins.

Harding, J (1992) Breaking the Barrier: Girls in Science Education. Paris: International Institute for Educational Planning, UNESCO.

Harnett, T, and W Heneveld (1993) Statistical Indicators of Female Participation in Education in sub-Saharan Africa. AFTHR Technical Note No.7. Washington, DC: World Bank, African Technical Department.

Jan, AS (2007) Exploring perceptions of parents and girls about girls' education in a slum area of Karachi. An unpublished master's dissertation. Karachi: Aga Khan University, Institute for Educational Development.

Jha, J (2007) Concept Note prepared for the Study on Gender Analysis of Classroom and Schooling Processes. London: Commonwealth Secretariat.

Jha, J (2007) An Annotated Bibliography on Gender in Secondary Education: Research from Selected Commonwealth Countries. London: Commonwealth Secretariat.

Jha, J and F Kelleher (2006) Boys' underachievement in education: an exploration in selected Commonwealth countries. London: Commonwealth Secretariat.

Kabeer, Naila (2001) 'Resources, Agency, Achievements: Reflections on the Measurements of Women's Empowerment'. In *Discussing Women's Empowerment: Theory and Practice*. Stockholm: SIDA Studies No. 3.

Khalid, HS, and EM Mukhtar (2002) The future of girls' education in Pakistan. Islamabad: UNICEF.

Koch, J, B Irby and G Brown (2002) 'Redefining gender equity' in J Koch and B Irby (eds.) *Defining and redefining gender equity in education*. Information Age Publishing.

Leach, F (1997a) 'Education and Training for Work: A Gender Perspective'. In J Lynch, C Modgil and S Modgil (eds.) *Equity and Excellence in Education for Development*: 41-52. London: Cassell.

Leach, F (1997b) Gender Implications of Donor Policies on Education and Training. Paper presented at the Oxford Conference on Education and Geopolitical Change: Marginalisation and Inclusion, 11-15 September 1997, Oxford.

Leach, F (2003a) *Practising Gender Analysis in Education*. London: Oxfam.

Leach, F (2003b) 'Learning to be Violent: The role of the School in Developing Adolescent Gendered Behaviour'. *Compare* 33 (3): 385-400.

Lee, Annie et al. (2002) English Form 4. PGI Cipta Sdn. Bhd., Malaysia.

Management and Information Systems Division (2004) Seychelles 2002 Census Report. Victoria, Seychelles.

Marohaini, Binti Yusoff et. al. (2004) *Bahasa Melayu*. Dewan Bahasa dan Pustaka, Malaysia.

Meleisea, M (1987a) *Lagaga: A short history of Western Samoa. Suva*: University of the South Pacific.

Meleisea, M (1987b) *The making of modern Samoa*. Suva: Institute of Pacific Studies, University of the South Pacific.

Miller, E (1992) *Men at Risk*. Mona, Jamaica: University of the West Indies Press.

Miller, E (1994) *The marginalization of the black male* (2nd ed.) Mona, Jamaica: Canoe Press.

Ministry of Education and Youth (2002) Gender differences in the Educational Achievement of Boys and Girls in Primary Schools in Seychelles. Victoria, Seychelles: Ministry of Education and Youth.

Ministry of Education and Youth (2001) National EFA Strategic Plan 2002-2015, Goal No. 5. Victoria, Seychelles: Ministry of Education and Youth.

Ministry of Education (2006) Directory of donors' assistance for Pakistan's education sector. Karachi: Government of Pakistan.

Ministry of Education and Youth (2000) Education for a Learning Society: Policy Statement of the Ministry of Education, Seychelles.

Ministry of Women, Family and Community Development (MWFCD) [online]. Accessed 27 December 2006 from: http://www.kpwkm.gov.my

Ministry of Women, Family and Community Development (2008) Statistics on Women, Family and Community. Kuala Lumpur, Malaysia: Salz-TERACHI Design Sdn.Bhd.

Mohammed, J, and C Keller (2007) Presentation at the One Day Symposium on Masculinities, Education and Criminal Justice. Voices from the Classroom: a gendered perspective on 15 June 2007. St Augustine: Univsersity of the West Indies, Centre for Gender and Development Studies.

Mohammed, J (1996) Career aspirations and expectations of fifth form students at a senior comprehensive school. Unpublished PhD thesis. St Augustine: University of the West Indies, School of Education.

Moinuddin, Ahmed (2006) Poor grades in education report card. *The Daily Dawn*. Retrieved 12 December 2006 from: http://www.dawn.com/2006/10/15/ebr18.htm

Morris, J (2002) 'Gender equity and schooling in Trinidad and Tobago'. In N Mustapha and R Brunton (eds.) *Issues in Education in Trinidad and Tobago*. St Augustine: University of the West Indies, School of Continuing Studies.

Mukhtar, EM (2006) Gender-aware policy appraisal: education sector. Retrieved 12 December 2006 from: http://www.grbi.gov.pk/documents/GAPA_Edu.pdf

Munns, Geoff (2005) Motivation and Engagement of Boys. Australian Government Quality Teacher Programme. Main Report. Australia.

Muoito, M (2004) Gender Equality in the Classroom: Reflections on Practice. Paper prepared for the Seminar on Pedagogic Strategies for Gender Equality and Quality Basic Education in Schools, Nairobi, Kenya.

Mustapha, N (2002) 'Education and stratification in Trinidad and Tobago'. In. N Mustapha and R Brunton (eds.) *Issues in Education in Trinidad and Tobago*. St Augustine: University of the West Indies, School of Continuing Studies.

Nambissan, GB (2004) Integrating Gender Concerns. *SEMINAR*, Issue No. 536.

National Council for Women's Organisations (NCWO) (2005) NGO Shadow Report on the Initial and Second Periodic Report of the Government of Malaysia. Malaysia: NCWO.

Niherst (2003) CXC and GCE 'A' level results 1998 and 2002. Port of Spain, Trinidad.

Nik, Hassan Shuhaimi et al. (2005) *Sejarah*. Dewan Bahasa dan Pustaka, Malaysia.

Nussbaum, MC (2000) Women and human development: the capabilities approach. The Seeley Lectures. Cambridge: Cambridge University Press.

Ooi, Jeffrey (2006) Kissing: Let's not mix up morality and law. Malaysiakini, 6 April 2006. Available from: www.malaysiakini.com [accessed 15 May 2009]

Parry, O (2000) *Male Underachievement in High School Education in Jamaica, Barbados and St Vincent and the Grenadines*. Kingston, Jamaica: Canoe Press.

Pasha, HA, HZ Ismail and MA Iqbal (1996) Continuation rates in primary education: A study of Pakistan. Karachi, Pakistan: Social Policy and Development Centre (SPDC).

Petana-Ioka, K (1995) Secondary education in Western Samoa: developments in the English curriculum, 1960s–1990s. Unpublished master's thesis. Dunedin: University of Otago.

Plummer, D (2005) 'Crimes Against Manhood: Homophobia as the Penalty for Betraying Hegemonic Masculinity'. In G Hawkes and J Scott (eds.) *Perspectives in Human Sexuality*: 218-232. South Melbourne: Oxford University Press.

Pratham (2005) Annual Status of Education Report (ASER). Mumbai: Pratham.

Rarieya, JF, B Dean, R Joldoshalieva, U Bano and A Hussinay (2006) How does Gender Affect the Processes of Teaching and Learning in Primary and Secondary School Contexts in Pakistan? A Situational Analysis. Karachi, Pakistan: Aga Khan University, Institute for Educational Development.

Rudduck, J (1994) Developing a Gender Policy in Secondary Schools. Buckingham: Open University.

Samoa National Human Development Report (2006)

Sawada, Y and Lokshin, M (2001) 'Household schooling decisions in rural Pakistan.' Policy Research Working Paper Series 2541. The World Bank.

Schmuck, P, C Brody and N Nagel (2002) 'Going beyond sex equity'. In J Koch and B Irby (eds.) *Defining and redefining gender equity in education*. Information Age Publishing.

Sen, A (2003) Keynote Speech delivered at the Commonwealth Education Ministers Conference in Edinburgh. Available from: http://www.guardian.co.uk/education/2003/oct/28/schools.uk4 [accessed 15 May 2009]

Sindh Education Foundation (2007) EFA: A critical review. Karachi, Pakistan: Sindh Education Foundation.

Stake, RE (2000) 'Case Studies'. In NK Denzin and YS Lincoln (eds.) *Handbook of Qualitative Research*: 435–454. London: Sage.

Sturman, A. (1997) 'Case Study Methods'. In JP Keeves (ed.) *Educational Research, Methodology, and Measurement: an International Handbook*: 61–65. Oxford: Pergamon Press.

SUHAKAM (2006) SUHAKAM's Report on the Human Rights Approach to the Millennium Development Goals. Malaysia: SUHAKAM.

Swada, Y and Lokshin, M (2001) Household schooling decision in rural Pakistan. Policy Research Working Paper. Washington, DC: World Bank.

Tuia, Tupu T (1999) Samoan culture and education in the European context: a case study based on one Samoan family from different generations. Unpublished master's thesis Brisbane: University of Queensland.

UNDP (2001) Trinidad and Tobago National Human Development Report, 2000: Youth at risk in Trinidad and Tobago. Port of Spain, Trinidad: UNDP.

United Nations Development Programme (UNDP) (2003) Human Development Report 2003. New York: Oxford University Press.

UNDP (2005) Malaysia Report on MDGs.

United Nations Development Programme (UNDP) (2008) Human Development Report 2007/8. Fighting Climate Change: Human Solidarity in a Divided World. New York: Palgrave Macmillan.

UN Educational, Scientific and Cultural Organization (UNESCO) (1995) A Report of the International Consultation on the Education of Girls and Women. Paris: UNESCO.

UNESCO (1995) United Nations Country Team, Malaysia: Achieving the Millennium Development Goals. Success and Challange. Kuala Lumpur: UNDP.

UNESCO (1997) Gender-sensitivity: A Training Manual. Paris: UNESCO.

UNESCO (2001), Malaysia: Education for All. Progress and Achievement in Elimination of Gender Gaps, 28–30 November, Japan. Available from: www.unescobkk.org/fileadmin/user_upload/appeal/gender/Malaysiaeducationforall.doc

UNESCO (2003) EFA Global Monitoring Report 2003/04. Education for All by 2015: Gender and Education for All: The Leap to Equality. Paris: UNESCO and Oxford: Oxford University Press.

UNESCO (2004) The Extent of the Problem. Available from: http://portal.unesco.org/education/en/ev.php-URL_ID=28702&URL_DO=DO_TOPIC&URL_SECTION=201.html [accessed 28 April 2004]

UNESCO (2005) Global Monitoring Report on Education for All, 2006. Paris: UNESCO Publishing.

UNESCO (2007) EFA Global Monitoring Report 2008. Education for All by 2015: Will We Make It? Paris: UNESCO and Oxford: Oxford University Press.

UNESCO (2009) EFA Global Monitoring Report 2009. Overcoming Inequality: Why Governance Matters. Paris: UNESCO and Oxford: Oxford University Press.

UN Children's Fund (UNICEF) and National Planning Commission (2001) Children's and Women's Rights in Nigeria: A Wake-Up Call. Abuja: National Planning Commission and UNICEF.

World Bank (2008). World Development Indicators, Washington DC.

Worrell, F (2006) 'Ethnic and gender differences in self-reported achievement and achievement – related attitudes in secondary school students in Trinidad'. *Caribbean Curriculum*, Vol.13, No.1:1–23.

Worrell, P and J Morris (2007) Presentation at the One Day Symposium on Masculinities, Education and Criminal Justice: Voices from the Classroom: a gendered perspective on 15 June 2007. St Augustine: University of the West Indies, Centre for Gender and Development Studies.

Yin, RK (1994) *Case Study Research: Design and Methods*. London: Sage.

Zafar, F and M Malik (2004) Dropout of girls from primary education in Punjab. Society for the Advancement of Education, UNESCO, Islamabad, Pakistan.

Zainulabidin, N (2007) Teachers' instructional practices in relation to their expectations of girls and boys in a co-educational primary school in Pakistan. An unpublished master's dissertation. Karachi, Pakistan: Aga Khan University, Institute for Educational Development.